"THE MAN WHO SAVED PARIS":

ROGER WEST'S RIDE 1914

"THE MAN WHO SAVED PARIS":

ROGER WEST'S RIDE 1914

MICHAEL CARRAGHER

UNIFORM

UNIFORM

Uniform
an imprint of Unicorn Publishing Group

Unicorn Publishing Group
101 Wardour Street
London W1F 0UG
www.unicornpublishing.org

First published by Uniform 2017
© Michael Carragher, Unicorn Publishing Group 2017

A CIP catalogue record for this book is available
from the British Library

ISBN 978-1-908487-05-6

All royalties from the sale of this book go to Help 4 Forgotten Allies
http://www.h4fa.org.uk/veterans

Printed and bound in the Great Britain

Table of Contents

Maps 6

Foreword 17

Preface 19

Introduction: The Contemptibles 23

Diary 31

Appendix 1: Note on BG Drummond 195

Appendix 2: March 8th 1916 196

Brief Biography 197

Glossary 225

Bibliography 227

Index 231

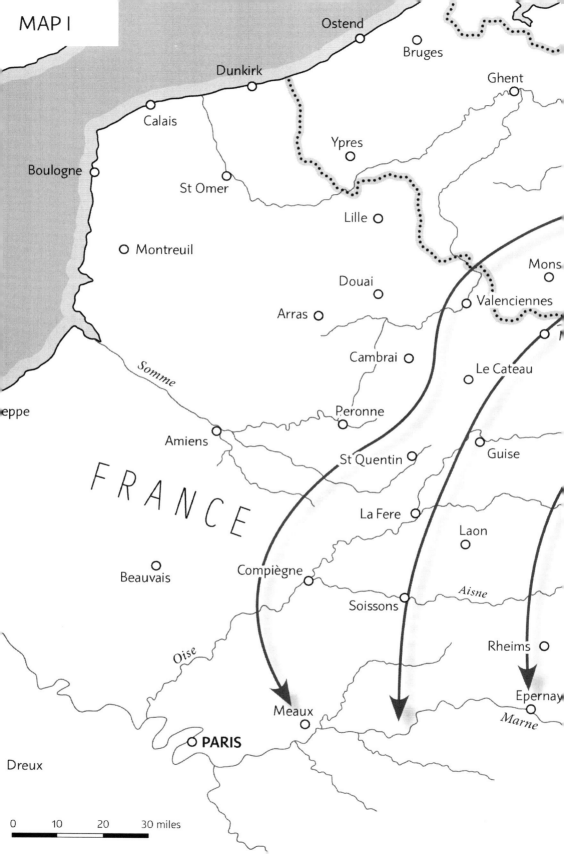

MAP I

Ostend
Bruges
Dunkirk
Ghent
Calais
Ypres
Boulogne
St Omer
Lille
Mons
Montreuil
Douai
Valenciennes
Arras
Cambrai
Le Cateau
Somme
Peronne
eppe
Amiens
St Quentin
Guise
F R A N C E
La Fere
Laon
Beauvais
Compiègne
Aisne
Soissons
Oise
Rheims
Meaux
Epernay
PARIS
Marne
Dreux

0   10   20   30 miles

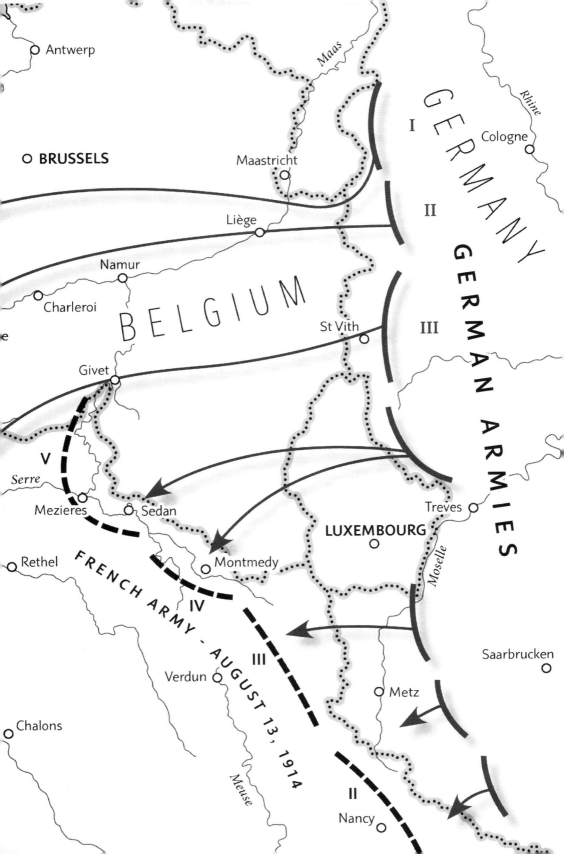

Antwerp

Maas

Rhine

GERMANY

I

Cologne

BRUSSELS

Maastricht

II

GERMAN ARMIES

Liège

Namur

BELGIUM

Charleroi

St Vith

III

Givet

V

Serre

Mezieres

Sedan

Treves

LUXEMBOURG

Rethel

Montmedy

FRENCH ARMY · AUGUST 13, 1914

IV

III

Moselle

Verdun

Saarbrucken

Chalons

Metz

Meuse

II

Nancy

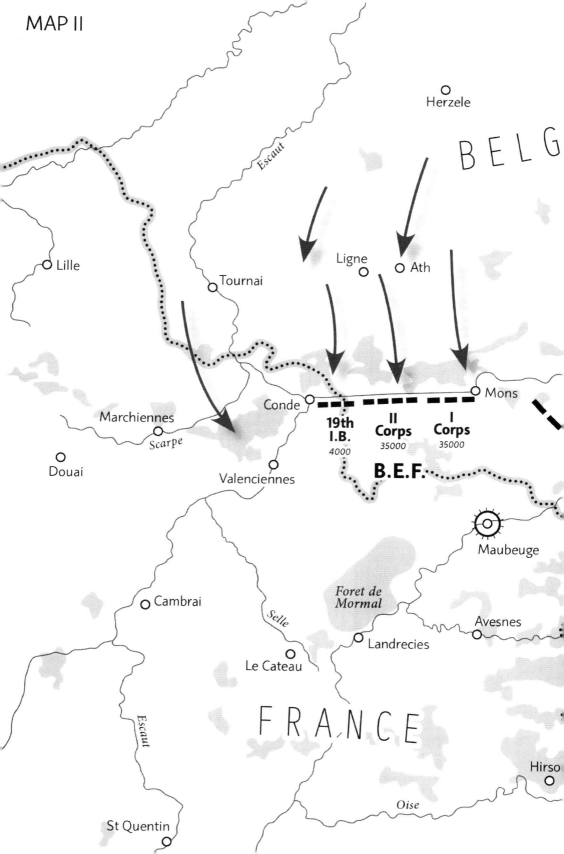

MAP II

Herzele

BELG

Escaut

Lille

Tournai

Ligne

Ath

Conde

Mons

Marchiennes

Scarpe

**19th
I.B.**
4000

**II
Corps**
35000

**I
Corps**
35000

Douai

B.E.F.

Valenciennes

Maubeuge

Cambrai

Selle

*Foret de
Mormal*

Avesnes

Landrecies

Le Cateau

F R A N C E

Escaut

Hirso

Oise

St Quentin

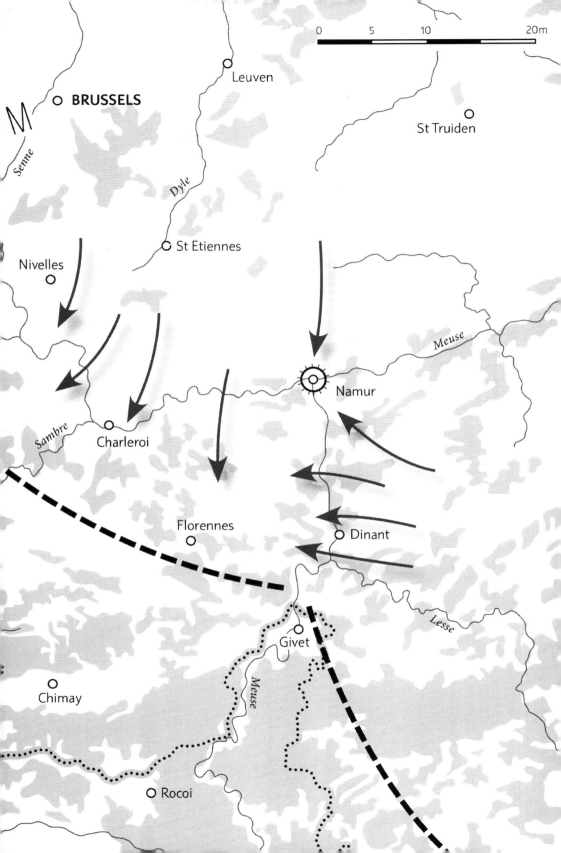

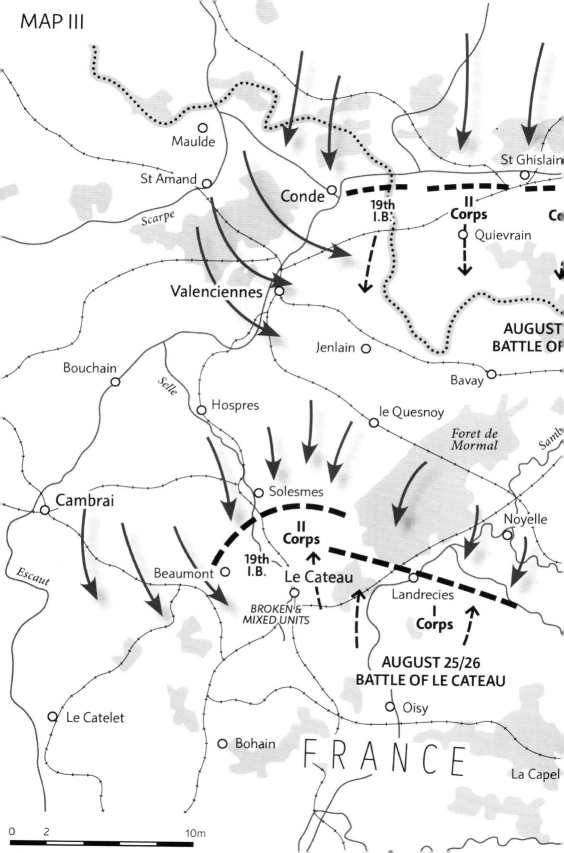

MAP III

Maulde

St Amand

Scarpe

Conde

19th
I.B.

II
Corps

Quievrain

St Ghislain

C

AUGUST
BATTLE OF

Valenciennes

Jenlain

Bavay

Bouchain

Selle

Hospres

le Quesnoy

Foret de
Mormal

Samb

Cambrai

Escaut

Beaumont

Solesmes

19th
I.B.

II
Corps

Le Cateau

BROKEN &
MIXED UNITS

Noyelle

Landrecies

Corps

AUGUST 25/26
BATTLE OF LE CATEAU

Le Catelet

Bohain

Oisy

F R A N C E

La Capel

0   2   10m

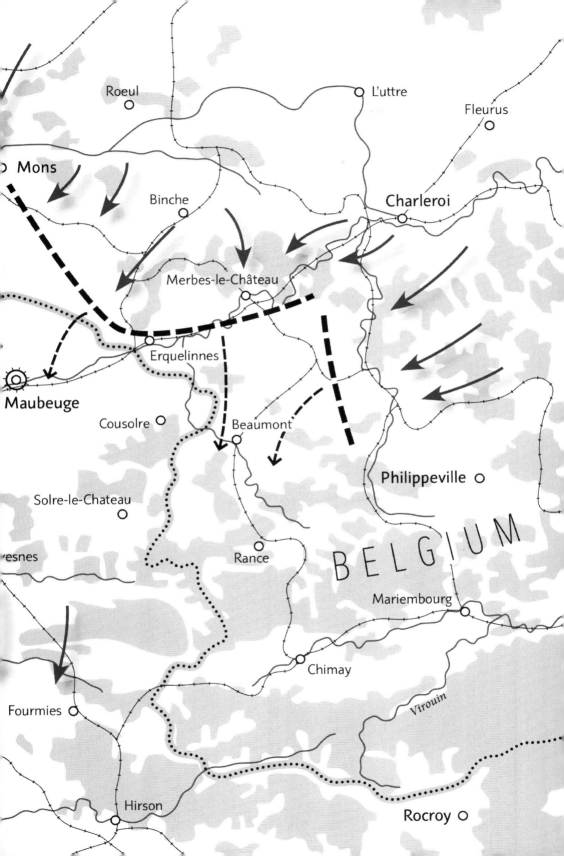

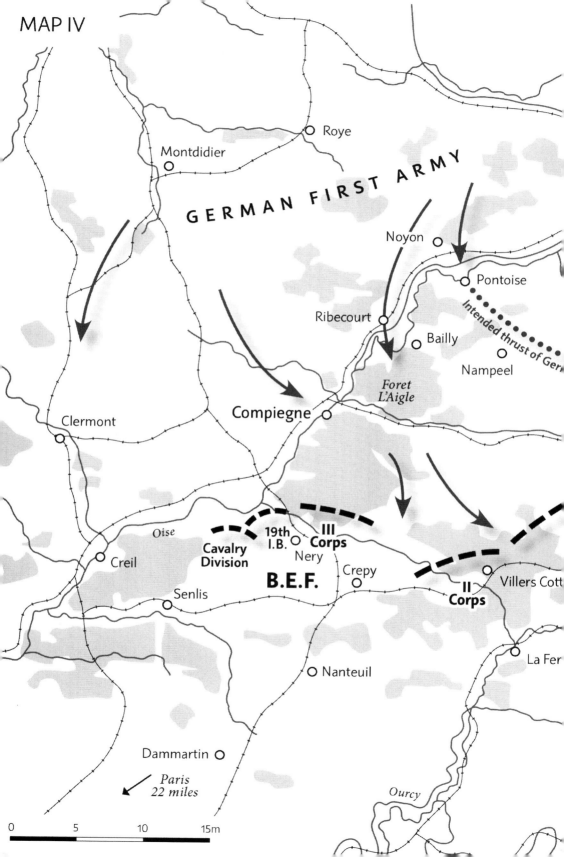

MAP IV

Roye

Montdidier

GERMAN FIRST ARMY

Noyon

Pontoise

Ribecourt

Bailly

Intended thrust of Ger

Nampeel

Clermont

*Foret
L'Aigle*

Compiegne

Oise

Creil

**Cavalry
Division**

19th
I.B.

Nery

**III
Corps**

Crepy

**II
Corps**

Villers Cott

Senlis

B.E.F.

Nanteuil

La Fer

Dammartin

↙ *Paris
22 miles*

Ourcy

0   5   10   15m

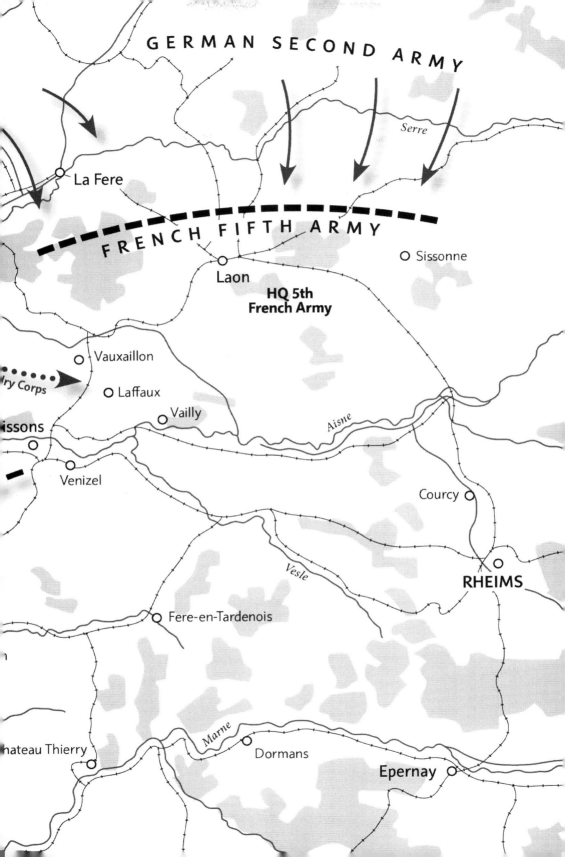

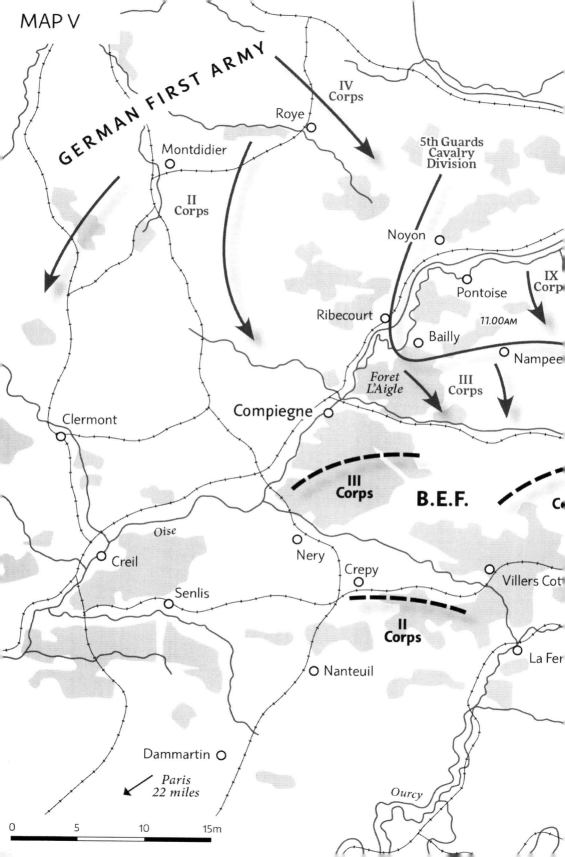

MAP V

GERMAN FIRST ARMY

IV
Corps

Roye

Montdidier

5th Guards
Cavalry
Division

II
Corps

Noyon

Pontoise

IX
Corp

11.00AM

Ribecourt

Bailly

Nampee

Foret
L'Aigle

III
Corps

Clermont

Compiegne

III
Corps

B.E.F.

C

Oise

Nery

Creil

Crepy

Villers Cot

Senlis

II
Corps

La Fer

Nanteuil

Dammartin

Paris
22 miles

Ourcy

0   5   10   15m

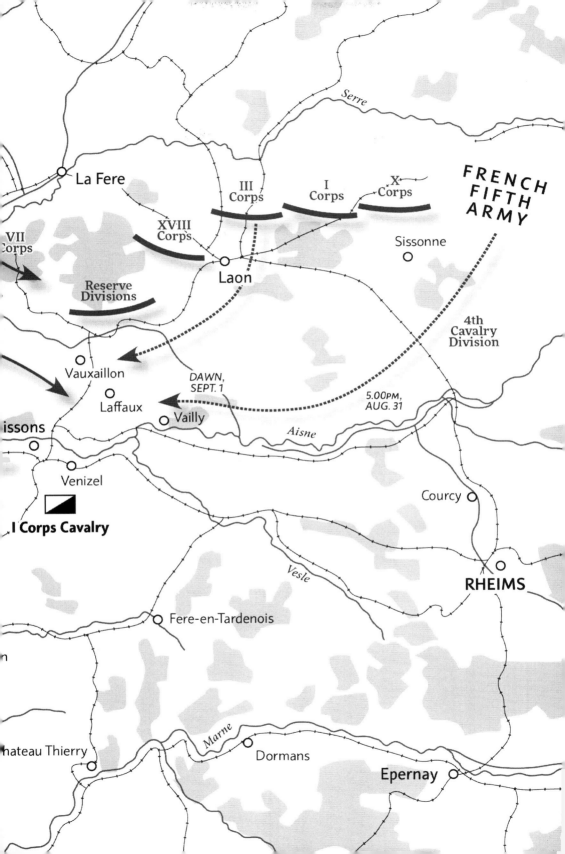

Serre

La Fere

III
Corps

I
Corps

X
Corps

FRENCH
FIFTH
ARMY

XVIII
Corps

VII
Corps

Sissonne

Reserve
Divisions

Laon

4th
Cavalry
Division

Vauxaillon

*DAWN,
SEPT. 1*

*5.00PM,
AUG. 31*

Laffaux

Vailly

issons

Aisne

Courcy

Venizel

I Corps Cavalry

Vesle

RHEIMS

Fere-en-Tardenois

hateau Thierry

Marne

Dormans

Epernay

Foreword

THESE DIARIES SHOW an eyewitness view of the opening phases of the First World War in the west by one who was deeply involved. They are, of course, only one man's view. But what they show is of much greater significance than might be supposed. Indeed, the action of this one man had a highly significant effect on the outcome of the Battle of the Marne. Had the Germans won that battle, they would no doubt have defeated France and achieved the result which in fact they did achieve in 1940.

The one man was Roger West. After an extraordinary motorcycle journey of over a thousand miles hither and thither seeking a means of joining up, and with scarcely any military training, he arrived in France as a so-called Intelligence Officer with a motorcycle on 13 August 1914. He kept a diary in the form of notes in the heat of battle and later wrote them up as a continuous narrative. This has now been skilfully edited by Michael Carragher and set in the context of the broader history of the period. It provides new insights which I believe are unique.

Dr Noble Frankland
CB, CBE, DFC

Preface

ON NOVEMBER 19ᵀᴴ, 1975, the *Monterey Peninsula Herald*, a California newspaper, reported the death, at age 84, of Roger Rolleston West. Mr West, the obituary noted, had been born in 1891 in England and had "served with the Intelligence Corps in the first contingent to leave England for the Continent in World War I". After combat in that war he worked as an aeronautical engineer in wind-tunnel development, and later as a seismologist, a petroleum geologist, a lecturer in engineering at the University of British Columbia and a technical advisor to Paramount Pictures. An impressive CV. But what made Lieutenant Roger West briefly famous was when, detailed as a despatch rider through the Great Retreat of August 1914, he blew up the bridge at Pontoise-lès-Noyon, in the face of the German advance. For this action he was awarded the Distinguished Service Order—the first decoration awarded to the newly-formed Intelligence Corps, and one very seldom bestowed on a subaltern in the British Army—and credited as "the man who saved Paris".

With the characteristic modesty of men of his class whose sense of duty was imperative, West discounted the accolade, the success of his mission being a good-news story when good news was in scant supply and understandably inflated in importance—though perhaps not all that much, as examination of the event in detail will reveal. He himself evaluated his experiences through the opening weeks of the Great War as merely those of "one individual in the midst of tremendous happenings".

But what tremendous happenings! And what an individual!

It feels like rather a cheek to take on to edit Roger West's diary, if only because no editing beyond transcription is strictly necessary. His account stands on its own merit and reads as easily as good fiction. I have placed events in the wider context of what was happening at the time, which no participant could have known, and also in the context in which we now understand the Great War; but even in that regard West has gone a good way to anticipate any editor in his "Introduction: The Contemptibles", which he wrote more than thirty years after the events he describes. While he revised his typescript more than once before he submitted it to the Imperial War Museum in 1967, his account was written up from events he had noted in a field pocketbook daily, so his account retains all the vividness of contemporary experience.

It is impossible not to be impressed with this man, and with the society that produced an engineer who could write better than many journalists a century later. If West was privileged—the son of a famous London hospital physician, an Old Rugbeian and graduate of Cambridge University—accounts by veterans of more humble backgrounds may be scarcely less fluent. And of course these men also defeated German militarism and secured European democracy against totalitarianism in discharge of their well-honed sense of duty.

It's long been fashionable to sneer at such sentiments and statements; to misconstrue them as defence of the indefensible; to pretend that the Great War was nothing but a squalid struggle of capitalists in which conscientious *duty* was degraded to a dirty euphemism for exploitation of the blinkered proletariat toward imperial vested interests. And indeed, human lives *were* squandered in badly-planned and -managed battles (something that angered and embittered West); and imperial rivalry *did* play a part, especially as the struggle dragged on and the Allies looked for ways to compensate themselves for the appalling costs of a war that had been imposed upon them. If the BEF did secure European democracy after the French mutinies of 1917 this was not why the force was despatched in 1914: Britain went to war to defend British interests, but preventing German hegemony in Europe fortuitously was congruent with national and democratic values. In 1914 what was at stake was neither the "light soil" of North Africa nor the steamy wealth of the Congo but the cosmopolitan integrity of France and Belgium,[1] Germany's aim being, among other things, dismemberment of the latter, whose neutrality she had guaranteed, and annexation of north-eastern France as far as the English Channel. British interests would have been unacceptably endangered by such hostile hegemony, and control of the Narrow Seas.

German victory came perilously close to being achieved. With the Belgians pulled back into the fastness of Antwerp, had the British Expeditionary Force been defeated in the opening weeks the left flank of the French Fifth Army was open to onslaught by the German First, while the Second pinned it frontally. Schieffen's plan—or Moltke's—to defeat France in six weeks might well have been realised, and Germany would have won the war.

What prevented such disaster was, to a significant extent, the despatch riders of the BEF, who kept the force coherent through that protracted Great Retreat from Mons to the Marne. Retreat is the most difficult and dangerous of military manoeuvres, and one must not take from the professionalism of the officers and men of that most professional of forces, the British Army of the time, who executed it. But without communication there can be no

---

[1] "Light soil": Lord Salisbury's dismissive evaluation of the empire of the Third Republic.

command and control, no coordination of forces, and it was despatch riders who provided that communication, most of them citizen soldiers like Roger West.[2] Though West had enlisted in the Intelligence Corps, almost immediately he was seconded as a despatch rider to the independent 19th Brigade, something of an "orphan" in the opening stages of the war.

By the end of the Great Retreat the 19th had done its most important work, for it operated alongside the II Corps, on the extreme left of the Allied line, and suffered constant assault and infiltration by German cavalry. So fluid was the situation in the first few days that one could never be sure whether friend or foe was on one's flank, behind or in front. West was within yards of the Germans more than once, and rode through their cavalry. His account may read like something from *Boy's Own*, but it's true; an important work of history; a gripping and vivid description of those weeks of "tremendous happenings". For all its author's modesty, his story deserves to be known; indeed, more than a century after his ride, and to restore memory of what he did, it all but needs to be told.

Frequent reference is made to "the Schlieffen Plan". Dr Terence Zuber has challenged the existence of this and there are strong grounds for believing that after the war German generals formulated an excuse for their defeat by blaming the safely-dead General von Moltke for ruining a foolproof plan for victory. But there certainly was a contingency plan, which was put into effect in August 1914. Schlieffen may have considered this more *ad hoc* than doctrinaire; Moltke's many departures from it suggest as much. Nevertheless, we may speak of what became known as the Schlieffen Plan as *de facto* German strategy in August-September 1914.

This book is divided according to the daily entries of West's "Diary of the War: Retreat from Mons to the Battle of the Aisne",[3] followed by a biographical note, with analysis of the consequences of his destruction of Pontoise-lès-Noyon and tentative evaluation of the action. Sometimes the pace was such that one day bled into another and where this is the case I indicate that I have done so. I try to place West's daily accounts in the context in which they occurred, but it is with a good deal of trepidation that I presume to intrude on the remarkable adventures of Lieutenant Roger Rolleston Fick West, DSO.

Having done so, I have to thank many people for their assistance. The staff of the Imperial War Museum are always helpful. Roger's great-nephews and -nieces were enthusiastic and encouraging since I first approached the family with the proposal to publish their uncle's "Diary of the War"; I am particularly grateful to John Bucknall and Sally Steen. In California Tony

---

[2] See Michael Carragher, "'Amateurs at a professional game': The Despatch Rider Corps in 1914" in *Stemming the Tide: Officers and Leadership in the British Expeditionary Force 1914*.

[3] Imperial War Museum document reference: 67/162/1.

Murphy and his daughter Dierdre tracked down Roger's old house in Carmel. Thanks above all to my wife, Consuelo, for her forbearance in this and all my other undertakings.

Michael Carragher
Dublin, September 2016

Introduction:
The Contemptibles

BY R ROLLESTON WEST, DSO

THIS IS NOT a military treatise on the fighting retreat from Mons to Paris at the start of the First World War. It is the personal experiences and journal of one individual in the midst of tremendous happenings.

The retreat from Mons was a defeat, even as the retreat from Dunkirk in the Second World War or the destruction of Pearl Harbor were defeats. But in none of these were the defeated beaten, and the retreat from Mons ranks among the epics of how victory was plucked from the jaws of disaster.

Speaking German and French I was nominally commissioned to the British Intelligence Corps, but soon found myself despatch riding, searching for lost regiments, and having to do anything else that came along as the vastly superior German forces crashed down on and nearly shattered the vital British flank of the allied armies.

It was on August 4th 1914 that Britain, acting on her written treaty with Belgium, declared war on Germany. Germany complained that Britain was going to war "just for a scrap of paper." Kaiser Wilhelm II, enraged at such an affront to his ideas of international ethics, ordered his generals to wipe out the "contemptible little British army."[4] His immense forces were led by highly-trained and efficient officers. But the rank and file consisted mostly of only moderately taught conscripts. They [the BEF] struck a small, but for its size probably one of the highest-trained bodies of experienced and professional soldiers that had ever been put into the field. Mere privates often had undergone many years of fighting on the Indian frontier, Africa and

---

[4] What the Kaiser said, or strictly, wrote in his order of the day for August 19th, was "General French's contemptibly small Army". Canny mistranslation rendered this as the "contemptible little army", and as such a statement certainly would have been congruent with Wilhelm's famous tact there was no problem in its being believed by all, and accepted by the "Old Contemptibles" as the challenge it was deliberately mistranslated to construe.

elsewhere, and they were just not to be wiped out. Had the British crumbled under the blow the whole allied armies would have been rolled up and the war would have had a very different ending.

In the midst of such a far-flung action few if any grasped the overall picture; others knew only what was personally happening to themselves. It was not till strategic histories had been written years after that the significance of individual experiences fell into place. It is necessary therefore as a background to this journal to get some idea of the general strategy of the operation as a whole.

The French view (see Map I), carefully prepared for many years, envisaged an attack along the Franco-German frontier from Switzerland in the south to the neutral Belgian border in the north. North of this they felt no cause for alarm, and Marshall Joffre, commanding the French, had massed his forces along the south against this anticipated attack.

Germany however, as is now old history, tore up her treaty with Belgium as another "scrap of paper" and violated Belgian neutrality; and while making only holding attacks in the south poured her vast hosts far to the north through Belgium. The forts of Liège put up a heroic defence, but were soon pulverised by the new German heavy howitzers. The German First, Second and Third Armies then swept aside the ill-prepared and poorly-armed Belgians to come in and around the left flank of the allied forces.

The French high command seemed unable to comprehend the blow that was being prepared in the north, and on the left General Lanrezac of the Fifth French Army, already far out on a limb, was ordered to advance.

Guarding his imperilled left flank lay the British Expeditionary Force under Field Marshal Sir John French. This consisted of only two corps totalling 70,000 men. To this was hastily added the 4,000 men of the 19th Brigade, to which I was attached, brought up from the lines of communication. This brigade was tacked onto the dangerous extreme left of the whole line. These troops extended the left flank along the Mons-Condé canal with Lanrezac fallen back on [the BEF's] right. Against them were frontally opposed (Map II) three German corps some 120,000 strong, with two more corps following close behind. Meanwhile away out beyond the 19th Brigade the German Cavalry Corps of some 16,000 horse, which alone outnumbered this brigade some four to one, was swinging in behind our left flank. Thus 74,000 British were confronted with about a quarter of a million enemy.

The brunt of this onslaught on August 22nd 1914 was taken by the 19th Brigade and the II Corps, while to the east General Lanrezac's Fifth French Army, though only moderately pressed, had precipitately retreated without notice, leaving even the right flank of the British exposed.

There was much misunderstanding and clash of temperament between Lanrezac and Sir John French. Lanrezac had probably a clearer view of the true situation than Joffre his commander-in-chief, and retreat was the only sensible action, but his complete disregard for the safety of his allies guarding his flank has come in for much argument and unfavourable comment. Wherever the fault lay, the fact remained that the British were left far to the north to fight it out alone.

There was no chance of victory against such insuperable odds, but the "contemptible little army" refused to be wiped out. They held on for one day more waiting for the expected support which never came. Then they fought their way back under heavy attack and frightful difficulties to Le Cateau. Here Sir Horace Smith-Dorrien, commanding the II Corps and the 19th Brigade, realised his troops were too exhausted to go on and he decided to stand and slug it out. Thus occurred the Battle of Le Cateau, one of the most extraordinary examples of dogged determination in the face of what seemed certain annihilation.

Some 55,000 tired troops, gallantly aided by Sordet's equally tired French cavalry, which at last had ridden 30 miles to support them, turned at bay against 150,000 men of von Kluck's First Army opposing them. Though out-gunned and outnumbered three-to-one they held up this vast German horde and fought it to a standstill. Then they retired in good order, "all that was left of them."[5] "Good order" is perhaps hardly the right phrase, for so many officers had fallen, and in the battle the shattered units had become mixed with each other, and had often lost touch with their commands. But they were a fighting force still, and had gained such a reputation for desperate fighting that the enemy who should have overwhelmed them were now chary of frontal attacks on even small packets of resistance.

Thus they retired on St Quentin, unbelievably tired, marching and fighting and marching again. There was little or no sleep and little or no food as the transport had frequently lost their units in the melee. At St Quentin they came to rest for a few hours and some respite was given them.

At last the defeatist or mistaken General Lanrezac promised and actually made a counter-attack at Guise to the east. This, though necessarily on the right flank and not the imperilled left, took some of the pressure off the sorely-tried British. In this [action] the British I Corps might have helped. But by now the strained relations between Sir John French and General Lanrezac, and the former's distrust of French promises, had gone too far and he [Sir John] refused to send the I Corps to participate.

It is a very human trait to distrust beyond redemption an apparent friend who has let one down in an emergency. The solid Anglo-Saxon temperament

---

[5] An allusion to Tennyson's poem. In fact the II Corps' losses at Le Cateau, like those of the Light Brigade at Balaklava, were not as heavy as at first believed; nor were they as heavily outnumbered as West thought, though they certainly were out-gunned.

of Sir John French found it impossible either to understand or to forgive what he considered his betrayal by the Gallic mind of General Lanrezac. The clash of temperament was as [that of] a dog and a cat. Sir John's army had taken tremendous knocks, but every call for aid had been brushed aside by Lanrezac with only a further French retreat as an answer.

So Sir John decided not to get involved in what might only prove to be another mythical French counter-attack. Instead he ordered a retreat, so as to be sure of getting at least level with or possibly south of the French armies on his right.

The third British corps of fresh troops from England had now been formed on the left flank,[6] but south of Compiègne together with remnants of the badly-mauled 19th Brigade. The shattered remains of the II Corps, also with mixed units of the 19th Brigade, were withdrawing towards Villers Cotterets, shortly, however, to be heavily pressed again by the enemy. The I Corps was retiring south-west of Soissons.

Admittedly this retirement, due to Sir John's perhaps understandable distrust of his allies, gave his tired troops some relief from the intolerable pressure they had undergone, yet it had gone too far and too fast. Conditions were now reversed, for already Lanrezac's army was dangerously exposed on his left, and the gap between the British and the French forces was rapidly widening.

The Germans strained every nerve to enter this gap in time, for if they succeeded they would cut the railways and roads of Lanrezac's supply lines, and trap his whole army north of Laon. It was a race to get the tired French troops back to hold the crossings of the Aillette and the River Aisne (see Map IV).

At this juncture in one of my fortuitous rangings I found the last bridge on this front over the Oise at Pontoise still intact, and a wide open road for the German thrust. I sped south to overtake the retreating British, and with an Engineer companion riding pillion was able to return in time to blow it up.

The great importance of this was at the time quite unknown to me, but it threw the German Guard Cavalry far to the west to find a crossing. The crucial moment was lost to the Germans and the French army escaped. I was surprised later to find myself decorated with the DSO for this act; and later was even more astonished when I heard the idea put about that I had saved Paris. This I think was a gross if enthusiastic overstatement, but the demolition of the bridge at Pontoise no doubt played some part in the outcome of events.

---

[6] III Corps was constituted from the 4th Division and the 19th Brigade on August 31st, under the command of General Sir William Pulteney.

By now the British army had retired due south, and the Germans who had lost touch with them, or maybe thought they were annihilated, concentrated on the outflanking of the French left wing. But Paris with its vast ring of fortresses, however old, spread away to the west of the German hordes. To von Kluck it was obviously impossible to outflank that as well, so he decided to strike south-eastwards away from Paris and drive into what he thought was a gap left by the destruction of the British army, and roll up the French to the western frontiers of Germany.

But he had made a sore miscalculation. The Sixth French Army from Paris came out in his rear, and he found at the bottom of the pocket a British army that was far from dead and which turned in behind him. Farther east again the French Fifth Army had come to life, no longer under the defeatist Lanrezac but commanded now by the dynamic General Franchet d'Espèrey who had replaced him. Farther east still they were held up by General Foch and the armies of the east.

The German Colossus raged against the bars of this trap which the genius of Joffre had improvised for them, and there was born out of the previous vast defeat the victory of the Battle of the Marne. The tide was turned, and to prevent complete encirclement the Germans retired with all speed and heavy casualties northwards again to the River Aisne.

At this point virtually the war was won, though it took four more years to finish it. Thereafter followed the race northward to the sea, each side trying to outflank the other. But neither side won. At last the opposing forces reached the sea, and the war of movement settled down to the murderous drab trench warfare, from Ostend to Verdun—four years of mud blood and horror, till by sheer attrition and lack of adequate numbers, particularly after the entry of America, the Germans collapsed.

It is with the first part of the war from Mons to Paris and back again to the River Aisne that the journal which follows is concerned. There has been little endeavour to edit the writings of a young man just out of college, and enough only has been done to hold the story together. It was written up immediately afterwards from scrappy notes jotted down in a field pocket book. Often as is natural the notes were fewest where the action was greatest, but it gives the bald experiences of one man flung suddenly into the midst of a great epic in world history.

Roger West wrote his "Diary of the War" many years after the event. Though he claims that "There has been little endeavour to edit the writings of a young man just out of college", textual analysis suggests that his account was transcribed from original notes sometime after 1930 and revisited after 1945 and perhaps several times up to 1967. Likely, though, his editing on every visit was on some point of detail; the most significant was his expansion on the personnel of the Intelligence Corps, which he seems to have gleaned from the Corps' official War Diary on a visit to Britain in his old age (he lived abroad for most of the post-war years).

West's Introduction shows an understanding of both scholarship of the Great War and capacity for objective analysis of his own role in this. "[I was] astonished when I heard the idea put about that I had saved Paris. This I think was a gross if enthusiastic overstatement, but the demolition of the bridge at Pontoise no doubt played some part in the outcome of events." Indeed it did: "it threw the German Guard Cavalry far to the west to find a crossing" and helped prevent the enemy cutting off General Lanrezac's retreat. "[I]f von Kluck's masses could be brought down upon the [Fifth Army's] flank, the whole French line would be rolled up and Paris entered after a victory such as history had never yet recorded."[7]

West demonstrates the critical importance of the French Fifth Army. It was this that would determine success or failure of the Schlieffen Plan. The BEF simply was too small to make a difference on its own strength, nor was its performance as gallant and glorious as has traditionally been portrayed. Yet in securing the flank of the Fifth Army, however imperfectly, the British served a vital role, and if the force was numerically small, its professionalism gave it disproportionate punch. Perhaps too much has been made of its achievements at Mons and Le Cateau, but these battles did help to grit the cogs of the German engine of war, and frustrate the Schlieffen Plan.[8]

The "sore miscalculation" of General von Kluck at the Marne, when he attempted to infiltrate a gap in the Allied line left by the over-hasty retreat of the BEF, was not the first such miscalculation by the leader of the German First Army. Kluck only learned of the BEF's position when he ran into it at Mons, and through the Retreat he was surprised more than once to find the British still intact and opposing his passage. His surprise was not completely down to hubris, but to communications difficulties (the Germans left themselves

---

[7] Sir Frederick Maurice, *Forty Days in 1914*, p. 136.

[8] The revisionists most critical of the BEF's performance are Terence Zuber, Adrian Gilbert and Peter Hart in, respectively, *The Mons Myth: A Reassessment of the Battle*; *Challenge of Battle: The Real Story of the British Army in 1914*, and *Fire and Movement: The British Expeditionary Force in the Campaign of 1914*. There is credit in these men's arguments, but they over- redress an historiographic imbalance. Zuber, extraordinarily, claims that "The British Cavalry Division was an operational liability" (p. 266); rather, for once it was the best in the field. A reviewer contends that "Hart perhaps goes a little too far in denigrating the performance of the BEF" (Adam D Johnson, *Intelligence and National Security*, April 2016, Vol 3, Issue 3, p. 452), and to claim, as Gilbert does, that Le Cateau was a German victory strains the facts. Strategically it was that, as it drove the British back, and much at a tactical level makes for uncomfortable reading. Yet Le Cateau may still be rated a British victory (of sorts), because it saved the BEF from being overwhelmed by superior forces and bought time to retreat, which was its tactical objective.

over-dependent on wireless and cable), and to very effective screening by British cavalry, without question the best in the field in 1914—for once. Much had been done since the embarrassments of the South African War, notably by General Michael Rimington, and much has been done in recent years to correct the "donkey walloper" view of British cavalry.[9] (And in fairness to Kluck, he acknowledges "This gallant British Army, with such excellent fighting qualities".[10])

West's harsh judgement of General Lanrezac is one that would have been shared by almost all Englishmen of his generation, and especially by men of the BEF. Lieutenant Louis Spears, liaison officer between the BEF and Lanrezac's Fifth Army and a vital witness to the opening days of the campaign, criticises the French general for "lack of faith in his own troops" and claims that "At Guise he manipulated his units with the consummate skill of an expert at the great game of war, but he played his hand without zest or faith".[11]

Once tipped—by Joffre himself—as a future commander-in-chief, Charles Lanrezac was perhaps more unfortunate than "defeatist", as West claims; rather than "without ... faith" he was what Napoleon might have called an "unlucky general". Ostensibly delegated to secure the left wing of an invading French force, he found himself instead bearing the brunt of an assault by elements of two, occasionally three, German armies, and, as West acknowledges, "had probably a clearer view of the true situation than Joffre" had. His support for and by the BEF was compromised by his bristly relationship with its commander in chief, the ironically-named Francophobe Sir John French. This caused problems—as if he didn't have enough with the Germans and his own GQG. If French was Francophobic, Lanrezac was Anglophobic, constantly suspecting Albion of perfidy, and the fact that each man spoke the other's language only poorly didn't help. When they first met and French asked what the Germans were doing on the north bank of the Meuse (they were expected to confine themselves to the south and east of that river, buttressing the flank of what was thought would be the main German attack through Lorraine) Lanrezac sarcastically answered "fishing". "The interview closed with 'flushed faces'". French, small-minded and vindictive, good at nursing grudges, never forgot. (His self-serving *1914* would be dismissed as "one of the most unfortunate books ever written".[12])

---

[9] See in particular Stephen Badsey, *Doctrine and Reform in the British Cavalry 1880-1918* (Ashgate, 2008) and David Kenyon, *Horsemen in No Man's Land: British Cavalry and Trench Warfare 1914-1918* (Pen & Sword Books, 2011); see also Major-General MF Rimington, *Our Cavalry* (London: Macmillan, 1912).

[10] Alexander von Kluck, *The March on Paris and the Battle of the Marne, 1914*, p. 79.

[11] Edward Spears, *Liaison 1914: A Narrative of the Great Retreat*, p. 269.

[12] Barbara Tuchman, *The Guns of August*, p. 250, Probably the "fishing" remark was made subsequently, and well out of French's hearing, but that it was made at all reflects how

That said, Lanrezac's precipitate withdrawal from the BEF's right was militarily inexplicable as well as personally dishonourable: had the BEF been defeated as a consequence, his own flank would have been exposed. But Sir John French's exposure of Lanrezac's left flank, by his own retreat a week later, after countermanding Sir Douglas Haig's offer of I Corps support to the French attack at Guise, was no less replete with the capacity for disaster, a disaster that was averted in no small measure by the initiative and courage of Roger West.

Something of a Gallic Cassandra, Lanrezac had foretold a German invasion through Belgium, only to have his warnings dismissed by General Joffre, who "conceived the whole duty of generals ... to be lions in action and dogs in obedience, an ideal to which Lanrezac, with a mind of his own and an urgent sense of danger, found it impossible to conform".[13] He knew that he would be called a *catastrophard* and blamed for the failure of Plan XVII, but his very lack of *cran* saved *La France* so that she could fight another day. His disengagement from the Battle of Charleroi prevented the Fifth Army from being enveloped by the German First, Second and Third, thereby denying the decisive victory that the Reich needed to win the war in the West. Later, he was the tactical victor of the Battle of Guise, though perceived as having been defeated because of the necessity to withdraw in the face of superior numbers. Joffre never forgave Lanrezac for having been right in his early distrust of Plan XVII, and right in his analysis of the situation in August when Joffre had been wrong, but the *Légion d'Honneur* that was eventually bestowed on him reflects belated recognition of Lanrezac's military virtues.

While "Desperate Frankie" (General Louis Franchet d'Espèrey), his erstwhile subordinate who replaced him, was more of a "thruster", Lanrezec really was scapegoated. His head was one of dozens that were to roll as Joffre ruthlessly cut back the dead wood of the French high command, and there can be no question that this culling was an essential component in containing the Germans at the Marne. Here d'Espèry, "a stranger to depression", as he appeared to President Poincaré, performed better than Lanrezac possibly could have, exhausted and demoralised as the latter was after his battles against the Germans, Sir John French and GQG, and the hardships and humiliations of prolonged retreat.

---

ill-tempered and portentous the first meeting of the two commanders was.

[13] Tuchman, op cit, pp. 237, 286.

Diary of the War

August 4th 1914.

War declared by England on Germany.

This economical entry is added in cursive to West's typescript and seems to have been inserted as a sort of formal baseline to the "tremendous happenings" in which he was to become involved.

In response to the British declaration of war General Helmuth von Moltke, Chief of the German General Staff, hubristically dismisses the *Kaiserliche Marine*'s offer to sink British troopships in the Channel as "not necessary"; that "it will even be of advantage [to] settle with the BEF at the same time as with French forces".[14]

German forces launch their assault on Liège and battles of encounter begin all along the Western Front (though "the "Battles of the Frontiers" is a term confined to the pitched battles of 20-23 August). The Third Balkan War has been transformed into European war and Erich von Falkenhayn, Prussian Minister for War and later Chief of the General staff, proclaims "Even if we go under as a result of this it was beautiful".[15]

In London, staff are appointed to the British Expeditionary Force and the Grand Fleet placed under command of Admiral Sir John Jellicoe. A naval

---

[14] Martin Gilbert, *The First World War: A Complete History*, p. 35.
[15] Max Hastings, *Catastrophe: Europe Goes To War 1914*, p. 118.

blockade of Germany is mooted to starve the enemy of vital resources, and the Royal Navy cuts German communication cables in the Channel.

As of today, the British Army owns "some 80 mechanical transport vehicles" (though many more are to be impressed into service on mobilisation under a government subsidy-purchase scheme), fifteen of them motorcycles,[16] but civilians are rushing to the colours, some with their own motorcycles, in answer to appeals from the War Office;[17] advertisements have been posted weeks earlier for "Several motor cyclists ... to act as despatch carriers on 28th July to 8th August next, and also on 3rd August to 8th August",[18] but this was merely for annual manoeuvres—*merely* indeed! The very need for civilians to perform in such a role reflects how amateur the British Army was when compared to the superb *millionenheer* forces of the Second Reich.

It also anticipates the need for a nation in arms to defeat German militarism.[19] British Neutrality Committee holds its first meeting.

August 5th 1914.

Declaration of war.
We arrived in Birmingham at last on the night of August 5th, and I wrote frantic notes to everybody, and tried to settle up my affairs generally. I let Tangyes know they would have to dispense with my services,[20] and arranged with Mrs Brightwell, with whom I was staying, for the removal of my goods and chattels if I did not return.

Today Prince Lichnowsky, the German ambassador, having denounced his government as "gangsters" and "swine", sorrowfully departs London. He is given a battleship escort across the Channel and the courtesy of a German flag, and later reports, "I was treated like a departing sovereign."[21] In Berlin the British ambassador is spat at as he leaves the embassy building and subsequently billed for the train that brings him to the Danish frontier.

British Neutrality Committee holds its last meeting and British War Council its first—in Downing Street. Yesterday's blockade proposals are shelved for the moment because of reluctance to disrupt trade and because it's expected

---

[16] *Statistics of the military effort of the British Empire during the Great War, 1914-1920*, p. 852.

[17] WHL Watson, *Adventures of a Despatch Rider*, p. 4.

[18] *The Motor Cycle*, July 9th, 1914, p. 56.

[19] Michael Carragher, "'Amateurs at a professional game': The Despatch Rider Corps in 1914".

[20] A Birmingham engineering firm which, more than a century after it had to dispense with Roger's services, and despite the travails of British industry in the interim, is still in business.

[21] The flag had to be hurriedly lowered when it attracted a shot over the bows from HMS *Amphion*, itself soon on its way to the bottom.

that the war will be too short for blockade to have any effect. Lord Kitchener and Sir John French favour concentrating the BEF at Amiens rather than at Maubeuge, which they feel is too far forward and likely to constrain the force's freedom of action—concentration at Amiens would enable it to reinforce the French wherever needed—but Francophile Sir Henry Wilson, Director of Military Operations, successfully argues for conformity with French plans.

While England's preparing, the Germans are marching. "Our advance in Belgium is certainly brutal," Moltke frankly admits; "but we are fighting for our lives and all who get in the way must take the consequences". The assault on the Liège forts gets into stride with "The dead piled up in ridges a yard high".[22]

August 6th.

> I got on my motorcycle to see where I could join up, and was directed to Captain Huxley, whom I found after some difficulty. He said he was sorry, but they were quite full up for motor cyclists, that I had better try London, and he gave me an address at Battersea. I went off there by train next day and arrived there in the morning, August 7th.

The war is spreading. Austria-Hungary declares war on Russia and Servia (as it still is called) on Germany.

The cruiser *Amphion* is sunk by a German mine, with the loss of 150 lives, including those of the German crew captured with the minelayer yesterday.

The British Cabinet recommends that four infantry and one cavalry division be sent to France, to the chagrin of Henry Wilson, who wants all six infantry divisions despatched.

In the war's first air raid, a Zepplin kills nine in Liège.

August 7th.

> The streets in all directions within about two hundred yards of the door were packed with motor cyclists and motor cycles of all descriptions and kinds. Machines were either to be bought by the government or, if unsuitable and they wanted the man alone, they supplied him with a machine; these were Triumphs, Premiers, Rudges and Douglases for the most part.[23]

---

[22] Tuchman, op cit, p. 199.

[23] It seems that the War Office officially "supplied Black 3½ hp Rudge Multis" to the Intelligence Corps (Martin Gegg, *War Bike: British Military Motorcycling 1899-1919*, p. 63) but West's account makes clear that the WO was struggling, here as everywhere else, and glad to take what it could get from any supplier. This is not the only instance where West's observations and experiences are at odds with the "official account".

I gave my qualifications, but hearing I was from Birmingham they said I should try up there again. This was a nuisance, but it would be absurd to turn back now. So I dashed off to Frankland,[24] via Wendover, and was driven up in a fly to see Mother and say "Good-bye." I found her and Ethel sewing on the chesterfield in the drawing-room, and told them I was going to the War. Mother was naturally a bit upset, and talked about the superior excellence of enlisting for Home Service. I told her that old England was on her beam ends, and wanted every man she could get. All this after being twice turned away. (Of course I don't pretend that this was really my opinion at the time, but unconsciously it was somewhat prophetic.) I could not stay, so said "Good-bye" and back to London again to catch the train to Birmingham, which place I reached that night.

West is a bit late. The scramble to become a despatch rider, to get into the war before it was over by Christmas, is very clear from his description. Even two days earlier the scramble had been evident, and by now the "lucky" ones, like Willie Watson, are being "drilled, lectured and given our kit" at Chatham.[25] More than 2,000 motorcyclists surplus to immediate requirements will present themselves for service by mid-August.

While Britons are enlisting, across the Channel men are dying. Erich Ludendorff leads a daring assault on Liège's citadel, winning the *Pour le Mérite* and taking the first steps to becoming de facto dictator of Germany. In Alsace French forces cross the border and prepare to liberate the province from the German "occupation" it has suffered since 1871.

Farther afield, HMS *Gloucester* exchanges fire with the *Göben* and the *Breslau* in the Peloponnese. None of the ships are damaged but the two Germans, after being harried across the Mediterranean, will soon seek refuge with the Sublime Porte, a staging post on Turkey's entry into the war in October.

On this day, too, Kitchener issues his famous appeal for what will become "the first hundred thousand". Though few except himself and Sir Douglas Haig believe it, Britain is in for a long war.

The Defence of the Realm Act (DORA) is passed, giving the government unprecedented control of the economy and people's lives. Things are to be rather "business as usual" for some time to come, but DORA marks the beginning of governmental intrusion that has remained with us ever since.

---

[24] The family home at St Leonards, near Tring, Herts. West was the grandson of Sir Edward Frankland and his father named the house that he built "Frankland" after his famous father-in-law; the house still stands.

[25] Watson, op cit, pp. 4, 6.

Entirely unnoticed by the enemy, the vanguard of the BEF lands in France, two weeks before the force will encounter the enemy at Mons. MI5 has done a fine job of rounding up enemy agents: over a period of ten days 120,000 men will cross the Channel without loss, and by the time the last disembarks the Germans still will not know of their whereabouts. The *Kaiserliche Marine*'s offer of August 4th to sink BEF troopships was as hubristic as Moltke's declination of the offer.

Today's vanguard comprises lines of communications (LC) troops, charged with establishing campsites and accommodation for the main body. They are all members of the 19th Brigade, unattached to any division, and it is while acting as a despatch rider with the 19th that West will earn fame.

As the BEF is landing in France, the first British shot of the First World War is fired far away by Ghanaian Lance Corporal Alhaji Grunshi in the short-lived Togoland Campaign. Grunshi will go on to be promoted to Sergeant Major and win the Military Medal in the *Ostafrika* campaign.

August 9th.

I woke early, and fled off to see Captain Huxley. Of course his list was as full as ever, but I thought I might try Cambridge, so thumped along there on my old Triumph. Somewhere between Bedford and my destination the clutch gave out, but I got it going again and reached Cambridge about 7 o'clock that night. There I met Ivor McClure (an old student friend of Cambridge days), also after a job. We dashed off to Corpus College and saw Captain Thornton, who gave us both fine testimonials to take to Chatham. We then went off to repair the Triumph, and though we were getting a bit tired by now we decided to make Chatham that night.

Starting about 11 o'clock we roared off at great speed down the Trumpington Road and on through Shelford, and so to Royston. There was no time to look up Dora, but I would have liked to have bidden farewell there as we had been good pals during the Cambridge days. Somewhere beyond Baldock the clutch gave out again. Darkness made repairs impossible, so I pushed it back to Baldock while Ivor went on and vanished into the night.

"Extraordinary thing," he said before he left, "to think that we are going out to a *real* proper war!"

That was the keynote of all my thoughts during that time, wondering what *real* war was like, real fighting, real lead slung at one, real fear, and how they differed from what one had read.

Stayed the night at Baldock, and the next morning, put the bicycle and all on the train for Chatham.

West's chronology is missing a day here. This is excusable, given that he has been running all over southern England and the Midlands, from Birmingham to London, back to Birmingham, thence to Cambridge, and on to London again, on a motorcycle that proves very unreliable (though the Triumph was the first truly reliable motorcycle, and through the war was to justify its moniker, *Trusty Triumph*).[26]

This is not the last West sees of his friend Ivor McClure, though by the time September 13th comes round and they meet by chance at Coulomniers, "It seemed about three years ago that he had left me that night at Baldock". Evidently McClure made it to Chatham in time to be attested as a DR— Chatham Barracks is the base of the Royal Engineers, to which the Despatch Rider Corps was attached in 1914; Willie Watson already is training there.

By now it is dawning on West just what "a *real* proper war" might be like.

Men fighting in Belgium and along the Franco-German border could tell him all about it. Battles are moving from encounter toward engagement—though today the French occupy Mulhouse without a fight. "Meanwhile at Essen the hideous fat black siege mortars" are loaded onto trains and despatched to reduce the fortresses of Liège. Berlin and Vienna, each as paranoid as the other, threaten to invade Italy if that country refuses to stand by its alleged obligations to the Triple Alliance (a defensive agreement that didn't bind Italy after Austro-German aggression; and besides, a clause had exempted her from making war against Britain in any event). In light of this enveloping threat and the spreading bloodstains in Belgium, Switzerland mobilises.[27] Switzerland has never been a great seafaring nation, and it's likely that the Swiss are less worried about taking broadsides from Royal Navy dreadnoughts than bombardments from their neighbours to the north and east.

Farther away, French and British forces have invaded Togoland and HMS *Astræa* bombards Dar es Salaam in response to commerce raiding by the *Königsberg* (which already has captured the SS *City of Winchester* in the *Kaiserliche Marine*'s first victory, and is to remain a nuisance until sunk in the Rufiji delta next year); forlorn hopes that the terms of the Berlin Conference might exclude Africa from European conflict are slipping away.

August 10th.

Arrived there [at Chatham] about mid-day and applied at the Royal Engineers' barracks. They were sorry to say they were full up, but there was

---

[26] See, for instance, David Minton, *The Triumph Story: Racing and production models from 1902 to the present day*, pp. 20-22.

[27] Tuchman, op cit, p. 206.

one more place going at the War Office if I hurried—I did. At the War Office I saw Captain EW Cox, and told him I had been over one thousand miles after this job, and he had got to give me something. Gave in my qualifications, and he took me on as the last of five spare men for the Intelligence Corps, for *six months* (!) or the duration of the war.

It was then about 2 PM and I was to report ready at 7 PM. The whole family had now come to town, and there followed the most frantic rush round to get kit. Officers' tunics were unobtainable, but at last I found one at Messrs Mosse Bros, Covent Garden, secondhand, and became the complete officer for 30/-! Thence on to the Army Ordnance, where I was given complete Tommy's outfit, though what for I don't know. Meanwhile the family had bought me a number of essentials, more especially a strong leather bag, and at 7 PM I reported at the War Office, and was told that I had until 7 PM the next day. This gave me a breather at last, and time to be a little uncertain whether I wanted to go.

As Ivor McClure successfully enlisted as a despatch rider, West seems to have just missed the cut. Instead he ended up in the Intelligence Corps, something that had been mooted in the Haldane reforms following the South African War but was only established on August 5th, less than a week before West joined it. The Corps was comprised of "academics, businessmen, journalists, writers, artists and others selected for expertise, linguistic (French or German) or other, useful for operations in France." However, "not all those called, or those who volunteered, were found suitable",[28] hence West, an eminently suitable man, found a place at the last minute. Quickly he is to find himself seconded to the 19th Brigade as a despatch rider.

The exclamation point in parentheses at the end of the first paragraph here is added in pencil to the typescript, evidence of West's revisiting his manuscript over time, and how fantastic, in retrospect, appears the delusion that the war might be over in six months.

The rush to the colours overwhelmed the country's ability to provide uniforms, even within a week of Britain's declaration of war. Obtaining one secondhand should not be surprising, however; almost 60 years later "Regiments tried to keep costs down by re-using second-hand uniforms wherever possible".[29] Moss Bros still maintain an outlet at Covent Gardens— West's mis-spelling of the name probably reflects the many years he spent far from London. Thirty shillings equates to £1.50, but its purchasing power was immensely greater a century ago, when a good pair of shoes cost about ten shillings.

---

[28] Anthony Clayton, *Forearmed: A History of the Intelligence Corps*, pp. 14, 16.

[29] Alastair Kerr, *Betrayal: The Murder of Robert Nairac GC*, pp. 214-15.

More elements of the BEF land in France, to find billets well set up by the LC troops. "That evening, to the sound of far-off summer thunder, the sun went down in a blood-red glow"—an ominous portent: ten Belgian civilians are murdered in Linsmeau. The Kaiser betrays the bombast behind his later dismissal of "General French's contemptibly small army" when he admits to the American ambassador, "The British change the whole situation—an obstinate nation. They will keep up the war".[30]

August 11th.

> Got photographed *en famille*, and reported to the War Office at 7 PM and went off from Waterloo Station with Drury and Richardson, and soon after Pilcher,[31] all of the Intelligence Corps. My sister Marjory and others came to see us off.
>
> Arrived at Southampton we went into rest camp, and I got a place in a tent with Sawyer and MacEwan. Of course I had too much luggage, and the next morning, August 12th, sent the greater part back.

"Of course I had too much luggage ..." A subaltern in the IC Corps was given a uniform and kit allowance of £50 and "The total weight of baggage and field kit allowed for each Intelligence Officer is 135 lbs which must not on any account be exceeded. Of this 100 lbs will be left at the Base, and 35 *lbs only taken into the field*".[32]

Abroad, the *Göben* and *Breslau* enter the Dardanelles on grounds of "military necessity", but already the Porte has agreed terms with Germany for support in the war, and the two ships are popularly regarded as compensation for the *Sultan Osman I* and the *Reshadieh*, the Ottoman-commissioned dreadnoughts impounded by order of Winston Churchill, then First Lord of the Admiralty, on the outbreak of war the previous week.

Closer to home, fighting along the frontiers continues. The Germans recover Mulhouse from the French, indicating an early unravelling of the Schlieffen Plan to defeat France quickly by containment on the German left wing, attack to be not here but on the right. Strategic objectives already are being sacrificed to tactical temptations. Moltke, nervous and insecure, agrees to these departures from the Plan.

---

[30] Tuchman, op cit, p. 230; Martin Gilbert, op cit, pp. 39, 41.

[31] None of these men appear in the list of Intelligence Corps personnel that West compiles in his entry for August 13th. Though West includes him here, Drury may not have joined the IC until August 15th. See WO 372/6/98049; also WO 372/16/8305.

[32] National Archives of Ireland, 1096/10/20; emphasis in original.

Sir John French's resolve is hardly strengthened when, still in England, he learns of German inclusion of reserves in front-line strength. But apart from Lanrezac, no one appreciates the size of the colossus marching down on the Allied left wing, or the extent of the peril. Aerial reconnaissance eventually will discover that menace, but it is only today that the first four squadrons of the RFC fly the Channel to their base in Amiens—it is barely five years since Louis Blériot won the *Daily Mail* prize for flying that recently-formidable body of water, and the pace of technological advance is going to accelerate enormously over the next four years, too often leaving generals and politicians struggling in its wake.

August 12th.

We were given motor cycles (a Premier in my case), also field glasses, first field dressings and other kit, and then moved off to the quays.

There were no rations issued, but we managed to raise sandwiches privately for lunch. I had written a line to Dora and curiously enough received a reply at Southampton, wishing me luck, though I don't know how they found me. We were to cross by SS "Olympia," but at the moment all quay space was occupied, and she could not come in until the evening. Troopships were leaving all day, and the songs of the soldiers on board faded slowly into the distance. As the ship entered the open sea someone from the quay shouted, "Are we downhearted?" A hoarse answering "No-o!" came back with a roar from the packed troops on board.

The sailing of the first Expeditionary Force to ports unknown.
At 5 o'clock the "Olympia" warped herself in to the quay, and cars, lorries, guns, limbers, waggons, crates of food, cases of ammunition, fodder for horses, spare gun and waggon wheels, and all imaginable war materials were slung on board by the fussy little steam cranes, and let down into the hold with a rattle of chains and tackle. Meanwhile horses and men and still more horses and men were streaming across the gangways, and the boat which had come in light with towering sides began to settle slowly in the water. We pushed our motor cycles up the gangway by relays, and got them settled on the lower deck.

It was towards dusk before all was ready and the ropes cast off. There was a rush to the shore side of the boat and messages were shouted back and forth. The messages were either purely personal, or instructions as to what to do with the Kaiser and the Germans! As the "Olympia" moved out someone struck up "God Save the King" and we all came to attention. It went with an earnestness and an intensity from some two thousand voices (battalions of Royal Sussex and Coldstream Guards) which lent a dignity to that oft-sung tune that I have never heard before.

It became dark as we moved down the Solent, and every now and then small boats would slide past us, showing a few lights in the gloom. Now and again we would be hailed by some old lighter drifting on the tide. "Are we downhearted?", and the answer always returned a raucous "NO-O!"

Finding real hot baths were obtainable down below I took advantage of the opportunity. Looking out of the port holes afterwards I found we were just entering the Channel. It was quite dark save for the great ray of a search-light from a chessboard fort barring the way across the Solent. We passed through this and on into the darkness, running without lights for the open sea. Then some watching war ship loomed up dimly, standing away to one side of our course, and a searchlight blinked out of the night, picked us up, looked for a while, and then passed by. We did not know whither we were bound, or for how long, or what we were to find when we got there, but the "Olympia" ploughed slowly on at half speed and, tired and excited, we went to sleep on the lower deck.

At the outbreak of war the Intelligence Corps, like the Despatch Rider Corps, was mounted on just about any motorcycles that could be obtained. While despatch riders enlisted with their motorcycles, machines for the Intelligence Corps were bought up hastily by the War Office, the initial idea being that Scout Officers in the IC would be deployed to the flanks in order to gather intelligence on the enemy which the high command then would use in devising battle plans of Napoleonic brilliance. The scale of the battlefield, compounded by problems of communication, relegated this notion, but personal mobility would remain an asset for such personnel so their motorcycles were retained. Besides, West and three of his colleagues were to become "despatch riders pure and simple" for weeks, three of the four motorcycle-mounted.

It must be acknowledged that General French greatly undervalued intelligence. In one disquieting episode that would seem to exemplify the Lions-led-by-Donkeys cliché, an improvised intelligence section of the cavalry established the position of the Germans in Belgium simply by making calls across the country from the telephone at Mons railway station; the excellent intelligence thus collated was ignored by GHQ.[33]

There was a great variety of motorcycles in the armed forces initially. In early 1914 the Army specified Triumphs and Douglases, the Air arms P&Ms, but it was only in early 1915 that the specified models were more-or-less-reliably delivered; other makes survived in service to the end, on home duties. The Premier on which West was mounted was a Coventry-manufactured

---

[33] Charles Messenger, *Call-to-Arms: The British Army 1914-1918*, p. 52.

single-cylinder 500cc machine, a very good motorcycle with advanced features like ball-race main bearings, gear-driven magneto and a rather ingenious tappet arrangement, which reduced valve-train wear.[34]

Not all Scout Officers were motorcycle mounted. James Marshall-Cornwall "somewhat untruthfully" claimed an ability to ride motorcycles, but was "fortunately allotted to the mounted section, and took over a fine chestnut gelding".[35]

West's description of the voyage is augmented by one from Major JL Baird (later Viscount Stonehaven): "The route across was patrolled by 3 lines of warships, so disposed that if a ship gets through one line in the dark, she cannot reach the third line before daylight. The ships were ten miles apart. A perfect sight! The lights on Southampton at sunset were a beautiful sight. We steamed very slowly."[36]

The war continues to spread. Britain and France declare war on Austria-Hungary, which finally invades Servia, the ostensible cause of the problem. Troops rape civilians in Sabac and murder 120 and by the end of the month about 3,500 Serb civilians will be dead.[37] Britain finally begins blockade of German ports, France that of Austria-Hungary's Adriatic coast.

Russian cavalry crosses into East Prussia, prompting German fears of Cossack depredation which leads to critical tinkering with the Schlieffen Plan. In France, Lanrezac proposes to face northeast, to meet the invaders, rather than east, to support an attack into the Ardennes; he is denied permission by GQG, fixated on smashing the German forces in Alsace-Lorraine. The French plan sees the Fifth Army merely buttressing the left wing, not taking the full frontal force of two German armies.

In Belgium 305mm Skodas and 420mm Krupps howitzers are brought into action against Liège. At Haelen General Georg von der Marwitz's cavalry (of which more later) suffers a setback in the Battle of the Silver Helmets, so called because of the number of cuirassier helmets left on the field. From Brussels, through *The Times*, Nurse Edith Cavell notifies the nation that British casualties will have to be catered for in Belgium, and appeals for support.

---

[34] Thanks to Mr Richard Rosenthal for information on the Premier.

[35] Messenger, op cit, p. 50.

[36] Clayton, op cit, p. 20.

[37] Martin Gilbert, op cit, p. 41; Max Hastings, *Catastrophe: Europe Goes To War 1914*, p. 149.

August 13th.

We arrived outside Havre, moving dead slow and finally stopped and waited for about two hours as all the landing space in the harbour was fully occupied. At last at 9 o'clock we got in amid many other transports and began to unload. The absolute completeness of it all was what most impressed me, everything and everybody being, as the Tommies say, "In the Pink." Lorries swung out, and started away with one turn of the handle; aeroplanes stood ready to take off; cars and motor cycles, brand new and in perfect condition, ready to move off on the first feel of solid ground beneath their wheels. I thought of my old motor cycle I had patched up somehow to bring me to London. But here nothing was makeshift, everything was 100 percent.

We had crossed with the Royal Sussex and the Coldstream Guards, and on arrival cycled up to Camp No 7 on the top of the hill above Harfleur. It was a hot dusty day, and we arrived with thirsts like nothing on earth. Bevan and I were first up and got a wonderful drink of sour red wine from a French *Piou-Piou*.[38] As for water there was hardly any, just one tap and since this was right on the top of the hill it would only dribble feebly.

The assembly of the BEF in France.
The following week had nothing worth recording other than what is in the official war diary. All I know is that everybody and everything conspired together to make us as uncomfortable as possible. The camp was filthy, there were no adequate arrangements for cooking, and I have never spent a more squalid week. If one had only been allowed to sleep in a hedge somewhere it would have been better. The complement of my tent consisted, as far as I remember, of Powell, GA Gladstone, WG Fletcher, RB Bourdillon, T Breen, WG Gabain, KF Gemmel, JT Seabrook. They were a fine crowd, well educated and all of them speaking several languages, German and French of course being essential in our organisation.

But such close quarters was stifling and I went and slept in a chaff loft. Seabrook (who was killed later on August 27th 1914) came along too, and later Breen. The chaff got into one's clothes and everything, and at night the rats burrowed in it and ran along the rafters. Anyway, one could spread out a bit.

Our bicycles had stood out in the open, but we finally got them under a barn. C Molyneux Smith and Montague Tanner Rogers looked after them more or less, that is to say when they were not chauffing [sic] for various officers.[39] The rest of what we did here, and all the beastly life we led, are they not written in the first page of the Official War Diary which here followeth?

---

[38] Slang term for infantryman. More about Bevan in list below.

[39] Few people could drive in 1914, and anyone who could might be called upon to chauffeur a staff car.

Taken from Official War Diary of the Intelligence Corps

August 12th: Intelligence Corps under Captain Torrie, 27th Indian Cavalry, left Southampton on SS "Olympia."

August 13th: Reached Le Havre 9 o'clock with Royal Sussex and Coldstream Guards. Camped above Harfleur. No arrangements of any sort made.

August 14th: Passed at Harfleur, completing equipment and instructions in reconnaissances. Hasty demolitions, etc. On the second day heavy rain fell and camp a sea of mud. Roads almost impassable for motor traffic, and caused great deal of delay to transport.

August 17th: Cyclists turned out at 2 AM with lamps to light Blackwatch [sic] transport out of camp. Leave "Sunbeam" behind.[40]

August 19th: Corps left for front. Mounted sections to Le Cateau by rail. Cycles to Le Cateau via Amiens for the night.

August 20th: At Amiens route changed from road via Cambrai to road via St Quentin owing to proximity of German cavalry to former route.

Intelligence Corps

Capt. TGJ Torrie[41]	27th Indian Cavalry (IA)
Capt. J Montgomery	7th Dragoon Guards
Capt. FW Hunt[42]	19th Cavalry (IA)
Capt. JA Dunnington Jefferson	Royal Fusiliers
Capt AEG MacCallum[43]	late 4th Hussars
Lieut. AH Lean	late Highland Light Infantry
Lieut. DCM Laurie	8th Hussars
Lieut. GH Bell	South Lancashire Regiment
Lieut. AH Smith Cumming	Seaforth Highlanders (killed in motor smash)[44]
Lieut. JHM Cornwall	Royal Field Artillery
Lieut. AC Grame Harrison	late 4th Hussars
Lieut. AM Nicholson	late 14th Hussars
2nd Lt. (temp) QMS AE Richardson	Rifle brigade

---

[40] Likely a Sunbeam motorcycle that was left for camp service.

[41] The IC Commandant, soon to be Major Torrie; he had been on leave from the Indian Army and was anxious not to miss the war through being posted back to India. Later he left the IC to command a cavalry squadron. He was killed at the Somme in 1916.

[42] Killed at Gheluvelt, First Ypres.

[43] Anthony Clayton lists this man as MacCullan (op cit, p. 261) but West uses MacCallum through his account.

[44] Near Meaux, 1914, in the course of the Great Retreat.

Scout Officers:

2nd Lieut. P Alsopp
"   " Lord B Blackwood[45]
"   " G Chapman
"   " P Cockerell, examiner of documents
"   " E de Trafford
"   " AJ Evans, examiner of documents
"   " F Hughes
"   " EH King, 19th Infantry Brigade[46]
"   " Sir M Monson
"   " CR Williams
"   " J Martin Smith (killed)[47]
"   " J Addison (Laissez Passer)[48]
"   " C Agnew, examiner of German prisoners
"   " EH Barker, 18th Hussars
"   " FH Bevan, 5th Independent Cavalry Brigade ([made] prisoner)[49]
"   " WL Blenner Hasset, EGP[50]
"   " LO Bosworth, Staff
"   " RB Bourdillon, examiner of documents 3 Army
"   " T Breen, examiner of documents ([made] prisoner)
"   " GE Bridges
"   " GMO Campbell, photographer
"   " W Chapman
"   " WD Drury (wounded)
"   " C Fairbairn (*Légion d'Honneur*)
"   " WG Fletcher, 19th Infantry Brigade and Royal Welsh Fusiliers (killed)[51]
"   " WG Gabain, Cavalry Division[52]
"   " KF Gemmel, 3rd Army Headquarters

---

[45] Killed at the Yser Canal, 1917.

[46] Killed at Third Ypres.

[47] Smith was killed a mere three weeks into the war, but at the very outset, at Mons on August 24th, he had, while attached to the 9th Lancers, volunteered to help save the six guns of 119 Field Battery, RFA. See Clayton, op cit, p. 22.

[48] Responsible for issuing and vetting *laissez passers*—identification papers with permits to move in the war zone. At a time of paranoia and "spy fever" these were essential documents, as West will discover.

[49] See West's entry for September 1st for more detail.

[50] EGP—Examiner of German Prisoners. Clayton has the more usual spelling, Blennerhasset, op cit, p. 262.

[51] Sniped near Neuve Chapelle, 20 March 1915. More on Fletcher later.

[52] Killed in Flanders, 1918.

"   " CA Gladstone, Royal Flying Corps ([made] prisoner)

"   " JV Hay (*Légion d'Honneur*)

"   " HW Le Grand ([made] prisoner)

"   " CL Lindenman

"   " JG Lumsden, 4th Cipher

"   " WL McEwan, 3rd Army Headquarters

"   " EW Powell, Royal Flying Corps

"   " MT Rogers, General Headquarters

"   " A Sang, 19th Infantry Brigade (wounded at the Marne, September 8th, 1914; died in hospital of wounds, October 26th, 1914)[53]

"   " EG Sawyer, Cavalry Division

"   " JT Seabrook, 8th Indian Cavalry Brigade (killed 10/9/14)

"   " RF Speir, Cavalry Division

"   " M Spicer, Royal Flying Corps

"   " RRF West, 19th Infantry Brigade

"   " H Wolf Murray, examiner of documents[54]

We find more small inconsistencies in West's account. According to Major Baird, the ship docked at 11:00 o'clock, but as West is working here not from his own notes but the Official War Diary of the IC he can hardly be blamed (and either time is as likely to be correct). The "fine crowd" were not all so well educated and proficient as West remembers: on August 11th "a French exam was held and 12 [men] 'plucked', i.e. sacked".[55]

Such minor factual inconsistency is congruent with truthful testimony. West dates the death of JT Seabrook initially as August 27th, but in his subsequent list he gives the date as September 10th, the correct one, as Seabrook was killed in action at the Battle of the Marne. Seabrook's Christian names were actually James Herbert, according to his obituary notice; Anthony Clayton, historian of the Intelligence Corps, claims that Seabrook died in Flanders, but Seabrook's obituary notice reveals that this is not correct. (Incidentally, his commanding officer, Lieutenant FF Blake, wrote to Seabrook's mother that he had "done splendid work for me and was immensely popular with all", before reassuring her that he must have died "very quickly and painlessly" as he was shot in the head—something that may or may not have been the case, as there was an understandable wish to mitigate loved ones' anguish.)

---

[53] Sang actually died on 2 October, in No 8 General Hospital, Rouen. His War Office file (PRO, WO 339/10578), in one document erroneously dates his death as 5 October, the confusion of war affecting more than a front-line soldier's understanding. More on Sang later.

[54] Wolfe-Murray.

[55] Clayton, op cit, p. 20.

The list of Intelligence Corps personnel is not a definitive one for the time, even by West's inadvertent admission: he fails to include here Drury, Richardson and Pilcher whom he mentions in his entry for August 11th (and subsequently in that for August 20th), and Lieutenant E Burney, alluded to on August 29th. The Hon Maurice Baring, a distinguished writer and diplomat, also joined in August 1914,[56] and Major Torrie soon was to be replaced by Captain Wavell (later Field Marshall Lord Wavell).[57] Another omission is Elliott Hotblack, who later won the MC and the DSO and "who in military career terms was the most successful of the 'originals' [of the IC]"—though he only was appointed in September,[58] which accounts for his absence from West's list. Also missing is the colourful Sigismund Payne Best, who crossed to France a week after West and was much later captured by the Gestapo in the Venlo Incident of 1939.[59] It's significant that Clayton does not list these men either. Despite a mistake or two in transcription, it's quite clear that he and West both drew on the Official History of the IC in compiling their accounts, so the Official History's list is incomplete. There may be good reasons for this. There may be room for investigation.

Later (August 20th) West summarises his colleagues as "scientists, stock-brokers and what-not", as one might expect of an Intelligence Corps, but there were some duds, in motorcycling ability as well as in linguistic skills. William Lewis Blenner Hasset, or Blennerhasset, as the name is usually spelled, "whose efforts on a motor cycle had been the standing joke of the camp", as West describes him, "and was constantly coming off", survived the war to become a stockbroker, and in 1933 embarrassed himself again by suing for libel over a claim that he "had gone stark, raving mad from diddling with yo-yos"—and losing, with costs.[60] One can imagine West chuckling at this news, when the London papers reached him (probably in British Columbia), for quite without a yo-yo Blennerhassett was mad enough. Of Irish and German parentage, he knew many of the Bavarian nobility, including Prince Rupprecht, commander of the German Sixth Army, but his German was "fluent but not very accurate", and he was regarded by his peers as anything from "slightly crazy" to "an extraordinary madman". His eccentricity did not take from Blennerhassett's war record, though, for he once crossed No Man's Land and persuaded several Germans to desert, and won the *Croix de Guerre*.[61]

---

[56] Clayton, op. cit. p. 22.

[57] JP Kelleher, *The Royal Fusiliers (the City of London Regiment) and the Intelligence Corps 1914-1920*.

[58] Jim Beach, *Haig's Intelligence: GHQ and the German Army, 1916-1918*, p. 71.

[59] Messenger, op cit, p. 51.

[60] Kelleher, op. cit.

[61] Beach, op cit, p. 70.

The list shows that several Intelligence Corps personnel were made prisoner, of whom one, it is alleged, was captured after he "was clever enough to fill his tank with water instead of petrol," for all his intelligence—see the account of despatch rider WH Tait.[62] However, one must not be too judgemental, or indeed underestimate the power of stories to grow legs, especially in time of war. West himself accidentally put water in his petrol tank—on the very day stipulated by Tait, August 25th, so possibly Tait heard a distorted version of this—and Willie Watson had a mechanic do the same to his motorcycle on September 2nd.[63] Neither man was captured, however, and one ought to treat Tait's account of this incident with some circumspection (though it is a fine and valuable account overall). The power of rumour and exaggeration are also illustrated by the case of Lieutenant Bevan, described in West's entry for September 1st.

Blennerhassett was not the only eager volunteer to exaggerate his motorcycling abilities. James Marshall-Cornwall has already been referred to in this regard; "I had never ridden a motorcycle. Being a field gunner I was fortunately allotted to the mounted section". Stanley Casson tried it on too, but he was rejected (though eventually commissioned elsewhere).[64]

The "motorcycles, brand new and in perfect condition," do not long remain thus; within three weeks—on August 30th—West speaks of his "old" Premier; later (on September 18th) he estimates the life of a motorcycle at the front as "only a matter of weeks".

West is inconsistent in his spelling, sometimes using "Head Quarters", sometimes "Headquarters", the inconsistency part of a pattern that shows he revisited his diary between jotting down events and submitting his typescript to the IWM; for consistency, "Headquarters" is used throughout here.

At the end of this list is the following: "(Note in diary.) *Spy Car?* 40 HP Grey Renault. With light body. 706XC"—presumably the registration number. This was a time of "spy mania" when everyone was seeing, or thought he was seeing, spies, and the closer the BEF gets to the action, the more paranoid everyone gets, justifiably or otherwise. Tom Bridges was uneasy on the eve of Mons when he observed many young men cycling northward toward the enemy.[65] "At that period German Staff Officers in plain clothes were working ahead, spreading false news and trying to create panics."[66] The fear of "spy

[62] IWM collection reference PP/MCR/161.
[63] Watson, op cit, p. 70.
[64] See entry for August 12th; Messenger, op. cit. p. 50; Stanley Casson, *Steady Drummer*, p. 33.
[65] Tom Bridges, *Alarums and Excursions: Reminiscences of a Soldier*, p. 76.
[66] JC Dunn, *The War the Infantry Knew 1914-1919: A Chronicle of Service in France and Belgium*, p. 38.

cars" could have tragic consequences and innocent people were killed at the wheel.[67] General Jack Seely was arrested by French officers at gunpoint very early in the campaign,[68] West himself almost fell victim of the paranoia on September 9th, while Paul Maze, another motorcyclist, serving with Hubert Gough's cavalry, had an even narrower squeak.[69] West's cryptic entry may be an uncompleted retrospective speculation on the "big grey car" West observes later on August 28th, its headlamps shining on the passing British troops and later reported "travelling rapidly northwards toward the Germans". Looking back from 1930 Lieutenant Spears mentions how "we all remember the 'blue' car full of spies or the 'red' car crammed with Huns that haunted the roads in those days",[70] but spies were active in the war zone, and one car, indeed a grey one, contained two spies disguised as British staff officers. These, though acknowledged to be "plucky fellows", were of course shot.[71]

Spies weren't very active in Britain. With most of their agents there interned since the opening of hostilities,[72] German intelligence falsely reports the BEF as having landed at Ostende, Calais and Dunkirk (the British have actually landed at Rouen, Boulogne and Le Havre); at the same time Prince Rupprecht, commander of the Sixth German Army, is informed that they have *not* landed and might not be deployed at all. The BEF is far ahead of the Germans in intelligence.

Fighting continues along the Franco-German border and in Belgium. Lanrezac grows more worried about his prospects.

The Times proclaims Britain's first naval victory in the war: the capture of a German gunboat on Lake Nyasa.

August 19th.

Advance to the front.

At last we got away from our abominable quarters. The mounted section entrained for Le Cateau, and the rest of us on motor cycles went by road via Yvetot to Amiens. It was a long ride, some two hundred or three hundred kilometres in all, but it was a good thing for some who were not used to

---

[67] Lyn Macdonald, *1914*, p. 226.

[68] Brough Scott, *Galloper Jack: The Remarkable Story of the Man who Rode a Real War Horse*, p. 172. While looking down a revolver Seely's *sang froid* companion, the Duke of Westminster, remarked, "It seems rather rough luck for these people to shoot us just when we have come such a long way to cheer them up."

[69] Paul Maze, *A Frenchman in Khaki*, p. 45.

[70] Spears, op cit, p. 18.

[71] A Corbett-Smith, *The Retreat from Mons*, p. 132.

[72] A few remained at large, notably Karl Lody.

their machines. Blenner Hasset, whose efforts on a motor cycle had been the standing joke of the camp, finally went by car. He had been seen one day pushing his machine up the Harfleur hill because, as he said, he "was looking for something". But actually I think he preferred to push it than ride it. He was constantly coming off, but was always game to take another try on a machine of any size, shape and power.

It was one long race, this ride. Everybody had brand new machines in tip-top order and "ran them in" properly. Nobody ever thought of going under forty miles per hour once they got the hang of the machines; in fact many went over forty without even knowing the elements of a motor cycle. The amazing part was there was only one smash, and that was when Fairbairn got his rifle in his front wheel and came a sprawler in the grass. He did not suffer appreciably but his rifle barrel was bent and twisted from the stock.

I shall always remember that ride. It was just in the rose season, and fruit was beginning to ripen. The inhabitants of the countryside lined the road for miles, and handed us roses, pears, apples, dahlias, and cigarettes, or if we were going too fast they just threw flowers at us—but had the discretion not to throw the fruit which might have been misinterpreted. The troops who had passed on ahead had had a similar reception. So it came about that we advanced up-country over roads literally strewn with "roses, roses all the way."

Nothing was too good for the British. Wherever they stopped red wine and food were immediately proffered. The dust rose chokingly from the columns as we passed, and the red wine tasted very good. Seabrook, Bosworth and I, on a Triumph, a Rudge and Premier respectively, had a tremendous race for miles and miles, passing and repassing. My Premier was the slowest on the level, but on the hills generally gained, but Bosworth's Rudge finally burned out a valve, and we passed him with many insulting remarks. We were advancing, though few could tell exactly where, and there was a sort of reckless exhilaration in the air.

The motor lorries were also being driven at a similarly crazy speed. They would go swaying and bumping on their solid tires down the long steep hills in clouds of dust and were perilous things to pass, as they were all over the road and one could hardly see for dust. Catastrophes were numerous, and many a fine lorry was seen in the ditch, or thoroughly worsted in an argument with a tree!

At last we reached Amiens, and those who had arrived got a meal at the Station Cafe. The Hotel de l'Universe was a Headquarters of some sort, and our billet was away in a school where we parked our motor cycles in the playground. Our quarters were more or less dirty, but we had plenty of straw in the hall, and settled ourselves in. Later we went for a walk up the Western road. Long columns of Mechanical Transport were now coming up, and the inhabitants of Amiens were out along the roadside welcoming them in. There was much surprise and delight at the marvellous equipment of the British Expeditionary Force, a force which obviously they had considered more in the light of a pretty and expensive toy than a fighting unit. (At that time I had no true conception of the relative sizes of our little Army compared with a continental one such as that of the French, and it was rather an eye-opener to find that we were not received as a gigantic and invincible force.) It may have been only my personal impression, but it seemed to me that as a whole the people of Amiens were not quite so friendly to the British as those of most towns we went through. But where everybody was so kind comparisons are odious and ungrateful.

Several days have passed since West's last entry, something he does not explain but which reflects the busy time the new Intelligence Corps was having. While West and his chums were joy-riding on their motorcycles, their colleagues were "spending two days developing a reporting system in and around Mons which provided useful information in the early stages of the retreat".[73] The fine work of the cavalry here has already been described and there can be little doubt that the most exclusive unit of the British Army collaborated with the very newest in securing this "useful information".

"... there was a sort of reckless exhilaration in the air": there's something poignant in this day's account, something innocent as well as reckless in the exhilaration; something of the lull before the storm. These were young men with young men's high spirits and subconscious feelings of invincibility, and many of them were not to grow much older. Housman's lines from "Here Dead Lie We" come to mind: "Life, to be sure, is nothing much to lose; / But young men think it is, and we were young."

That the French "had the discretion not to throw fruit" at passing soldiers is the sort of understated dry wit these patrician young men would have considered "good form", and which West occasionally indulges.

The performance of West's Premier on hills can be credited to its unusual system of exhaust-gas scavenging, barrel-ports feeding into a secondary manifold. Quite radical designs had characterised Edwardian engineering experimentation, and the Premier is an example. A friend's 1911 model "certainly has more power on hills than a contemporary 500 Triumph" thanks to the Premier's unique feature.[74] Exhaust-valve failure was a common fault on side-valve engines at the time—and almost all motorcycles used side valves,

[73] Clayton, op cit, pp. 20-21.

[74] Thanks to Mr Richard Rosenthal for information on the Premier. Auxiliary ports for both intake and exhaust had featured in engine design through the Edwardian age, e.g. the Dorman aero engine (see E Charles Vivian, *A History of Aeronautics*, p. 409) but by now were being abandoned for straightforward poppet-valve design.

overhead valves being rather exotic and far less reliable—but valves are easily replaced with this design.

As a rule DRs did not carry rifles, because these were cumbrous, as Fairbairn's experience shows, and besides DRs, being non-combatant troops—as a rule—were unlikely to need them. Sidearms were issued, but few DRs had occasion to use them. At the time, though, there was much variation from division to division, and West was in the IC, just two weeks old and still finding its feet.

French "surprise and delight at the marvellous equipment of the British Expeditionary Force" is a reminder that the BEF was, relatively speaking, the most mechanised army in the world in 1914—though most cars and lorries were commercial vehicles that had been subsidised by government and subject to commandeering. A couple of days later a French officer with liaison officer Lieutenant Louis Spears—whom West will meet on September 1st—will be "rendered almost speechless by the sight of these fighting men".[75]

That "it was rather an eye-opener to find that we were not received as a gigantic and invincible force" is a reminder of the imperious attitude of the time: "Fog on the Channel; Continent isolated". However arrogant and infuriating it may have been to subject-peoples, to what extent was the British superiority complex responsible for eventual victory? People of West's station seem to have been literally incapable of conceiving defeat of the Land of Hope and Glory, and the "lower orders" took their cue from their "betters".

West's spelling "tire" reflects his many years spent in America. The fact that "tires" is a cursive insertion, and the fact that elsewhere in the typescript he uses British spelling such as "tyre" and "waggon", along with other such clues, indicates that his account was revisited and revised over a good long while.

In the six days of West's silence a lot has been happening.

On the 14th Sir John French lands in France and the BEF begins to march toward its proposed area of concentration around Maubeuge; it's "roses all the way" from the French,[76] wildly relieved to have their *ennemi ancien* stand with them now against the *sale Boche* of more recent and more bitter memory—though some, Lanrezac notably, continue to suspect Albion of perfidy, and one Old Contemptible was "informed ... that the opinion of the upper and middle classes of Rouen was that Great Britain had only come into the War for what she could make out of it, and that if she could see there was nothing to be gained she would soon withdraw her army".[77]

---

[75] Spears, op cit, p. 120.

[76] Barbara Tuchman as well as West quotes the phrase—op cit, p. 233.

[77] Frank Richards, *Old Soldiers Never Die*, p. 12.

This day Lanrezac, unconvinced that the British will fight at all, personally pleads with Joffre to be allowed to turn the Fifth Army to face the German forces marching on his flank, rather than toward the Ardennes. Joffre refuses, being committed to an offensive in Lorraine, and all-out assault along the frontier, assuming that the German First and Second Armies will confine themselves to east of the Meuse, as flank support to the other German armies as the Fifth is meant to be supportive of the other French armies. Joffre holds onto this delusion even as General Manfred von Richthofen's cavalry advances on Dinant to secure a Meuse crossing. But now Lanrezac's apprehensions are beginning to be shared by others, most notably Joseph Gallieni, a studious-looking old soldier soon to become famous for his role at the Marne, and the Fifth Army arrives in time to contest Richthofen's crossing.

On the 15th Japan declares for the Entente, freeing large numbers of Russian soldiers for deployment on the Eastern Front, to German concern about the Eighth Army's prospects and creating something close to panic in Berlin. People of social and political importance begin to importune the Kaiser to reinforce East Prussia; this will have consequences for events in France.

In Paris Sir John French meets the French government and GQG; smiles all round until he announces that the BEF will be unable to take the field until the 24th—the French had expected him to join forces with Lanrezac by the 21st. Sir John's lack of urgency and enterprise ought to be read in light of the fact that he is not told of the size of the force bearing down on him and Lanrezac—indeed, he is given to understand that he will be facing no more than two corps and a division of cavalry, rather than about a quarter of a million men. He will continue to dismay his ally, though, and suitably dismayed now, Joffre deploys three territorial divisions under General Albert d'Amade to string the gap between Maubeuge and the Channel. This force, somewhat overlooked by history, will help prevent the II Corps from being outflanked at Le Cateau. More importantly, Joffre at last authorises Lanrezac to turn to meet the invading forces on the Sambre. With almost 80 miles to march, Lanrezac sets out, filled with foreboding.

On the 16th an artist of circumscribed ability on the run from military service in Austria enlists in a Bavarian regiment. Of more immediate relevance to world affairs than the activities of Adolf Hitler, the last Liège fort falls. The Kaiser and OHL move to Coblenz, the better to direct battle and hoping to ameliorate by relative proximity to the front the enormous problems in wireless communication in which they've placed almost total reliance. But the length and convexity of the German front mandates that in order to coordinate activities along it OHL be positioned much farther behind it than the Allies' GHQ and GQG. Distance "blunts the curve" of wireless transmission and causes ultimately fatal communications problems. On the bright side, however, distance from the front means that the Kaiser can do relatively little damage to command and control.

Further problems are now to emerge as strategic objectives are compromised by tactical temptations. The French are attacking in Lorraine with all the *élan* they can muster and Prince Rupprecht, commander of the German Sixth—and effectively Seventh—Army, begins to convince himself that rather than draw them into a "sack", as mandated by Schlieffen, he rather ought to counter-attack and bring about a double-envelopment of the enemy in a battle of Cannae-like decisiveness and magnificence. In his ambition, he discounts Lorraine's geomorphological obstacles to such envelopment.

On the 17th Rupprecht demands permission of OHL to counterattack—granted. Meanwhile Russian General Rennenkamf''s infantry follows earlier cavalry incursions into East Prussia, while Samsonov's Second Army moves from Russian Poland in the south, increasing OHL nervousness about the Eighth Army's ability to hold off the Russian hordes. The Germans attack at Stallupönen, rather than contain the invaders. Schlieffen's grand scheme, never much more than wishful thinking, is crumbling.

Back in the West, General von Kluck, commander of the German First Army, is subordinated to the more cautious von Bülow of the Second. This is to prevent the courageous but impetuous Kluck from opening a gap between the two armies, but it compromises his ability to envelop any enemy encountered, and envelopment is both traditional Prussian strategy and at the heart of the Schlieffen Plan.

The Belgian army falls back on Antwerp, breaking contact with Anglo-French forces but frustrating German designs to smash it in the field, and instead becoming a threat to Kluck's lines of communication and supply. Lanrezac's dread of being overwhelmed by superior forces is dismissed by GQG as "premature". Prematurely and to British disappointment, General Sir James Grierson dies. His linguistic skills and expertise on the German armies will be greatly missed but the pace of the Retreat likely would have killed him anyway, overweight and out of condition as he was (his favourite joke was that he fought his best campaigns with a knife and fork). He is replaced as commander of the II Corps by Sir Horace Smith-Dorrien, famous for his temper but "a straight, honourable gentleman"; "Never was a British general less hidebound by the traditions and prejudices of the Regular Army".[78] But this formidable man is appointed much against the wishes of Sir John French, who now has another grudge to add to his collection and a

---

[78] Spencer Jones and Steven J Corvi, "'A Commander of Rare and Unusual Coolness': General Sir Horace Lockwood Smith-Dorrien", in *Stemming the Tide: Officers and Leadership in the British Expeditionary Force 1914*, pp. 157, 154.

strong-willed hothead with a history of insubordination to keep his mind off fighting Germans.

Up to 63 Serbian peasants are bayoneted to death—"In order not to upset [Austrian] soldiers by [the sound of] shooting"—and fourteen hanged.[79] Photographs of the corpses are distributed as warning not to resist the Austrian invasion.

On the 18th Joffre's Order 13 directs his Third and Fourth Armies to attack into the Ardennes, difficult country to fight in, with support from Lanrezac's Fifth. Lanrezac, marching toward the Sambre to try to stop the German First and Second Armies, is placed in an invidious, even impossible position by this latest directive, which is at utter odds with his previous one; but GQG cheers him up: "If the Germans commit the imprudence of an enveloping manoeuvre through northern Belgium, so much the better! ... the easier it will be for us to break through their centre".[80] No doubt adding to Lanrezac's foreboding, though of some encouragement to Sir John French, General Sordet's cavalry is detached in order to support the British left flank—where, with d'Amade's Territorial forces, it will prove to be needed.

On the 19th the French counterattack the Germans at Mulhouse, opening the "official" Battles of the Frontiers. Looking on in mounting horror, Lieutenant Louis Spears concludes: "only despair and the strength of despair could furnish the motive force" for such violence.[81] The first French general, Plessier, dies of *cran*.

French cavalry, saddle-callused, shod-worn and spurred skinny, enter Brussels, followed by a few British officers in motor cars. They are far too late: the government has fled to Antwerp and the Germans are about to invest the city. Lanrezac is informed that Namur, shockingly, is about to fall—it had been believed capable of holding out for six months.

Problems with German communications are exacerbated by civilian sabotage—time for a little more *schrecklichkeit* ("frightfulness"). A series of "severe and inexorable reprisals" is initiated; 20 Belgian POWs and 76 civilians are murdered in Aerschott and the town is burned. General von Hausen, commander of the Third Army, is unaccountably puzzled by "the hostility of the Belgian people" he encounters afterward. The Kaiser proclaims his infamous dismissal of the BEF—to the great mirth of the "Old Contemptibles" he's dared to disdain, now moving up to meet the "Huns" Wilhelm prides himself on commanding, their own British complacency and certitude of invincibility soon to be sorely tried.[82]

---

[79] Hastings, op cit, p. 148.

[80] Tuchman, op. cit, p. 253.

[81] Spears, op cit, p. 106.

[82] Tuchman, op cit, pp. 255-56; Hastings, op cit, p. 190.

Schrecklichkeit is justified by Clausewitz's endorsement of terror as a legitimate way to shorten wars and thereby save lives. (At the time of the South African War a German officer allegedly remarked, "With us terror is our greatest weapon".[83]) Shortage of troops to garrison towns along attenuated supply lines would make it acceptable and logical to army commanders, so acceptable—indeed, in Clausewitz's way of looking at things so humane— that its use is proclaimed to the world as warning without any sense of shame. The rector of Louvain University observes that in the destruction of the great library there "The Germans ... definitely broke with wisdom and with civilisation", but during the sack of the town a German officer cordially encourages an observer to take photographs: "go ahead. You will find some beautiful things over there on the corner in the house they are getting ready to burn".[84]

Elsewhere, overcoming minor setback at Stallupönen, the Russians have invaded East Prussia, to great alarm in Berlin, and in Galicia they're scaring the superciliousness out of Conrad von Hötzendorff, Chief of Staff of the Austrian *Armeeoberkommando* (AOK). Far off in *Ostafrika*, General Paul von Lettow-Vorbeck has disregarded the palliative directives of Governor Heinrich Schnee and invaded the Belgian Congo and British East Africa, occupying Taveta. In response, Indian Expeditionary Force C is despatched to sort him out; but Lettow-Vorbeck is to lead combined British, Belgian and Portuguese forces a merry dance for over four years, only surrendering on November 25th, 1918.

August 20th.

We rode down to the Eastern Road in the morning with our voluminous kit piled high on the carriers. Here we were served out ammunition, and Captain MacCallum, a regular Army officer, endeavoured to put the fear of the Lord in his flock of irregulars with terrible tales of the Germans we were going to meet. He was a bit of a wag and I don't think anybody took him very seriously.

We were told to go on to Le Cateau via Cambrai. This route, however, was changed as the German cavalry was out on the warpath at Cambrai, and it was not considered advisable to hurl members of the Intelligence Corps, consisting of scientists, stockbrokers and what-not, into a bloody battle without further training! So we detoured through St Quentin. With

---

[83] Corbett-Smith, op cit, p. 65.

[84] Jeff Lipkes, *Rehearsals: The German Army in Belgium, August 1914*, p. 537. For more on the Belgian atrocities see Larry Zuckerman's *The Rape of Belgium: The Untold Story of World War I*, and John Horne and Alan Kramer's *German Atrocities 1914: A History of Denial*.

occasional misdirection, occasional breakdowns, and always an everlasting thirst and dust, we reached Le Cateau at last. Passing in front of the school with its big stone arch we roared up the hill and round to the left at the top. Here I met Sergeant E Longley, a Regular Army sergeant attached to Cambridge University Officers Training Corps, Royal Engineers, also on a motor cycle. Thence we turned to the right, and so down to a rotten little billet in an empty house with no trace of anything except the floor to sleep on. Fairbairn, MacEwan and others got a much better billet across the way, with numerous spare beds. By now our nerves were probably more highly strung than we knew, and it was only after a lengthy palaver with Fairbairn that I got a mattress on the floor next to Pilcher. Gabain was just across the road, also Gladstone and various others.

The British are far ahead of the Germans in intelligence, aware of the enemy presence miles away at Cambrai two days before Kluck bumps into the BEF at Mons. The "everlasting thirst and dust" is to be the least of West's problems, though problems they remain—until the dust changes to mud. In an age of tarmac it's almost impossible to conceive the hazard and discomfort that dust was on the unsealed roads of a century ago, especially for despatch riders. The "rotten little billet" is something upon which many may have looked back wistfully through the Great Retreat, when a field might be the only place to sleep and many despatch riders would find themselves in the saddle round the clock.

The last Belgian forces reach the fastness of Antwerp. German troops, "their ranks closed to eliminate the gaps left by the missing" and wearing "expressions of studied scorn", occupy Brussels, just a day behind schedule; they impose on the people an indemnity of 50 million francs and give them ten days to come up with it. At Morhange further German outrages follow an engagement.[85]

The Battles of the Frontiers are raging now. Labouring under the deluded virtue of *élan à outrance*, the French not merely have disdained anything heavier than the *soixante-quinze* to support field troops (in 1909 a staff officer had reported to the Chamber of Deputies, "Thank God we have none [no heavy artillery]"), their Plan XVII has gone so far as to stipulate that even the 75mm may be used only in direct support of infantry attacks—no preliminary bombardment. Unsurprisingly, their First and Second Armies are cut to ribbons by Rupprecht's much heavier artillery long before their poor *poilous* get a chance to blood their bayonets, for in addition to artillery superiority, the

---

[85] Tuchman, op cit, pp. 258-59.

Germans have taken defensive positions on tactically advantageous ground, forcing the French to attack across open country.

But his very success is to lead Prince Rupprecht to compromise the Schlieffen Plan further than he's persuaded OHL to depart from it already. Rupprecht, a personable German with a "sensible" moustache—sensible alongside his Kaiser's, certainly—comes from a "less eccentric branch of the [Wittelsbach] family" than the one that gave the world Mad King Ludwig. A descendant of Louis XIV, he also will fall heir to the Stuart claim to British monarchy, but with defeat of the Second Reich he will forgo even the Bavarian throne.[86]

After taking Brussels, the Germans move toward the Franco-Belgian border, their anxiety to knock France out of the war quickly and deal with the Russian Bear at relative leisure all the greater with Russian troops on Prussian soil. But Lanrezac has reached the Sambre now, to contest passage. GQG assures him that "Reports on German forces in Belgium are greatly exaggerated. There is no reason to get excited." Not much: only two armies to beat, plus elements of a third. GQG's encouragement is wasted on Lanrezac, who rather is plunged deeper into gloom by such self-deceiving nonsense. Joffre, by contrast, and inconsistent with his dismissal of reports of them as exaggerated, relishes the prospect of large German forces advancing on the Fifth because it increases the likelihood of the Fourth Army's assault through the Ardennes breaking the enemy's "hinge" and cutting off from their communications- and supply-lines the German First and Second Armies. This assault is a core component of French Plan XVII. No one has appreciated the scale and significance of the Germans' incorporation of reservists in the front line.[87]

Farther south the French re-take much-contested Mulhouse, but in face of the threat from Rupprecht's armies, withdraw from the rest of Alsace, encouraging Rupprecht to delude himself further of enveloping the French right wing as Kluck envelops its left.

Fifty women, children and elderly men are murdered in Nomeny and the town is burned; as many are killed at Seilles. The town of Ardenne likewise is razed and possibly 211 civilians killed. Looking toward Charleroi, Lieutenant Spears sees "the whole horizon burst into flames.... A chill of horror came

---

[86] Tuchman, op cit, pp. 235-36. Rupprecht was one of the good Germans. With the end of Wittelsbach rule in 1918, the man who would have been King of Bavaria seems to have turned from killing people to curing them. According to Paddy Fermor, Rupprecht had an "unassuming demeanour" and by 1933 was "a distinguished doctor in Munich, and much loved" by his erstwhile subjects—see Patrick Leigh Fermor, *A Time of Gifts*, p. 136. (Like West, Fermor was in the Intelligence Corps and would be awarded the DSO for a daring venture, in his case kidnapping General Heinreich Kriepe in Crete during the next war.)

[87] Tuchman, op cit, pp. 259-60.

over us. War seemed suddenly to have assumed a merciless, ruthless aspect that we had not realised till then."[88]

Off to the east, encouraged by minor victory at Stallupönen, General *der Dicke* von Prittwitz, incompetent, foolish and fat, attacks Rennenkampf's Russian First Army at Gumbinnen; defeat, and the threat from Samsonov's Second Army advancing from the south, unnerves him. This is to lead to his replacement by Paul von Hindenburg and Erich Ludendorff, and the transfer of two full corps from the Western to the Eastern front. The Schlieffen Plan is further compromised.

The Allies have their first land victory when the Austrians retreat in panic from Mount Cer after suffering 28,000 casualties.[89]

August 21st.

The next morning we trooped across to the original billet where were Jock Lean, Cumming, Bell and all the rest of the Intelligence Corps assembled. Here we were allotted our jobs in groups, putting if possible one man of mechanical mind with two others. Powell, Fletcher and Gladstone wanted to get together, but Fletcher was finally fixed up with Sang and Bourdillon, neither of whom he knew, and was very morose about it. Finally Bourdillon was changed and I got his job. We were posted to the 19th Infantry Brigade, at that time back at Amiens, and officially assigned to communications only. This depressed us all as we thought that we would not see any of the war before it was all over. However Fletcher, Sang and I got our things together and rode off to Bussigny.

At Bussigny we entrained and railed back to Amiens, and again went to the school and dumped our goods. The 2nd Royal Welsh Fusiliers were now billeted in another part of the buildings. Up till the time we left, those in authority had impressed us with the fact that, though we had received commissions, we were never under any circumstances to consider ourselves officers,[90] so we were always herded into the most abominable billets, and given even fewer privileges than the Tommies. But we had left that crowd now, and we managed to spread ourselves fairly comfortably in the school hall, where we had plenty of straw, though it was full of fleas.

---

[88] Tuchman, op cit, pp. 263, 351; Ian Senior, *Home Before the Leaves Fall: A New History of the German Invasion of 1914*, p. 66; Spears, op cit, p. 106.

[89] Hastings, op cit, p. 151.

[90] Strictly, West and his colleagues held the "temporary rank of Second Lieutenant". See *Supplement to the London Gazette*, 23 September 1914, p. 7567.

The remarkable 19th Brigade

There's rich irony in the fears of West and his three chums who have been detailed to the 19th Brigade that they "would not see any of the war before it was all over". The 19th had been in charge of lines of communications and the "absolute completeness" of the preparations that so impressed West when he landed at Le Havre was due to the efforts of the brigade to which he was soon seconded. With key points along the advance to Mons prepared, and billets and campsites organised, the Brigade was now free for less pedestrian work.

Through the first days of the Great Retreat the 19th Infantry Brigade formed the extreme left wing of the retreating BEF and, with the cavalry, secured this against German probing attacks. Though fighting alongside the II Corps, the 19th Brigade was, for the moment, under the independent command of Major-General JG Drummond, who suffered breakdown after Le Cateau, as West recounts later. Its Captain James Jack, referred to through West's account, describes the brigade as "nobody's child" until its "permanent attachment" to the 4th Division. "Permanent" often is relative in war, however, and after the BEF moved to Flanders the 19th Brigade was reassigned to the 6th Division. Jack summarises its activities up to First Ypres: "The 19th Brigade was formed practically on the battlefield and short of equipment; was (like others) constantly on the move or in action; was attached seven times to different headquarters, which greatly increased the Staff Captain's administrative duties. It had three changes of commander and three of Brigade Major...."[91]

At Mons "The [19th] Brigade formed, with the possible exception of a couple of cavalry vedettes, the extreme left of the Allied line".[92] Under GHQ control until then, it should have been delegated to Smith-Dorrien's command, especially in light of its position, but instead was seconded to Allenby's; thereby "the Cavalry Division was now tethered somewhat by a force that could only move at the speed of a marching boot".[93] This may be an unfair judgement, for the cavalry's performance was not so compromised that it failed to give a sometimes-splendid account of itself. "For two days it [the 19th Brigade] was to be the Infantry Support in the running fight in which Allenby's Cavalry Division foiled the efforts of the First German Army to envelop the left of the BEF."[94] The Brigade was involved at Mons only late in the afternoon, and had few casualties, as may be gathered from West's

---

[91] James L Jack, *General Jack's Diary*, pp. 47, 58, 61, 77.

[92] Dunn, op cit, p. 18.

[93] Allan Mallinson, *1914: Fight the Good Fight: Britain, the Army & the Coming of the First World War*, p. 302.

[94] Dunn, op cit, p. 19.

account. At Le Cateau, however, it had been transferred to Smith-Dorrien's command and, along with "the 3rd Division and the Cavalry Division to their left … bore the brunt of Kluck's frontal and flank attacks, and the rearguards were in a running fight for much of the day … stumbling into Le Cateau itself at midnight with German cavalry still on their heels". Later two battalions, the 1/Cameronians and 2/Royal Welsh Fusiliers, were positioned along the Le Cateau-Maretz road to cover the II Corps' withdrawal.[95]

Between Mons and Le Cateau the 5th and 3rd Divisions had been swapped over on the march, the 19th Brigade along with the 5th Division, so that at Le Cateau the 19th was on the right wing of the II Corps, which now bore the brunt of the German assault. The two battalions engaged, the 1/Middlesex and 2/Argyll & Sutherland Highlanders, suffered between them 477 casualties: "quality could only tell as far as it could stretch". The 19th retired toward Maurois and helped cover the disengagement of the 5th Division despite its own losses, supported on the left wing by Sordet's cavalry and d'Amade's Territorials.[96]

Not only was it short of equipment, the "orphan brigade" had no despatch riders, hence the secondment of four Scout Officers from the Intelligence Corps, a horseman and three motorcyclists. In a parenthetical and tangential addendum to his entry for September 1st West accounts for the 19th Brigade thus: "The six regular divisions of three brigades each made eighteen brigades. The 19th Brigade was formed in a hurry before Mons from lines of communications troops, and was given a roving commission, an unwanted child [echoing Jack's 'nobody's child'] of the 6th Division [into which it would become incorporated] and generally given the dirty work of any division it was temporarily attached to. Anyway we thought so!"[97]

The diary of 2/Royal Welsh Fusiliers observes "that the 19th Brigade, hurriedly formed as it was and having been on lines of communication, was even more highly tried than the units who had marched up to Mons from the concentration area." Despite this "There was never a murmur of complaint, and the footsore men, and those tired by carrying their packs, stuck it out magnificently". Elsewhere this diary remarks that the brigade—quite apart from its "orphan" status—"must have been at a disadvantage compared to the other Brigades, owing to the number of Reservists we had in the ranks, who had recently re-joined." These constituted at least half of the force marching on Mons, and they were more likely to become footsore both because of their relatively poor condition (in those days before the welfare state, soldiers often fell on hard times after leaving the service), and because their new boots, stiff

---

[95] Mallinson, op cit, pp. 339, 362, 366.

[96] Mallinson, op cit, pp. 366, 382.

[97] This is a cursive afterthought annotated to p. 75 of West's "Diary of the War".

as hob-nailed leather soles could make them, had to be broken in. Despite this, though, "the footsore men, and those tired out by carrying their packs, stuck it out magnificently."[98]

Right through the Retreat the Brigade gives a good account of itself.

> Divisional Generals at that time did not seem to have heard of the 19th Infantry Brigade. The materialization of a "perfectly good" battalion at an unexpected moment, apparently at no one's orders, and at the disposal of the first General Officer who could lay hands on it, had given much satisfaction, if only momentary, to the GOC 3rd Division on the 26th, 5th Division on the 27th and subsequent days, and now [September 1st] the 4th Division was to be similarly blessed.[99]

In fact, by September 1st, the 19th Brigade strictly was no longer an "orphan", the III Corps having been formed on August 31st from the Brigade and the 4th and 6th Divisions, but clearly things were still in flux.

The fleas in the straw are to have consequences for West. Though he himself doesn't complain at being told "never under any circumstances to consider [himself an] officer" or at having "even fewer privileges than the Tommies", some of his colleagues were not impressed: at the very outset there was "Some grousing among Intelligence Corps owing to men who thought they had joined as officers being told they must look after their own horses".[100]

To the BEF's right, in reluctant obedience to orders, Lanrezac prepares to attack Bülow's Second Army across the Sambre, despite the French Fifth Army's having been weakened by the transfer of troops to Lorraine; but Bülow beats him to the punch and opens the Battle of Charleroi. At Tamines the Germans advance behind Belgian human shields. Seven French soldiers are murdered after surrendering, an event that, with others, will become the subject of a war-crimes trial at Leipzig in 1921.

Lanrezac is not the only commander whose forces are weakened: Joffre has formed the Army of Lorraine to meet the onslaught there, stripping three divisions from General Pierre Ruffey's Third Army. Ruffey, regarded by GQG as a nuisance since his earlier warnings of an enemy attack through Belgium, and something of a lunatic for his belief in things like aerial reconnaissance, heavy

---

[98] National Archives, WO95/1365/3/. See also George Coward, *Coward's War: An Old Contemptible's View of the Great War*, p. 17.

[99] Dunn, op cit, pp. 42-43.

[100] Clayton, op cit, pp. 19-20.

artillery and the presence of strong German forces in his front, explodes: "You people at GQG ... are as ignorant as an oyster ... operations are worse than 1870".[101] Next week he will be replaced by Maurice Sarrail.

Rupprecht attacks the French Second Army at Morhange, knocking out its field guns with heavier artillery and then assaulting the infantry. With the Second Army driven back, the First's flank is exposed and it too is forced to retreat. Shortage of heavy artillery is not the only French problem: sky-blue and scarlet uniforms are a giveaway, "quite impractical for modern warfare", as West observes on September 2nd, the *feldgrau* of the foe further camouflaged by thick fog in the Ardennes.[102] Casualties are horrifying. So dense are the dead that they're stacked standing up, "bodies lying in rows on top of each other in an ascending arc from the horizontal to an angle of 60 degrees". The survivor of one regiment that loses half its strength illustrates the power of German artillery: "And [all these losses] even without seeing the enemy! I tell you, we haven't even seen a single German!" But French *élan* persists, with disastrous consequences, generals leading from in front rather than directing from the rear and being cut down "perform[ing] the functions of corporals, not commanders". General Édourd de Castelnau, who had opposed the invasion of Lorraine, receives condolences on the death of his son (one of 10,000 casualties in a single action near Morhange) and responds, "We will continue, gentlemen".[103]

The scale of death is due in part to the low level of training that many French soldiers have received, as well as GQG's extraordinary disdain for heavy artillery. Since 1905 the Two Year Service law has increased the proportion of first-year conscripts and reservists to veterans and the 1913 Three Year Law, while it has increased the raw numbers of recruits, has done nothing to improve their professionalism. Rather, the consequent shortage of training in fire-and-movement means that close-order battlefield tactics are employed. The same tragic outcome of these tactics will be seen in October with the *Kindermord zu Ypern*, and again almost two years later, when the necessity to save the French from going under at Verdun will see the partially-trained Kitchener's Armies slaughtered at the Somme.

Three French battalions are sent to support Namur—far too little; far too late.

Farther off, forces from *Südwestafrika* invade the white Dominion of South Africa.

---

[101] Tuchman, op cit, pp. 270, 272-74.

[102] Some years previously, when debating the proposal to exchange sky-blue-and-scarlet for horizon blue uniforms, a Deputy in the Chamber had protested, "*Le pantalon rouge c'est la France!*"

[103] Tuchman, op cit, pp. 272-74,385, 264; Janet Robinson & Joe Robinson, *Handbook of Imperial Germany*, p. 299.

August 22nd.

Found that the animals above-mentioned [fleas in the straw] had taken complete possession of my left foot, and spoilt it for most walking purposes! We did nothing all day except wander round and curse and send off a few field post cards, as letters were apparently not allowed. At 7 o'clock we went down to the station with EH King of the Mounted Section, IC, and entrained. We had no idea where we were going, and only knew that the Germans were out on the war-path, and we were going to butt into them somewhere. After some delay the train started, ran for a mile, and stopped for half an hour. Then it started again and trundled very slowly along towards the north-east. I suppose we went through Albert, Bapaume and Cambrai, but it was getting dusk and we were tired, so I really don't know.

Fletcher, King, Sang and myself had at least got a carriage to ourselves, and were fairly comfortable, but I could not sleep except for short dozes. It was now quite dark and the train was still rolling on, while the engine uttered long and mournful hoots at intervals of about thirty seconds. Thus we ran on all night, and the hooting of the engine wove itself into my dreams, travelling out into the unknown. (I cannot explain how peculiarly that whistle impressed me, but hearing an exactly similar whistle more than a year later in St Omer I was suddenly carried right back to that night when we lay huddled in the dark railway carriage, running slowly northward to take part in the first shock of the first world war.)

Aerial reconnaissance reveals a German corps marching to outflank the BEF; the report is dismissed as "exaggerated"—that word again—by Sir Henry Wilson, Director of Military Operations, as jolly, devious and tall as Basil Fawlty and with all of Basil's unerring sense of judgment. His "marvellous incapacity to admit error that was to make him ultimately a Field Marshal" will lead Sir Henry to a sticky end when he brings a sword to a gunfight with the IRA, perhaps imagining the danger to mortal flesh from large-calibre revolver-bullets to be as exaggerated as that from a German Army to four mere divisions eight years earlier.[104]

On the very eve of Mons a fifth division, the 4th, arrives, but without artillery and indeed without "the very essentials for a modern battle" so its effectiveness is compromised.[105] Its lack of a Signals Corps will impose an extra workload on the already-overworked despatch riders of the 3rd and 5th Divisions and the 19th Brigade. British strength now constitutes five divisions of infantry and one of cavalry—plus the 19th Brigade.

---

[104] Tuchman, op cit, p. 291.

[105] Mallinson, op cit, p. 350.

A cavalry patrol kills a few Uhlans in Soignies. An RFC plane brings down a German Albatross, but two British planes are shot down over Enghien, at last alerting Kluck to the BEF presence in his front. He requests permission for a westward sweep to envelop the British left flank but instead is instructed to swing eastward to pin the French Fifth Army against Bülow's forces (a manoeuvre Kluck will try again, on his own initiative, on August 31th, only to find that West has beaten him to a critical bridge). Angrily, he requests OHL to release him from Bülow's command in order to pursue the British, but this is refused, and with good reason: the BEF is a minor force; the key to German success is the French Fifth Army. If this can be defeated, the whole French line can be rolled up, the tiny BEF isolated and screened off.

No more good news. The bloodletting of the Battles of the Frontiers continues. This will prove the most sanguinary day of the entire war, with 27,000 Frenchmen alone dead by sundown. At Charleroi Bülow's Second Army attacks Lanrezac's Fifth while the German Third Army tears the Fifth's right flank, exposed by the French Fourth Army's having been driven back in the Battle of Ardennes. At Rossignol the 3rd Colonial Division suffers 4,000 dead and 6,000 wounded or captured, a casualty rate of over 60 percent. At Virton the dead are "stacked like folding chairs". General Foch's only son, and his son-in-law, are killed in action. Deaths beget deaths as the French shoot their own panicked soldiers who flee rather than offer their bodies on Mars' altar. The Germans suffer too: out of then-obscure *Leutant* Ernst Röhm's platoon, "Only three men are still unscathed".[106]

To the south, Rupprecht hectors Moltke into approving "Case 3", a modification of the Schlieffen Plan by which the Sixth and Seventh German Armies attack the French fortress line, the aim being breakthrough and envelopment.[107]

The by-now frantic French try to get the Russians to take pressure off. Samsonov, despite shortages of everything, food and fodder not least, and beset with communications problems, nevertheless crosses the border from Russian Poland into East Prussia. OHL, hardly less frantic at the prospect of two Russian armies annihilating the German Eighth, despatches Erich Ludendorff, "the hero of Liège", to take control of all German forces in the east.

At Tamines up to 384 civilians are killed, the youngest thirteen, the oldest 84, the largest mass-murder of civilians by the Germans until 1939. The Belgians evacuate Namur. Edith Cavell declines a German offer of safe conduct to the Netherlands.

---

[106] Hastings, op cit, p. 180-81; Hew Strachan, *The First World War*, pp. 54-55.

[107] Tuchman, op cit, pp. 353, 265.

The Catholic Austro-Hungarian Empire declares war on Little Catholic Belgium. Russia prohibits alcohol in an attempt to improve performance of army and industry, but thereby deprives itself of about a third of its revenue.

Corporal Edward Thomas, of the Royal Irish Dragoon Guards, fires the first shot in British anger on the Continent in 99 years. Lieutenant Roger West, his foot beginning to swell, has no idea what he's in for.

August 23rd.

Detrainment south of Mons and advance to Mons.

We detrained at Valenciennes, and the 19th Infantry Brigade Headquarters was set up in the First Class Waiting Room at the station, with quite a good restaurant attached. Here we had breakfast, while our cycles stood ready outside, piled high with our belongings.

Like a stranger newly introduced to a party of old friends it was hard for me to take them all in at once. But the staff of the 19th Brigade consisted of the following. First there was General Drummond, a rather distant figure in the Olympian heights to which a mere despatch rider did not aspire.[108] Brigade Major Johnson, a rather quiet personality, but always ready with a word of appreciation for a deed well done. Then there was our staff captain, Jack of the Cameronians, a tall good-looking man of considerable charm, and a distinct sense of humour, which seemed to us irregulars rather a rare quality among the regulars.

Commandant du Vignaux of the French Army acted as our liaison and billeting officer, and was also frequently called upon by the staff to act as interpreter. He was a big burly Frenchman, very affable and amusing, but with that volatility that is popularly attributed to Frenchmen was prepared to explode suddenly in noisy expostulations at any annoyance, followed almost immediately by a large hearty laugh. He drove a large Peugeot car, and his particular grievance was that people thought that it would run without essence, tyres or repairs.[109]

Then there were King of the Mounted Section Intelligence Corps, and G Fletcher, A Sang and myself, also of the Intelligence Corps, but armed with motor cycles and attached nominally as Intelligence Officers, virtually as despatch riders. Also Churchill of the Signals.

EH King was a slight, well set up man, with that indescribable something that is sometimes called "horsey." I think he had been in Canada, and that he had a certain direct way of speaking and looking at one that made one like

---

[108] For more on General Drummond, see Appendix 1.

[109] Du Vignaux's "grievance" proves well-founded, as West discovers when the two meet again on September 15th. By "essence" West means petrol.

him at once. Also he gave the impression of having a completely calm and objective outlook on any problem with resources and enterprise to back his judgment. I do not know what happened to King afterwards, but I felt he had that quality that makes for a leader of men.

WG Fletcher was an Oxford graduate, rather quiet and reserved to the strangers he found himself among, but opened up after he knew them better. I felt he hated this war more than most, his erudite academic mind being torn apart by the sudden impact of the rough and tumble that followed, and his sensitive nature was horrified by the carnage and beastliness of war. He told me once that he could not stand the loneliness of our job as solitary despatch riders, others were part of a unit always with companions to back them up, and that was what he craved. Yet one felt that he had innate courage, and all the more to be admired in that he was afraid. His later extraordinary deeds of bravery for which he was decorated proved this. He was killed about a year later carrying out some dangerous missions with his men in no man's land near Ypres.

A Sang was older than any of us, I suppose about 35. A swarthy rather small figure with a dark intelligent face. He spoke French like a native, and had spent many years as a travelling salesman in Northern France. He seemed to know every little village we came to, and the names of the Mayor and Councillors, who he was often disappointed to find had fled before our arrival. His quick amusing conversation should have been a key to his character, but one often sensed a dark cloud hanging over him and a kind of bitterness against the world. He hated motorcycles and motorcycling, but was always rushing into the most foolhardy situations in the face of the enemy, as if he just did not care. I think I knew him better than the others, and one day I asked him why he did such crazy things. For a long while he said nothing, and then his reserve broke, and the words tumbled out in a hurry, as if he was scared he would not finish before he broke down. His wife (or was it his fiancée?) had left him, and it was right, he just did not care, he did not care. He would welcome death in this war. What did anything matter? Then he got up from the road bank where we were sitting, and said he was sorry for this outburst, and the cloud of reserve fell back over him, never I think to lift till he was killed at the battle of the Marne a few weeks later.

As for the fourth member of our Brigade Intelligence Corps, namely myself, the gods never gave me or anyone else the "giftie to see ourselves as others see us." So I will endeavour no description except statistically. My grandfather Sir Edward Frankland had married a very sweet German lady which accounted for our always talking German in the family. My father was a physician of 15 Wimpole Street, London, a fierce Victorian parent, very near both geographically and psychologically to the "Barretts of Wimpole

Street."[110] I had spent a period each in Wurzburg and Bonn Universities, and had graduated a year before the war at King's College Cambridge in Engineering sciences. And the idea therefore was that in addition to talking German I might be of use to the other members of the Intelligence Corps in repairing their mounts—except of course King's horse.

From Valenciennes Major Johnson sent me out with orders to the four battalions of the Brigade, the Middlesex, the Argyll and Sutherland Highlanders, the Cameronians (Scottish Rifles) and the 2nd Royal Welsh Fusiliers. These were now marching out along the road to the north-east, which extends straight from Valenciennes to Mons. I caught up with 2nd Lieutenant Fitzroy of the Royal Welsh Fusiliers at Onnaing, and shortly afterwards the others, and delivered my message to each in turn. The troops were a fine sight, bronzed and fit, swinging along the dusty road, their arms and equipment flashing in the sun, everything right to the last button. (I would never then have believed that within a fortnight that same body of men, reduced in numbers, would have been staggering along the roads one hundred miles south, gaunt from want of food and sleep, their kit in tatters, and marching somehow by the power of will over bodies long since exhausted.)

Apparently the idea was that we were to travel up the Valenciennes-Mons road till we contacted the left of the II Corps. We were then to push north, cleaning up any odd cavalry patrols that got in the way, and hold a position south of the Mons-Condé canal.

I rode back to Headquarters for orders and was sent out again to our extreme right to see if we had got into touch with the II Corps yet. I found that we had fallen in with some of Allenby's cavalry at Quivrain just over the Belgian border.

Headquarters had now set up in St Saulve, just outside Valenciennes. Major Johnson, who was always very considerate, asked me to come in and have lunch at the headquarters mess, it being now 2 o'clock.

After lunch I went off again to keep in touch with the advance patrols who were now pushing up towards the canal. The whole country here is a huge marsh, cut by a bewildering network of dykes. Along the banks grow endless lines of willows, and it is quite impossible to see what is around the next corner. The "roads", marked so beautifully red on the map, are really no more than a series of paths, almost lost in the overhanging willows.

---

[110] *The Barretts of Wimpole Street* was a play written by Rudolf Bessier in 1930, proof that West's "Diary" was revisited after being "written up immediately afterwards from scrappy notes jotted down in a field pocket book" as he claims in his Introduction. The typescript certainly dates from after 1930.

Just beyond Vicq I fell in with Captain Vandeleur of the Cameronians on a horse. He was standing in a little glade almost hidden by willows growing along the deep ditches. He and some of his infantry had just run into two or three German mounted scouts who, much to their chagrin, had bolted precipitately. For my part, after running around these paths for some time, armed with a second-hand Belgian revolver of doubtful safety, I found nothing so returned to Headquarters.

All I saw of the Battle of Mons.

These had been moved up again to Quarouble. I was given a message to take to the Middlesex who were going to hold the bridge across the Mons-Condé canal at St Aybert. I became rather lost in the marshes and finally entered Thivencelles from the west, where the bridge was guarded by French Territorials. They were armed with antique hand cannons of enormous bore, and dressed according to individual taste. In one respect only were they in uniform—they all wore very ill-fitting trousers. They were most cordial and told me that some *"Anglais"* had passed that way and had gone on to the canal, so I sped off along the field track to the west.

A party of Middlesex had just arrived at St Aybert and were scraping some sort of cover and mining the bridge. (At that time my ideas as to who was doing the attacking and who the defending were rather mixed. I discovered long after this was the beginning of the famous battle of Mons.)

After a while a few German cavalry came out of a wood on our right front and looked round. Shots were fired and the cavalry fled back again. Somewhere away on our right some shells came over, but I don't quite know where they went. The Officer Commanding the Middlesex there said they were going to blow up the bridge and fall back. There did not seem much reason for this sudden retirement. (Of course I knew nothing of the German hordes at that moment pouring round our left flank, reaching later even as far west as Amiens.) Thinking this rather a feeble sort of war if that was all there was to it, I got on my motor cycle and trekked away to the south again. The Middlesex apparently blew up the bridge shortly afterwards and retired. Sole casualty—one slightly wounded, who was silly enough to be standing on it when it went up![111]

I got back to the main Valenciennes-Mons road and found Headquarters now set up at Quiévrechain. My left foot, which had got thoroughly poisoned, was one huge blister, the boot not having been taken off for two days. Fletched got 2nd Lieutenant Sproule, RAMC, attached to the Welsh Fusiliers, to come up and see me in our billet. He suggested wearing a carpet slipper and keeping it up for two days and doing nothing. So Sang very kindly ran

---

[111] We meet this man briefly on August 25th.

out and bought me a pair of wonderful carpet slippers, the finest product of Quiévrechain. They were about fifteen inches long and six or seven broad!

First news of German outflanking movement, causing the ultimate retreat.

The sun had now set and shortly afterwards I hobbled out into the dark street. There was an indefinable feeling of tension in the air. It is extraordinary how these things spread, but though nothing was said it was soon clear that something had gone desperately wrong, and our position was very grave. Captain Jack came out and told us to be ready to move at any moment. Sang and Fletcher, who maintained that they had not had much to do all day, kindly said they would do all the work, and I had better go and get to sleep in the billet. Soon after Fletcher was sent off post haste into the night, followed very shortly by Sang. I told Churchill where to find me, and went back to the billet across the road. It was now about 11 o'clock, but I could not think of sleep, so sitting down on the doorstep opposite Headquarters I waited.

An unexplainable shadow of coming disaster seemed cast over all. Officers from the staff were conversing in low tones, and orderlies were dashing off on errands. Small parties would emerge from the blackness into the flare of the lanterns and disappear again up the road to Mons, and guns and limbers and transport came slinking by in the darkness, all in the same direction. After a time I pulled myself together, went upstairs and lay down for a bit and tried to sleep, but almost immediately Churchill came up and said that there was a most important despatch—would I take it? Sleep being out of the question, I was rather glad to have something to do.

My instructions were to run down the road from Valenciennes southward to Solesmes, and to meet the 19th Brigade Transport which was coming up that way. They were to turn back and take the road from Solesmes through Le Quesnoy to Bavai. The German cavalry was out to the south-west of Valenciennes and all the transport would get massacred if not warned in time.

Here we meet some of West's colleagues, of whom the most intriguing may be Alfred Sang—who was not, strictly, killed at the Marne but succumbed to wounds received there. According to his War Office file Sang died on October 2nd of "gunshot wound, head". His "lawful widow and relict" was Sarah Alice Sang, née—remarkably—Stang, whom he had married on the last Valentine's Day of the last century and by whom he had three children, all of whom he must have been missing as well as his wife, who was living in St Cloud, west of Paris, when her husband was mortally wounded a few miles to the north. The portents on Sang's wedding day must have seemed splendid and fifteen years later his "bitterness against the world" is understandable; "What [could] anything matter" to one so bereft of all he loved most?

WG Fletcher is no less remarkable a character. West's speculation that "he hated this war more than most" may be based on his observation of August 28th that Fletcher "was very upset over the frightful things he had seen [at Le Cateau and Solesmes]—of which it is almost impossible to write". But the former Eton schoolmaster, nicknamed "the Don" by his new rough-and-tumble chums, didn't let such upset interfere with his duty as a soldier. At First Ypres he used his fluent German to halt an enemy assault and then lure the attackers into the line of British fire. West's feeling "that he had innate courage" was not misplaced:

> Pyers Mostyn and Fletcher were the most indefatigable and adven-turous of patrollers. Either singly, or with a NCO and a couple of men, they would be out almost every night that the Battalion [the Royal Welsh Fusiliers, to which Fletcher was attached] was in the line if the weather was not quite impossible.... Fletcher's knowl-edge of German led him to spend much time listening under the German parapet.

Fletcher was killed by a sniper—near to Neuve Chapelle, not Ypres, as West claims—on March 20th, 1915. Captain Attwater, of the RWF, mourned: "He will be a great loss, not only for his gallantry, but for his personality and his conversation at Mess".[112] It is possible that West maintained contact with Fletcher's family, for according to the woman he later married they met "at the Fletchers' dances" (though this may have been a different family).[113]

All three motorcycle DRs of the 19th Brigade, clearly, were impressive, dutiful, courageous men.

"Jack of the Cameronians, a tall good-looking man of considerable charm", was James L Jack, *Légion d'Honneur*, DSO and bar, later commander of the 28th Infantry Brigade; later still, author of *General Jack's Diary 1914-18*. He's in charge of ammunition and supply columns for the 19th Division now. That his "distinct sense of humour … seemed to us irregulars rather a rare quality among the regulars" may say much about the prejudiced views of civilians toward soldiers at the time: "a crowd of slavish wastrels and empty-headed slackers", Willie Watson, another civilian-soldier, another despatch rider—with the 5th Division in his case—regarded them until he got to know them better.[114]

West's description of General d'Amade's Territorials, however brief, gives some telling details about this overlooked force and an insight into how

---

[112] Dunn, op cit, pp. 87, 120, 125.

[113] See "Brief Biography", p. 197 See p. 205.

[114] Watson, op cit, p. 6.

hard-pressed the French were to contain the German assault. D'Amade's men, hastily mustered a week before, were shabbily uniformed and armed with "antique hand-cannons of enormous bore", probably Gras rifles dating back to the 1870s, dug out of storage. The single-shot Gras was an old Chassepot modified to take an 11mm brass-cartridge bullet propelled by black-powder, the equivalent of a Mauser M1871 or a Martini-Henry .450 and not a weapon to bring to a gunfight in which the enemy is armed with *Gewehr* 98s. But these ill-armed Territorials were all that stood between the BEF and the Channel and they would play a significant role at Le Cateau.[115]

The British are blooded on this historic day, the Germans dismayed. "They apparently knew something about war, these cursed English", complains Captain Walter Bloem, explaining: "Our first battle is a heavy, an unheard of heavy defeat, and against the English—the English we had laughed at". But no one is laughing now. If the BEF has inflicted such damage that the Germans imagine their rifles to be machineguns, they have hardly been victorious and the enemy has put up a better show than British history will credit them; German defeats are localised, and while the BEF's own losses are fewer overall they can be less afforded and the force's small size makes it impossible to follow up its "victory", so German fears of a counterattack, which "would simply run over us", are unfounded.[116]

West's 19th Brigade arrives at Mons as the BEF is beginning to disengage; "the men went straight off the trains into the thick of the fight", their effectiveness compromised by their being placed, for the moment, under the command of the Cavalry Division, rather than under the II Corps.[117]

Disengagement after Mons disgusts many of the Old Contemptibles: haven't they just beaten the Hun? Why not press the advantage: counter-attack and drive him back across the Rhine! But for those growing aware of the scale of the German juggernaut steamrolling down over Flanders—and DRs knew more than most, even more than many officers, thanks to all the messages to which they were privy—the "unexplainable shadow of coming disaster" has been cast. Lanrezac's disengagement has been without consultation with the British, both of whose flanks are now in peril.

The Great Retreat begins. In its confusion the 19th Brigade is to incorporate more than its four regiments—the 1/Middlesex, 2/Argyll & Sutherland

---

[115] At the St Quentin conference of August 26th there was mention of the need to have d'Amade's men "properly equipped with guns and machine-guns"—Spears, op cit, p. 231. While "guns" likely meant the *soixante-quinze*, in light of West's observation, it may also have meant modern rifles.

[116] Robin Neillands, *The Old Contemptibles: The British Expeditionary Force 1914*, p. 125; Tuchman, op cit, p. 290; Martin Gilbert, op cit, p. 58.

[117] Corbett-Smith, op cit, p. 115; Mallinson, op cit, p. 302.

Highlanders, 1/Cameronians (Scottish Rifles) and 2/Royal Welsh Fusiliers—for after Le Cateau, "2 companies of the Royal Scots Fusiliers, which had lost touch with the headquarters of their battalion ... were temporarily attached to the 19th Bde", along with many just "hoping for something to eat".[118]

Dinant is burned, and 644 civilians killed, the youngest three weeks old. Of another atrocity—Louvain—an officer boasts: "For generations people will come here to see what we have done".[119] Kurt Reisler, advisor to Bethmann Hollweg, who will draft the latter's September Programme, is less sanguine: "After this war, we will have a reputation as the worst barbarians, and we won't be able to show our faces anywhere abroad".[120]

The carnage over the past three days is compounded now when Rupprecht attacks in pursuance of Case 3, approved yesterday. His Sixth and Seventh Armies are supported by the Fifth, commanded, nominally at any rate, by the Crown Prince, soon to be acclaimed "the hero of Longwy". With a weak chin and much less imposing in appearance than his fine-looking fatuous father, "Little Willie" is possessed of more sanity than one expects in a Hohenzolleran; but if he isn't as stupid as he's often portrayed not even a Marxist show-trial could find him guilty of being an intellectual and his previous command was limited to colonelcy of the Death's Head Hussars. Could he have foreseen such a philandering lotus-eater even nominally in charge of one of his precious armies Schlieffen would have despaired. But his plan is rolling toward ruin now.

Meanwhile Ludendorff has arrived in East Prussia to salvage the situation there, along with *Junker* Paul von Hindenburg—who is to earn the sobriquet General-what-do-you-say from constant deferral to his nominal subordinate. In further sabotage of his predecessor's plan, and against Ludendorff's wishes, Moltke will strip two full corps from the critical right wing to send after this portentous duo.

The Russians urge Samsonov to attack the flank of the Eighth Army, supposing the Germans to be in retreat after Gummbinen; but Rennenkamf has broken contact and his renewed advance now is missing his foe. Yet he still could destroy the Eighth Army if he should discovered and fall on its rear, so it's a nervous Ludendorff who marches to meet Samsonov.

---

[118] Diary of the Argyll and Sutherland Highlanders, 26 August 1914; the National Archives, Catalogue Reference: WO/95/1365; Jack, op cit, p. 33.

[119] Lipkes, op cit, p. 537.

[120] Letter to his fiancée, Käthe Liebermann, August 29, 1914; Jaffé-Richthofen family correspondence, Leo Baecke Institute, New York.

August 24th.

The British Army outflanked.

A glance at the map (see Map III) will show what that message meant [that the 19th Brigade's transport "would get massacred if not warned" of rampaging German cavalry]. The previous day, for it was now past midnight, we had been facing the Germans at St Aybert and Thivencelles. Now we learnt that they were right around and behind our left flank. Valenciennes had been our railhead, and the line by which we had come up must now be in the enemy's hands; and the main road to the south from Valenciennes was, if not yet actually held by them, in immediate danger of being cut. So I wasted no time, but got away at once, as it seemed that the longer the delay, the more likely I was to have trouble down the Valenciennes-Solesmes road.

There were many French sentries out all the way to Valenciennes, but the town itself was asleep, and I tore through the deserted streets, and so away to the south. It was a dark night and no moon visible, but I thought it best to run without lights. Mounting the hill I rode into the dark little village of Famars. There were no lights in the houses, but out in the green lay a lot of horse transport waggons, apparently quite deserted. I stopped and beat at the door of the biggest cottage, and after a long time a frightened woman's voice asked "*Qui est là?*", the window being opened about half an inch for the purpose. She was not very reassured when I said "*Officier Anglais*", and asked her where the owners of the transport were. She was either too frightened or didn't understand—anyway I never found out. Besides it was evidently not the 19th Brigade transport, and so no concern of mine, and I rode on rapidly and under the railway bridge, where a sleepy French sentry waved a lantern at me. We had no official passes and they never asked for them.

After that not a soul was seen down the road for several miles. I was running as quickly and as quietly as is possible with a motor cycle, as I expected to meet the German cavalry at any moment. Once or twice I stopped and listened, but it was dead still, so still that the silence seemed to roar in one's ears. Then on starting again the motor cycle would make such a jarring noise that one thought it must be heard for miles.

I ran into Vendegies. Here were many roads and I laid out my map and compass to get right when suddenly I heard horses' hoofs ringing in the distance on the road. I drew the cycle quickly into a little court between two cottages and waited—seemingly for a year or so. It was impossible to tell where in the village they were, or in which direction they were going. The sounds got louder, and then began gradually to recede. I leaned the cycle against the house and tiptoed quietly into the street. They seemed to be away to the north, and then, when I crossed the road they seemed to be to the south. Finally they disappeared altogether and I went back to the cycle and started it up. I must have been rather strung up at the time, as I never remember a cycle making such an appalling roar.

I got away on the right road and off to the south. Somewhere beyond Maison Bleue, on the downward slope, I suddenly came upon a lorry trying to turn round in the narrow road. There was a young officer with it who was doing a powerful amount of swearing, and asked me where the --- I had come from, and how the --- I had got through. They had apparently been held up and fired on from the north-west, so that I must, without knowing it, have run right through a party of the enemy, who were luckily not actually on the road at the time. I told him that this was just what I had come for, namely to tell him not to come along that road at all as the German cavalry was out all over the country. He had that lorry round at once and dashed off down the road. I managed to squeeze past him and raced on ahead to Solesmes.

Here was parked a large amount of Mechanical Transport round the station, but none belonged to the 19th Brigade, and nobody seemed to know anything. So I warned them against the north road to Valenciennes, and acting only on the flimsy suggestion of some officers in a car that they thought some transport had gone along to Bavai, and it *might* be that of the 19th, I went out that way. They wanted to go there too, and were not sure of the road, so I offered to lead them.

We started in the darkness and ran through the town. I rode on about three hundred yards ahead of the car, revolver in hand. The officers in the car were likewise ready as we rather expected trouble. The first light of a misty morning was beginning dimly to outline the sleeping countryside and it was bitterly cold. At last we reached a little hamlet, and at the foot of the hill lay a petrol supplies lorry upset in the ditch, and a man unloading it. Dead tired, hungry and cold. The car I was accompanying disappeared somewhere, but I went on and found an old woman awake in a cottage and managed to get some coffee. A few civilians, refugees from the north, passed through the village in the grey dawn.

Leaving the village I passed a long train of lorries and went on east into the sunrise. The lorries were soon left behind and I reached at last what must have been Beaudignies, but somehow I had left the main road and was rather at a loss. My compass needle was stuck and I could not yet get my bearings from the sun, which was still hidden behind a cold silvery mist; so drawn up against a white stone wall at the cross-roads I waited in the twilight. It was dead still and I was slowly dozing off, when suddenly I was wide awake. Somewhere in the eastern end of the village there was a noise of a scuffle and footsteps on the *pavé*. No doubt the correct procedure would have been to draw my Belgian blunderbuss and see it through, whatever it was, but as my sole interests at the time were for peace and quiet and somewhere to sleep, I was off and out of that village in no time.

Soon I fell in with the lorry train again and ran back with them by the main road into Beaudignies, but suddenly my back tyre went flat, and I had to wheel the wretched machine into the village and push it into a little walled churchyard. The lorries turned west in the village, towards the Germans, but I could not go after them now to warn them, so started mending the puncture instead. Suddenly another motor cyclist came flying back down the road the lorries had taken. A shot was fired at him from a spinney about one hundred and fifty yards off, but he dashed straight on round the corner in the village and away to the south. It did not seem a healthy quarter to be held up with a crippled machine, and I kept my revolver conveniently ready, and got busy with the puncture behind the wall. At last it was ready and wheeled out into the road, when back came the lorries and halted in the village to take their bearings. The men said they had been on their way west when they butted into the Germans, were fired on and had been compelled to turn round without delay and come back. By now my back tyre had again gone flat, so some of the men helped me heave it onto one of the lorries, where it lay on its side dribbling petrol out over everything. The lorries now moved off to the north-east, and I got on board and slept among the jolting boxes.

The fighting retreat starts.

I do not know exactly where we went, but whenever we stopped for bearings we could hear a distant cannonade. It was about four or five o'clock in the morning when the lorries came to a final halt just outside Jenlain. None of the drivers or anybody seemed to know anything about the 19th Brigade, or where I was likely to find them again, and there were apparently no officers with the column. They said they were moving off again southward as soon as they had dumped their freight, so they lifted the bicycle off for me, and I pushed it into a farmyard and started to mend the puncture. There was an old woman and two little children awake and moving about the farm. She got me some brandy, raw eggs and some coffee, which made life more possible, the last proper meal having been lunch with the Headquarters mess at St Saulve the day before.

The gunning we had heard is now developing into a terrific bombardment, coming nearer rapidly. Two German aeroplanes are passing over the farm with their wings turned back like gigantic pigeons, and the great black crosses painted beneath. The farm people are astir and running about frightened, collecting their belongings to put into their waggons ready for flight. Hear some cavalry trotting past outside the farm—whose? Shortly afterwards a car passes, and I look out through the door to find it is a British staff officer's car.

The cycle was now mended again, and I raced after that car to find out how and where to join my brigade. The car ran down in the direction of Solesmes, but somehow I missed it and went down another road to the south. Gave it up after a bit and returned and then fell in with the same or another staff officer's car, and this time they could give me some satisfaction regarding the 19th Brigade. Apparently it had orders to retire through Quarouble on to Rombies, and I should find it somewhere in that district.

I went off north through, I think, Wargnies and Eth, but I was rather lost as the roads were little more than tracks. Somewhere near Sebourg, it must have been, I came across some of our cavalry under Major Ing. I found Major Ing himself on the hill, sitting under the trees by a little shrine. He did not know where the 19th Brigade was, but gave me some directions as to Rombies. But the old French maps we were served out with were very inaccurate, and I was soon lost again in the maze of tracks.

Reaching Sebourg or Sebourquiaux, I again asked the way of a party of villagers. They were standing in the road crying and frightened at the terrific bombardment that was in progress. A tall, nice-looking girl came out of one of the cottages, and finding me struggling to get information ran up to me; "Speak English", she said, and explained the way to Rombies very clearly. The rest of the villagers were quite incoherent. Their only question was repeated over and over again, "Are the Germans coming?" "Are the Germans coming?" I don't know. Who knows? I got on again and started the engine. Some of the women came up and clung to my hand, as if I could offer them any protection. The English-speaking girl came forward and shook hands firmly, though her eyes were full of tears, and as I moved off she called after me, "God bless you! God bless you!" and so I left them for the north.

At last I fell in with the 19th Brigade and reported to General Drummond and Major Johnson. I expected the latter would have thought me lost, but instead he seemed rather surprised to see me back so soon. I was just about ready for a huge meal—I suppose it would have been about 8 or 9 o'clock in the morning—but we moved off right away. There was nothing to do except to keep with the column and we trekked down, I think, through Estreux, Saultain and Preseau to Maresches.

Every now and then a great Taube would come sailing over, circle round once or twice, and turn back to report. The German aircraft was undoubtedly excellent. I can rarely remember seeing any of our aeroplanes, but always the great hawk-like machines of the enemy hovering over us, and pointing the way of our retreat to the advancing armies. They came down absurdly low, and now and then when we were resting beside the road, we would loose off ragged irregular volleys at them, but they sailed on glistening in the sun.

So we toiled on through the dust to Sepmeries and down into the Roman road from Cambrai to Bavai. At the cross-roads on the hilltop about one kilometre to the west, the Brigade Staff stopped and got off their horses for a rest. Here I met Fletcher and Churchill again. Major Johnson had a despatch for me to carry down ahead to the south. He advised me to go down the main Roman road through St Aubert, as the troops would be travelling south through Bermerain, and I might find some difficulty getting past.

After a while, the Brigade moved off south, as he had said, and I started off down the St Aubert road with my despatch. I ran along for about three miles or so crossing the Valenciennes-Solesmes road, and so over a hill, when I saw some cavalry trotting rapidly towards me about half a mile away. I rode on, when suddenly I noticed they wore darker clothes than our men, and stopping the cycle I had a look at them with my glasses. They were now quite close, about two hundred yards or so, and I could see by their *Pickelhauben* and carbines that they were German dragoons, fourteen of them. They had seen me, and came on at a gallop. I switched the bicycle round and started back. Suddenly to my right front as I was going now, four of our cavalry appeared over the rise. This was easier prey, thought the dragoons, than one motor cyclist who was obviously too fast to catch. So they swung off the road and charged over the fields. Our four fellows held their ground sportingly, and there followed a splutter of rifle fire, but I was out of sight now in the banked road. Then suddenly about forty of our troopers appeared over the rise. This was a nasty jar to the gallant Boche, and he turned tail and bolted incontinently for the horizon. Our troops reined in, and though some of their horses gibbed and plunged a bit they let fly at the fleeing Germans with their rifles.

Unfortunately this German patrol had gone straight down the road I was to take, and it was obviously not expedient to chase them along on a motor cycle, so I turned back to the cross-roads, and reported to Major Johnson that the cavalry was out on that road, and I would take the other through Bermerain. He said it was all right, and I had better stay with the column as they might have something more important for me later.

I was thinking it was about time to eat and ran on beside the column through Bermerain to St Martin and a short way up the Valenciennes road in search of food. As I rode up, along came a limousine towards me driven at a crazy speed, and rocking down the hill. I swung into the side of the road and got my revolver handy, for they were coming straight from the Germans, but a French soldier appeared on the step and waved to me as the car came to a stop about forty yards away. There were two French majors and one soldier besides the driver. All except the driver were wounded, and the car panels were plugged full of bullet-holes. They were delighted to meet the English at last. They had been about the last to escape from Valenciennes, and had run the gauntlet through the German cavalry. By the merest chance the driver alone had not been hit, and had brought them all through to safety.

The retreat.

From now on there was nothing for it but to trek away to the south in a seemingly never-ending retreat. Never any rest, rarely any food, a series of nightmare days and nights, when the dust-grimed columns moved on and on. Our guns hopelessly out-numbered stayed behind and guarded the tired infantry, till the last moment, when they would limber up and toil on to the next position, and come into action again.

So we came to a little village—I cannot place it on the map. Here we found some miserable little trenches about one foot deep, dug by somebody who had gone on before. It was no position, but the troops must have rest; some of the Argyll and Sutherlands manned them, and waited there for about half an hour. For my part I got into an orchard and bathed my foot which was becoming rather impossible. Then we moved off again, and trekked on into another little village about two miles farther south. Two batteries Royal Field Artillery, who were following on and fighting rearguard, stopped behind and lined the road, firing *due east*. The Germans could be seen advancing across the fields on our right flank and *rear*, and the guns were now "giving them Hell." Our batteries kept the fight up to the last moment, till our shells were bursting actually in the next field, and only then limbered up, and came trotting in after us. How much we owed to the guns may never be known, for they stayed behind and fought alone, and there was no one to report their deeds.

I rode on ahead of the brigade to the next village, and entered a cottage to get some food. There was a shrivelled-up old woman and a little girl about twelve years old. They managed to make me some coffee and an omelette. "Better the English should take all than save anything for the Prussian," they said, and refused to be paid. Then I went out to wait till the troops came up, and sitting down on the cobbled pavement was asleep in a moment. I was awakened shortly by King, who got off his horse. He sat down too, and was soon also asleep, while his horse stood wearily by with drooping head.

It was dusk when the brigade arrived, and King was off arranging billets for the general, and also for us. Soon a field ambulance came in and set up in a garden near by. They were desperately busy, as there were many wounded and few staff, but I got something for my foot. There seemed to be only two ambulance waggons, and the place was full of wounded. How many could walk I cannot say, but they could not all get a lift when we had to move again.

Walked back to billet, and found King had managed to raise a sort of meal for Fletcher, Sang and myself. King was invaluable; I believe he would have found a meal and a billet in the middle of the Sahara. The people were most kind, and did everything they could for us, even giving up their beds, while they slept somehow in the kitchen. The bed was wasted on me, however, as I was asleep before I ever got into it!

West provides an excellent insight into the confusion of the first days of the Great Retreat, the menace of enemy cavalry and the importance of the Royal Field Artillery. He also reveals that for all the dangers that beset them then and afterward, despatch riders have a cushy war compared with the infantry. The "sort of meal" that King rustles up was better fare than Tommy Atkins gets today, after marching more than 20 miles. The diary of the Argyll and Sutherland Highlanders reports: "No supplies received so men without food"; eventually "biscuits and tea" arrived at 10:00 PM, but the troops only broke their fast at 1:00 AM next morning.[121] "Biscuits" meant tooth-breaking hard-tack that might have been in storage for years.

How well West discharges his duty on this dangerous day is best illustrated by comparison. His efforts to save the very same column contrast to those of an RAC car-driver, also detailed "to await one of the transport trains of the 19th Brigade" and who, on sight of an Uhlan patrol, "jumped into his car and tore away for Solesmes, leaving the transport train of the 19th Brigade to whatever fate may have overtaken it".[122] This is not to censure the driver, but to counterpoint the stern courage of West and his conscientious discharge of his duty. (The brigade and its transport were reunited on the 28th at Pontoise. "We were greatly pleased to see each other, for each had heard that the other had been taken prisoner.")[123]

That despatch riders "had no official passes and they never asked for them" is surprising, given that spy mania was rampant and that one of West's IC colleagues, Lieutenant Addison, was responsible for issuing them; presumably there were more pressing concerns just then. By October at the latest such passes were universal, but by then West had been returned to the Intelligence Corps.

That he has a map to consult is also slightly surprising, because maps were in short supply and this caused countless problems for commanders and despatch riders. So certain did victory seem in August 1914 that all British army units had to surrender their maps of France when they crossed into Belgium, so retreat saw them marching into territory charted only on outdated and inaccurate French maps—utterly inadequate, as it emerges from West's account. No wonder he uses "off the map" as a metaphor for unavailability of such things as breakfast.

---

[121] National Archives, WO/95/1365. See also Jack, op cit, p. 32.

[122] Frederic Coleman, *From Mons to Ypres with French*, pp. 10-11.

[123] Dunn, op cit, pp. 32, 36-37.

To find "a man unloading" a petrol lorry would have been commonplace, for tankers were unknown back then, all petrol being supplied in cans—which, later in the war, were used to bring water up to the trenches, the taint of petrol lending an unpleasant taste.

The "few civilians" West encounters early today are to become a road-choking exodus as the smoke of burning towns and villages to the north warns people to get out of the way of *schrecklichkeit*—see, for example, his entry for September 2nd. Countless British soldiers are affected by the plight of refugees: on this day another despatch rider reports meeting a family of three generations

and [he and his companion] gave them all our spare food and the eldest daughter [about sixteen] seemed so tearful and sad that I told her in my best French to buck up and all would be well. She just flung her arms around my neck and kissed me again and again, hard and sobbingly—and her lips were cracked and dry. I sobbed for the next mile or two myself and so did Taylor—it was all too much.[124]

There's an interesting parallel here with the "English speaking girl" West meets, and the emotion in the two encounters. On the morrow another despatch rider reports: "We are unable to assure them of safety, and the crying of the women and children does not tend to remove the depressed feeling we are most of us obsessed with".[125]

Nor are congested roads and "depressed feelings" the only problems DRs encounter: *pavé* is a very real hazard. West's cursive annotation: "cobbles" is a reasonably accurate yet for a despatch rider an inadequate translation, as *pavé* was a very solid road for four-wheel transport, but a precarious one for two-wheels. Despatch riders heartily cursed its big lumpy stones, its slippery nature and typically steep camber, even as they acknowledged its durability and essential value to supplying armies in the field.[126] It also quickly wore out horseshoes, a significant factor over the retreat, when horseshoes, like everything else, were in short supply, and when von Richthofen's cavalry, at the very end of August, could perhaps have tilted victory toward the Germans had its horses been better shod. "It was awful to see the number of horses that had gone lame for want of shoes, and had to be left on the road."[127]

Taube was a whimsical name for German monoplanes of this early phase of the war, drawn from the resemblance of their swept-back wings to pigeons

---

[124] WH Tait, IWM document PP/MCR/161, 24 August 1914.

[125] AJ Sproston, "Four Months Under Fire", 25 August 1914.

[126] Michael Carragher, *San Fairy Ann*, p. 104 and passim.

[127] Dunn, op cit, p. 47.

in flight; but they were whimsical doves, the terror they induced in civilians suggesting that *falkes* would have been a better name.

West's emphasis that the RFA batteries were "firing *due east*" illustrates the danger of being outflanked on both sides, now that Lanrezac's uncoordinated retreat has left the BEF's two flanks "in the air". Successful enemy action at this point could have broken the BEF, Uhlans then scattering the survivors. That this disaster was averted was thanks to both artillery, West very properly crediting the RFA—"they stayed behind and fought alone, and there was no one to report their deeds"—and to cavalry, which proved far superior to the German in scouting and screening the open flanks and rear, and in their dismounted firepower. Mutual support is evident when the 9th Lancers help move RHA guns, under heavy fire—Francis Grenfell gains his VC in this action and West's colleague, Lieutenant J Martin Smith, also distinguishes himself. The better care the British take of their horses is observed on the morrow; so bad were the French in this regard that sometimes their horses' saddle-sores actually stank.[128]

The Despatch Rider Corps too played a vital role in holding the BEF together, as they were the linchpin of communications, and thereby enabled effective command and control.[129]

Lanrezac breaks off the Battle of Charleroi and the Battle of the Ardennes also ends. The French withdraw from Mulhouse, not to set foot in it again until the armistice. Closer to the British, they evacuate Lille. Joffre has got the message after suffering 140,000 casualties in four days; he issues General Order No 2 and begins to pull his armies back onto the defensive, provisionally along the Somme, from which to launch a renewed attack. He also plans a new army, the Sixth, on the left of the BEF, to defend Paris and buttress the Allied line. Over Flanders hangs "the smell of half a million unwashed men", to say nothing of carcasses and corpses. The Germans enter "impregnable" Namur after just four days' bombardment.[130]

Today, "Shrapnel Monday"—so called because artillery played a salient role in allowing the troops to disengage from Mons[131]—British cavalry attack the Germans in an ill-judged action at Audreignies. Eighty casualties are the consequence of a charge against guns across a mile of ground traversed by barbed wire and a sunken road. The mercurial Sir John French becomes convinced that the war is lost. Bitterly, he blames the French and decides that

[128] Mallinson, op cit, p. 280. See also Spears, op cit, pp. 100-02, for discussion of French cavalry.
[129] Carragher, *San Fairy Ann* p. 245; "'Amateurs at a Professional Game'", p. 342.
[130] Tuchman, op cit, p. 293.
[131] The term seems to be of recent coinage.

British interests will be best served if he pulls the BEF out of the line across the Seine or farther west. Even the Francophile Wilson sees how "exaggerated" the German threat is now and shares the alarm and depression. GHQ retreats to St Quentin.

In East Prussia intercepted wireless broadcasts reassure Ludendorff that Rennenkamf has led the First Russian Army too far off to be a threat, so he brings the full force of his own army against Samsonov—who attacks, with encouraging success.

Thirty Serb civilians are forced to dig their own graves and then bayoneted into them and buried with some still alive. "Our men behaved like savages", one Austrian officer complains; "I could not stand the sight, and left them to it."[132]

Much farther eastward, the first units of Indian Expeditionary Force A embark for France.

August 25th.

At about three o'clock I woke up from a feverish doze and got to bed, but at 3:15 enter Churchill, who tells us to be ready to start. Got ready and limped out into the street dully alive to the fact that the whole war was unlimited Hell.

Sang was already outside on his motor cycle, and people were busy everywhere collecting their traps and preparing for a further move. Madeleine, the daughter of our host, was walking about in tears, as were most of the villagers. She gave us some *vin bouché*. Our trenches, such as they were round the town, had now been evacuated, and the rearguard withdrawn, as the main body was already trooping out of the village to the south-west. One wounded Middlesex was standing at a street corner, with a smashed knee, and unable to go further. He had apparently been standing at the bridge at St Aybert near Mons when it went up, and was now likely to be left behind. Got him onto a limber finally, as all other vehicles were piled high with stuff.

By now everybody had left the town and Sang, who was always looking for trouble, ran down to our deserted trenches, and reported that the German cavalry had now arrived and was crossing them for the village. We started our motor cycles, and moved on to St Vaast, or anyway down the St Vaast road[133].

About a mile out we came across the bivouacs of Allenby's cavalry. They were making ready to start as we came up, and by the time we had fixed our direction on the map they were already on the move. The horses were still in good condition. (Even after their worst hammerings and hardest times

---

[132] Hastings, op cit, p. 148.

[133] West means St Waast.

the British horses were always in far better trim than the French. The British cavalry man certainly understands horses, not merely how to ride them.)

I kept with the column most of the day, and ran various messages, losing my cap on the way, which was always flying off. However, a grey bandanna was much more comfortable, so I did not worry very much about that. I was sent off in the afternoon to find the second line transport again for the 19th Infantry Brigade. This was supposed to be at Forest.[134] No luck there, so I went on and finally landed at Le Cateau. Here General Headquarters had been set up in the big schools, and the lorries parked in the gravel yard. I went in through the stone arch and purloined a tin of petrol. The petrol proved to be water, so the joke was on me. But I managed to get most of it out again, and then tried to find somebody in the staff who knew where on earth the 19th Brigade transport had got to. Here I was told I would find it at Montay, so off I went again north cursing the transport heartily.

The exhaustion of the troops makes it essential to make a stand, leading to the Battle of Le Cateau.

The roads were blocked for miles with English troops, transport, both horse and mechanical, guns and limbers all inextricably mixed up. It looked like the beginning of a complete break up. The troops were dead weary and were hobbling along singly or in couples, sitting down on the road bank when they could go no further, and taking off their boots to ease their feet. Now and then, however, a small body of men, headed perhaps by an officer or maybe only a lance corporal, would come swinging along in step, and making a brave show. The old regimental spirit was strong, and those of the same unit who saw them pass would get up, fall in behind and carry on. Groups of French dragoons came trotting now and again along the top of the bank, with their picturesque peaked helmets and the long horsehair plumes streaming down their backs. At intervals guns of various calibres would pass by, ranging from a battery of heavy "cow guns" to the little rickety French 75mm.[135] The French 75mm field gun much belies its appearance, which is most inoffensive and unimpressive.

There was no sign of the 19th Infantry Brigade Transport at Montay, although I asked everybody who could possibly have known, so I ran back to Le Cateau to get further directions in case they had moved. Here I met Fletcher who had discovered them somewhere. The drivers were apparently all inside an estaminet drinking, and their lorries in a farm yard, so how he found them I don't know.

---

[134] Forêt-en-Cambrésis.

[135] "Cow guns": 60-pounders made by Coventry Ordnance Works.

Fletcher was just going back to Brigade Headquarters and left me, while I went and fed, in, I think, the Cafe Continental up the hill on the left from the square. Here I met Lieutenant Cumming of the Seaforths and was heavily told off for not wearing regulation head and foot gear. It is funny what little things seem to count with some people at such a time as this. Not two miles up the road from the cafe door were thousands of men with no kit at all, and torn uniforms, and further north still many more who would never have any further use for either. This sort of spirit at the same time, however, was the backbone and the bane of the old Regular Army.

The 19th Brigade was now said to be at Solesmes, and I started back to find them. I heard that Solesmes was unapproachable and under fire, but I found it all right and full of the Argyll and Sutherlands, and also some Middlesex. After a while I discovered General Drummond, Major Johnson and Churchill, and reported. There was nothing much going on, except chaos and congestion in the narrow roads, and we trekked slowly back and stopped, I think, at Neiuvilly, a long straggling village on the way.

Our methods of drawing rations were non-existent, and for my part I lived purely on the country, as did also Fletcher and Sang. Officially, I suppose, we belonged to the Headquarters mess, but we were never on the spot at the right time, so we just ate where and when we could. One could almost always get eggs and bread from the people, but meat was quite unprocurable, and the former is not very sustaining.

It was now 4 o'clock in the afternoon, I suppose, and I was beginning to be deadly tired. However there was nothing to do but keep moving. Trekked back to Le Cateau with the troops now a mere rabble of mixed units. At Montay a French column was crossing us from the north-east, and the most expert point-duty policeman could not have controlled the traffic. At this junction there was very soon a mass of mixed transport standing wheel to wheel and facing in all directions. Bits of this muddle managed to detach themselves and go on their way, but there were always more and more coming in.

After a long time I reached Le Cateau, when a tall Staff Officer of General Headquarters seized upon me and asked me to run towards Cambrai and get into touch with the French. There was not very much difficulty in getting into touch with them, as after the cross-roads of Pont des Vaux the column which had crossed ours came pouring in and the whole road through Beaumont to Beauvois and beyond was packed with French troops of all arms.

I turned back and slowly made my way past them into Le Cateau where I reported and found General Drummond. He sent me out right away to find Major Johnson at St Python and tell the Middlesex to retire at once into Solesmes. I had no map and asked my way to Solesmes from various bodies of fleeing troops. They all had the same story, namely, that it was no use trying as the whole town was "done in," and the Germans all round it. However, I got there all right and went through towards St Python as directed, but apparently took the wrong road to the north, as I found St Python was down on the left, and quite un-get-at-able by road. So I left the bike and started to walk across the fields.

From here one gets a long view across the rolling landscape to the north-west. Over this the German cavalry was now pouring, and our ubiquitous troopers were flying around the country, hopelessly outnumbered, but endeavouring to create checks at every point against the oncoming tide.

I was cut off from St Python, and had to turn back to the road, trusting to luck that the Middlesex had had sufficient sense to leave the village. This I afterwards found they had done, as I met them later in Solesmes. On the road I fell in with one horseman and an infantryman, when suddenly a shot was fired at us from about a hundred and fifty to two hundred yards by a German who had somehow got up into a hedge far in advance of the main body. Fearfully bad shot, however, as we must have presented a target about twenty yards long as we stood, and the bullet went about another twenty yards to the right! One of the Middlesex very shortly afterwards stuck his bayonet into this gentleman as a reprisal.

We retired to a cutting. Soon half a battery of three field guns came in and took up position under the road bank, facing *due west*, and then about one hundred cavalry collected here under cover. Beaumont and Beauvois already in flames. The French—God knows where! The Germans all down our left flank for miles.

A huge phalanx of cavalry appears over a rise to the left. The gunners get their glasses on them and just as they disappear in a fold they are seen to be German. The range is taken of the nearer rise, about one thousand yards away, and over comes the cavalry and down towards us. Our guns let fly 1-2-3. Range and direction absolutely exact. The phalanx scatters in disorder and flies back to cover, while riderless horses are left careering about the ridge. The Germans get into the spinney on our left flank and a ragged fire ensues, but our guns cannot join in as the position is not clear, so stand by ready for developments. More and more Germans are coming up. What are some hundred and fifty men against so many? The sun now going down and Beaumont and Beauvois show lurid and red in the sky on our left rear.

So we retired and passed on south through Solesmes joining up with some of the Middlesex and Argyll and Sutherlands from St Python.

It got dark by the time we reached Montay. All the roads were blocked with the retreating troops. The crush here was such as I have never seen before or since. I dismounted, it being impossible to ride, and pushed the cycle along with a rabble of guns, horses, infantry, cyclists, horse transport, motor lorries, peasant carts and refugees. Girls brought up in luxury in some of the large towns in the north, who had perhaps never been any distance without a car, were now glad of a hand-hold on some transport waggon, and staggered on with the rest, ready to drop from fatigue. For my part, I was nearly through, having had only a few hours' sleep since leaving the Mons-Condé Canal, but we all moved on somehow with a sort of fixed and unquestioning idea that that was all we ever could or ever were meant to do.

A peasant cart stuck across the road, hopelessly interlocked with a GS waggon.[136] There was no possible room to manoeuvre and the column must keep going. The cart was demolished where it stood and the tide moved on. Had the Germans been able to bring up even one gun at this juncture they could have created absolute slaughter in the walled road, as nobody could move above a crawl.

At last in the dark we reached Le Cateau. Captain Jack was standing in the square, lit up by the fitful light of flares and a small bonfire. I reported and threw my cycle and part of my luggage into the school yard. The rest I took over to a cafe and tried to get some sleep.

I have only just settled in when I am called up to go down to the station at once. The cycle absolutely refuses to fire although I run it right down the street. Curse it and push it back to the square and tell Captain Jack. He advises sleep, so I go off again to the cafe which has now filled with soldiers. I manage to find a place under the stairs, and try to sleep on the floor with a blanket and mattress, amongst the dirt, the cooking, and the fleas.

Just after noon today the 19th Brigade is placed under the II Corps' command, but its commanders are out of contact and don't get word for hours. Following this, the Brigade forms the II Corps' reserve.

West's feverishness is a reminder that he's got a badly infected foot, something that is to cripple him to the end of the Retreat, and makes his dedication to duty and his historic accomplishment all the more impressive.

Favourable comparison of British with French cavalry is a reminder that the "donkey-walloper" caricature of incompetent, out-of-touch hippophile British generals has been thoroughly scotched in recent years. After a disastrous showing against the Boers British cavalry upped its game and was a notable beneficiary of the army reforms carried out in the wake of the embarrassing South African War, and an exemplary manual had been written,[137] so that in 1914 what had been something of an international joke was probably the finest body of horseman in the world—if, like everything else about the British armed forces, pitifully small and not beyond criticism, as yesterday's performance at Audreignies shows.

---

[136] General Service waggon.

[137] Rimington, op cit.

The "exhaustion of the troops" is not helped by the rain that falls today, so heavily that in places it damages roads, making retreat all the more miserable. After West locates them, the Argyll and Sutherlands march out of Solesmes toward Le Cateau at 3:30 PM, "arriving at 8:00 PM after very trying march in the rain".[138]

Throughout his account West describes how eggs are regular fare, however "not very sustaining". From other accounts, egg and chips seem to constitute Tommy Atkins' most regular meal out of the line. The cheapness and easy availability of meat is one of the many commonplace differences between ours and the Great War generation, whose main source of protein would have been eggs and dairy produce (plus bland bully beef and unappetising Maconochie stew for soldiers).[139]

Part of the reason for congestion today is the French Fifth Army's retreat, after breaking off the Battle of Charleroi, along a route that overlaps that of the BEF. Where "there was very soon a mass of mixed transport standing wheel to wheel and facing in all directions" is today the junction where the D932—along which the French were retreating—crosses the D955—along which West was riding. Congestion has become a real problem for command and control, and even for despatch riders, as shown by West's having to dismount and push his motorcycle. Today is particularly bad around Bavai and on the morrow Lieutenant KFB Tower of 4/Royal Fusiliers, attached to the Third Division, reports: "The scene on the road baffles any description I can give of it. It was a veritable rout—men, horses, guns, refugees and wagons struggling along in disorder to get away at all costs. Progress was naturally slow and all roads seemed to be blocked in the same way".[140] Another officer reports:

> An extraordinary state of affairs. Hardly a single formed body of troops and every field full of wagons and transport ready to turn into the column which was already miles long. The inevitable block and I thought we should probably be cut off by the Germans…. We would go on for 100 yards and halt for a minute then on again only to halt 50 yards further.[141]

It's worth remembering that West is negotiating all this with a swollen, infected foot, on a primitive motorcycle whose transmission does not take kindly to stop-go progress.

---

[138] Tuchman, op cit, p. 398; the National Archives, document WO/95/1365.

[139] French soldiers "clamoured for more vegetables" in preference to the meat the British called for—Spears, op cit, p. 70.

[140] Lyn Macdonald, *1914-1918: Voices and Images of the Great War*, p. 22.

[141] Jolyon Jackson, *Family at War: The Foljambe Family and the Great War*, p. 68.

The pressure on Smith-Dorrien's forces validates his decision to fight the Battle of Le Cateau in order to effect his retreat. All down the left flank "German cavalry was now pouring, and our ubiquitous troopers were flying around the country, hopelessly outnumbered, but endeavouring to create checks at every point against the oncoming tide". The diary of the Argyll and Sutherland Highlanders elaborates: "hostile cavalry and guns forced our Cavalry back and the Brigade fell in and lined the ridge [northwest of Haussy] to oppose any attack".[142] "The 3rd Division and the 19th Brigade and the Cavalry Division on the left … bore the brunt of Kluck's frontal and flank attacks, and the rearguards were in a running fight for much of the day" to try to break clear of pursuit. It was a "Cavalry Division Field Day",[143] but artillery was no less essential to saving the II Corps and 19th Brigade. Recent criticisms of Smith-Dorrien's choice of ground on which to fight need to be tempered by awareness of the enormous pressures upon him and the limitations these, and the darkness, imposed upon that choice.

The 14th Brigade has been detailed to help secure the imperilled left wing, but German pressure is such that the II Corps is nearly trapped at Solesmes. Smith-Dorrien reports to GHQ that so hot is pursuit he must pause in his retreat and fight a delaying battle if his troops are not to be overtaken on the march and overwhelmed. Appalled by this news, aware by now of the scale of the forces bearing down on the BEF, Sir John French braces himself to lose half his army.

Meanwhile to the east General Haig's I Corps is attacked at Landrecies, creating a situation that the normally-cool Haig describes as "very critical". Hearing this, and believing the I Corps about to be overwhelmed on its right flank—which Lanrezac's retreat has left open—French directs Haig to retreat immediately toward the south. This direction will lead to the two corps becoming separated by the River Oise for more than a week, greatly complicating communications and increasing the workload of despatch riders.

The Battles of the Frontiers have run down, but GQG can no longer ignore the menace to the northeast and makes plans to meet it. The scale of the disaster can no longer be hidden behind brave words and Joffre's imperturbable calm; government, never very firm through the Third Republic, begins to crack. General Gallieni, dying of prostatitis but still vigorous, beyond personal ambition and with no time left for fools, is placed in charge of the Paris garrison, which has been largely stripped to supply d'Amade's territorial force to the north, while the city's defences have been utterly run down.

---

[142] The National Archives, WO/95/1365.
[143] Mallinson, op cit, pp. 339-40.

In East Prussia further wireless intercepts assure Ludendorff that he has a free hand against Samsonov, so he turns yesterday's frontal resistance to a double-envelopment manoeuvre around the Russian flanks—classic Prussian tactics. Samsonov at last realises that it is not elements of an army in retreat he is facing, but the whole German Eighth Army.

But if Ludendorff's nerve has steadied, Moltke's has not, and he plans to send six corps to defend East Prussia; now that Namur has fallen they can be spared, or so he justifies his proposition. Ludendorff protests strongly, angrily denying the need for them, but populist and political fears of Berlin being over-run by Cossacks are too strong to be resisted by a man of such slender nerve as Helmuth von Moltke.

In the end, only two corps are despatched eastward, but they are two too many; and today Bülow leaves a corps of the Second Army behind to invest Maubeuge. Schlieffen's critical right hook is weakened further.

August 26th.

Extrication of the BEF from its dangerous position. Retirement from Le Cateau.

Up almost as soon as asleep. Still dead tired. Mechanically I threw the blanket into a roll and ran out into the square. All the transport was gone, and I had relied on getting my cycle on a waggon. Suddenly one came struggling up from the station, piled high with a tottering mass of things. The drivers were half asleep, having evidently had a stiff time like the rest of us. I forced them to put the cycle on board; my belongings and myself also getting on somehow, we moved off after the column as rapidly as the tired and overloaded horses could take us.

We went out along the road to the west and turned off after about half a mile to the south. Here we caught up the column and I transferred my luggage to another waggon, and at last, it being impossible to cling on on top of the waggon, I got off and walked along behind, holding onto the back in the dark.

The sun comes out by degrees. I don't know any longer where I am going, and don't care. Walking on and on with this damnable foot and ceasing to wonder when it is going to end.

Slowly the transport drew away and left me, and I fell in with some Tommies, and we pottered along together to the best of our varying abilities. Found some biscuits on the roadside—a broken case left behind by the Army Service Corps. We all devoured them ravenously, breakfast being quite "off the map." After a time we came up with the transport again, and I here met Captain Yates, quartermaster of the Royal Welsh Fusiliers, who made me a place on one of the waggons. A kindly Argyll and Sutherland corporal, talking the broadest Highland, looked after me. We moved on again, and stopped shortly afterwards near a few roadside houses for breakfast. A cottage woman cooked some eggs for Yates, the Cameronian quartermaster and myself, while the drivers and others fixed up a meal outside.

Then we pushed on through Maretz, and while we were there some of our cavalry came through. The exact unit I do not remember, but it might have been the 9th Lancers. There was one man to every two or three horses, and we heard they had been frightfully cut up farther north. Many of the lead horses were wounded. Some Argyll and Sutherlands had got up into the church spire of Maretz to look out for the Germans. They were seen from below and caused an immediate spy panic. Nobody, however, fired at them, and by the time we had mobilised to turn them out they had come down and been identified.

While here a corporal suddenly came up to me and said, "Are you Lieutenant West of the 19th Infantry Brigade?" I said "Yes." "There are some letters for you, then," and he handed me a small budget of three or four. He had evidently a better memory for faces than I had, as I didn't remember having seen him before. I identified him afterwards as Corporal Hodgkinson, attached to the Brigade Headquarters. It was an extraordinary time to get letters, and the first I had heard from home since leaving for France. There was one from Ken and from Marjory,[144] and a post card or so. I wondered what they thought in England of how things were going. I read them through a few times and then, acting on our rigid instructions, burnt them and stamped on the ash.

About two miles behind us the villages were burning, and great columns of smoke were rising into the sky, marking the rapid progress of the advancing Germans. We moved off down a side road, but after a mile suddenly stopped and turned back into Maretz, for some reason I did not know. In Maretz again we took stock of ourselves, and found that three or four transport waggons of our column had not come back. Since we had apparently been heading for the Germans at that time, these were probably "scuppered" as they did not turn up again. Then we turned off down another road and got mixed up with a column of motor lorries, miscellaneous transport units, and odd batches of infantry.

After a time we came upon an ammunition column parked in a field beside the road. Just on the sky line a few miles back was a village burning and nothing between us and the enemy. As we passed we cursed them for not coming on, but they said they had their orders to stay there till the battery arrived, and they were not going to move. This was very laud-able obedience to orders, but it might have been tempered with a little

---

[144] West's brother and sister.

commonsense. However, we trekked on and left them as we could not stop to argue. Half an hour afterwards we were caught up by a horseman, flying like hell after us on a draft horse, with the traces dangling and whipping up the dust. As he passed he shouted something about the ammunition column being "in the hands of the Germans, and scuppered and burnt." Panic seized our column. The drivers whipped up their horses and in a moment the whole line was thundering along at a gallop. Some of the Argyll and Sutherlands ran alongside and handed up their rifles and we pulled them up into the waggons as well. At the bottom of the hill one GS waggon mounted a heap of stones on the side of the road and turned right over, smashing to pieces. The rest of them somehow swerved out into the field, or scraped by on the road without mishap. Up the steep hill on the other side the column perforce had to slow up, and at last came to a standstill. Captain Moulton Barrett (nephew of Elizabeth Barrett Browning) of the Argyll and Sutherland Highlanders rallied the men, and having a rifle I volunteered to do any scrapping, being somewhat ashamed of having so heartily taken part in the panic just before.

In this turmoil some of the motor lorries had gone over the bank higher up the hill, and had to be abandoned. Any such were dismantled and then smashed with pickaxes, so as to render them useless. One, however, we left behind with its crew refusing to give in. It had slid backwards down the bank just on the edge of the road, and the men were digging and swearing and trying to get some purchase for the wildly-revolving wheels.

We crawled down to within four miles of St Quentin and called a halt—I suppose somewhere near Lesdins. It was said that the column was going to stay there all night. So I got the cycle off and the luggage, both of which took a lot of finding in the mixed-up traffic, and pushed it along towards St Quentin.

After about a mile a lorry suddenly came up from behind and stopped to give me a tow. It was full of wounded men, and turned out to be the same lorry that we had left behind stuck on the bank. They had, they said, stayed and worked till the last moment when the Germans were almost upon them, before the wheels suddenly got a grip. They had been able to collect various wounded beside the road and come on after us. This was a gallant piece of work and I hope they got some credit for it.

It had begun to drizzle as we neared St Quentin. I pushed the cycle the last bit and found a mechanic in a small garage on the outskirts of the town, but he could not get it to go. He went on fiddling with it and trying to find the trouble, and I very ungraciously stood by and cursed him and the cycle, and all his ancestors and everything to do with him or the war. Finally I left him and limped into the town, hanging onto the stirrup leather of a transport officer. Felt like crying from sheer weariness and hunger. Arrange dinner with the transport officer at the Hotel-du-Cygne, but he does not arrive, and finally dine alone and take a room there.

> There was a vague but very persistent rumour throughout the town that
> the Germans had received a big defeat somewhere. Place and time were
> not specified. But whether true or just officially started, it certainly put new
> heart into the jaded and tired troops. Real sleep in a real bed! Glorious!

At the Battle of Le Cateau (see Map III) the 19th Brigade was "the only infantry
reserve of the II Corps", and today the regimental diary of the Welsh Fusiliers
states: "XIX Brigade reinforced R flank then covered retreat of L flank". This
explains the busy and exciting day West had, despite being "Still dead tired"
on waking that morning. So tired, too, were the overloaded horses even this
early in the retreat that the previous day (August 25th) the Argyll & Sutherland
Highlanders' diary reports: "Transport moved slowly as the horses were very
done[; they] wouldn't pull so traces were cut and wagons set alight". As a
measure of how "mixed up" the traffic was, "Capt Hyslop was ordered to take
out the teams and lead them, abandoning 1 Water Cart, 5 SAA Carts, and 1
GS Limbered Wagon".[145]

The broken box of biscuit West discovers by the roadside has been dropped
there not by accident but by design: the retreat is so fraught and unpredictable
that the best the QMG, the admirable Sir William—"Wully—Robertson, can
do to supply the troops is roadside dumps.

The *schrecklichkeit* observed today is not the last reference West makes to
villages and houses being burned by the Germans; the Belgians are no longer
the sole beneficiaries of *Kultur* and West is not the only contemporary to
remark on this. In some cases the destruction may have been a consequence of
shelling rather than malicious pyromania or terrorism, but most of it was. A
corporal of the Royal Dublin Fusiliers reports:

> The whole countryside was like a half moon on fire—villages and
> farm houses were burning and illuminating the country for miles
> around, and some of the houses at least I know could not have been
> set on fire by the shells. Every night it was the same old game, and
> our lads used to look forward every evening to what they called the
> fireworks.[146]

In his account Captain Jack speaks of "tall, handsome" *Colonel* Moulton-
Barrett, and the diary of the Argyll and Sutherland Highlanders describes how
"Col Moulton-Barrett had collected a small force ... and took up a position
on a ridge to the E of REUMONT". West, strictly a non-combatant, made
himself a volunteer member of this "small force". Yet the fact that he "felt

---

[145] Jack, op cit, p. 35; National Archives, WO/95/1365.
[146] *Kildare Observer*, 12 September 1914, pp. 3, 5.

like crying from sheer weariness and hunger" is a reminder that while he was made of stern stuff, he was no more immune to the strain of warfare than any man. This account may read like something of a ripping yarn betimes, but war is always horror, and courage is never the absence of fear but the overcoming of it.[147]

Le Cateau is another impressive performance by the BEF, though not beyond criticism,[148] and the British might have been overwhelmed had Kluck not been constrained in sweeping westward to outflank them by orders from Bülow, and had d'Amade's territorial force not impeded German probing of the flank in the afternoon, when the British were withdrawing. British losses come to about 8,000 men and almost 40 guns, more than twice the casualty rate of Mons—about 20 percent. A great many men straggled in over the following days, making losses less serious than they were at first thought, but the encounter was imagined to be calamitous at the time: GHQ gives the II Corps up for lost. August 26th "was perhaps the worst day of all at GHQ. Nerves were bad, morale was low, and there was much confusion.... Many officers collapsed completely." GQG believes "Battle lost by British Army, which seems to have lost all cohesion".[149] Kluck, believing the same, orders a halt to deal with his own considerable losses, and consolidate his forces, after which he pursues in the wrong direction. The BEF gets away, and Smith-Dorrien, arriving at GHQ almost alarmingly alive, is chastised by Johnny French for suffering from cheerfulness in the face of grave developments. In a self-serving brazen lie French later will accuse Smith-Dorrien of being "depressed" and offering "a council of despair".[150]

Earlier that morning, at a hastily-convened conference at St Quentin, French meets Lanrezac and Joffre to be advised of Joffre's Order No 2. He complains bitterly—and justifiably—of Lanrezac's exposure of the BEF's right flank, and Anglo-French relations are not improved by the Frenchman's insolent shrugs of response. Perhaps in part out of spite, but convinced more than ever of the need to pull the BEF out of line, French refuses to agree to joint action, and moves GHQ back to Noyon, evacuating St Quentin, which Joffre has designated as the mustering point for the new Sixth Army, created to defend Paris and buttress the critical left wing of the Entente forces. Paris

---

[147] Jack, op cit, p. 39. As an old man West remarked to his great-nephew, "You do that which you fear most". Delmé-Radcliffe, however impressive he appears today, will succumb to nervous collapse long before West does.

[148] See, for instance, Terence Zuber and Adrian Gilbert, op cit.

[149] Spears, op cit, p. 233-35.

[150] Sir John French, *1914*, p. 95. ("Suffering from cheerfulness" is an expression coined later in the war, but it seems to apply to Horace's relatively up-beat mood now, a mood that by and large was shared by the rank and file though not the high command.)

still has no adequate garrison, and Gallieni is creating a defensive zone around it—a day after this was supposed to have been finished.[151]

In the east, Ludendorff continues to attack Samsonov. In Galicia, the Russian Fourth and Fifth Armies advance against the Austrians.

German forces in Togoland surrender.

The German cruiser *Magdeburg* runs aground on the Russian Baltic coast, leading to capture of *Signalbuch der Kaiserlichen Marine* along with an encryption key. This will enable the Allies to intercept enemy coded messages, rather as cracking Enigma will in the next war.

The rumour that the Germans have "received a big defeat somewhere" likely is stimulated by word of temporary repulse of Rupprecht's offensive in Alsace. Closer to where West is, the Germans infamously have been sacking and burning the town and great library of Louvain, in a rampage that lasts five days and causes outcry across the world. In response to this, the "Manifesto of the Ninety-Three", all prominent scientists and artists, will deny any German wrongdoing in this or any other aspect of the war, and defend *Kultur*. Attitudes harden: a nation of such "Huns" must be comprehensively crushed.

August 27th.

Up 7 o'clock and hurry down to find several officers in the *salle-à-manger* at breakfast. They were all wounded, one in the head, another in the arm, and another in the wrist, and their caps and clothes generally ripped by bullets. From their conversation I gathered they had evidently had a hot time at short range. When these had finished and departed a Red Cross (RAMC) major came down and sat opposite me. A perfectly delightful little waitress in black was quite too much for him. "I say! Tell her I think she is a topper." I do so to the best of my ability, but am rather at a loss as to the Gallic equivalent of "topper." The major, a thorough sportsman, does not really require any interpreting from me. He, too, had had a very hot time under fire the day before, but finally got away all right, though he told me they had left many wounded behind. He was angry at the way they [the Germans] fired on the Red Cross, but put it down to their inability to see who was who.

The Germans were now known to be advancing on the town, and I went to see if my cycle was all right. I found it nearly in the same condition as before, but being in a bit more reasonable frame of mind after the night's rest, I decided to try another mechanic in the same town whom the first mechanic knew, so he took me along. In the lower square I found Fletcher sitting in the fountain beside his cycle, but I could not stop my spluttering machine or

---

[151] Sir Horace Smith-Dorrien, *Memories of Forty-Eight Years' Service*, p. 409; Tuchman, op cit, pp. 400-02.

it would never have started again, so passed on. The new mechanic found the fault at once, namely, magneto points too far apart, and had it right in no time. I don't think I ever loved a man more than I did that old bearded Frenchman. I gave him a handful of money, and it might have been all gold for all I cared, but he would not take it, and only after an argument accepted a couple of francs. I had quite expected to abandon the cycle, luggage and all, as I had no proper haversack for carrying my kit on foot.

When I returned to the main square I found Captain EW Cox in a car outside the Town Hall. The troops were all rapidly moving out of the town, but when he saw me he jumped out. "Go back at once," he said, "and find the rearguard, remember the lives of all these people may depend on your finding it. I want to know the exact position. You *must* get there." Captain Cox, a very fine officer, was perhaps more rhetorical than this occasion proved. But how was I to know that then? However, I was delighted to oblige and so away like smoke.

About seven kilometres out near Fontaine I met some French cavalry, about four or five of them. They reported that the Germans were now in Bohain and Fresnoy-le-Grand and everywhere else north of St Quentin. But I ran on fast, if warily, into the village of Fresnoy-le-Grand and found all clear, and then dashed on along the clear open road northwards towards Bohain.

At the railway bridge I stopped and interrogated a family of French people who were standing outside their cottage. Had they seen any British troops? No? Had they seen any Germans? Yes! And they went off into an excited tirade about them, from which I gathered that a patrol of German cavalry passed through Bohain that morning, and went off south-east towards Guise. They thought some Germans were in Bohain at that moment. One of the women volunteered to walk on into the village and wave a handkerchief for me if they were there, so I left my cycle at the foot, and scrambled up onto the railway embankment, and covered by the long grass found I had a good view of the village beyond. Very soon twenty-one German dragoons came slowly out of the town, and trekked towards me along the road. I left the embankment and rode out towards them to identify them, as it was dead ground here and they were still about a thousand yards away. At the top of the rise I met a refugee cart which stopped at my approach, and on looking around the occupants caught sight of the Germans some way behind. At this they all jumped out, dashed into a barn and hid under the straw. The cart was left in the middle of the road to wander where it pleased!

I climbed back up the embankment again and looked over with my glasses. The patrol came on slowly and I could see that both men and horses were very tired. When they reached the cart they shooed it out of the way and turned towards the railway bridge. The road here bends sharply under the bridge so I knew I could get away unseen. But now they were uncomfortably close and it was time for a decision. In my Lee Enfield rifle I had 11 cartridges, 10 in the magazine and one in the chamber. After many successful rifle competitions I had always flattered myself that I could hit anything in range moving or stationary. So here were 21 cavalry as large as life in an open field at 200 yards or less; and myself prone in the long grass above them alongside the bridge parapet. I sighted on the leader and then another and another. Eleven of them at least were sitting ducks, and as good as dead, and maybe all 21 before they could reach any sort of cover. It was my duty to kill them. Or was it? But for once in the impersonality of war I could see them close to as fellow men, such men as I had met and been friends with at Bonn University before the war.

The horses slopped along with heavy feet, and the leader's head was bowed on his chest from sheer exhaustion. So they had been having a hard time too. I squeezed the trigger lightly but not enough to fire, and then crawled back down the bank to my cycle.

As I fled away south to the cross-roads at Fresnoy-le-Grand I tried to rationalise it all to myself. My rifle was probably full of dust and would have jammed. Besides, after my hectic ride I was probably unsteady and might have missed. And in any case I had been sent out to find the rearguard, and not to fight the whole German army. But I knew in my heart I could not have murdered those men.

In Fresnoy-le-Grand I heard that the English rearguards was up at Brancourt, so I started off thither to the north-west, but at the top of the hill I met two boys on bicycles riding hard in the opposite direction. They said three hundred Germans were in Brancourt. This didn't sound cheerful, but they were rather excited and might have been imagining things. I went on to the top of the hill and looked over. From here I could see a few German cavalry cavorting about to the north of the town, so it was evidently no place for me. I then had an unpleasant thought that the first patrol I had seen must by now be near to Fresnoy, and would cut off my line of retreat to St Quentin unless I hurried back. So I turned about and raced for Fresnoy. As I reached the village the German horses were clattering on the cobbles down the north-east street. But I reached the cross-roads first and turned sharp for St Quentin.

After about two kilometres I stopped at Maricourt,[152] and again enquired about the rearguard or any British troops. The whole hamlet turned out and all spoke at once and quite unintelligibly. However, I gathered that some British might be in Ramicourt, so having been told I must find them at all costs I laboured out there over mere tracks. On arrival the inhabitants told me that an English battery had passed out that morning to the south.

---

[152] West writes "Mericourt", but this is some 40 miles north of where he is today.

As there were no Germans as yet in Ramicourt, I went off south to Sequehart. Here I came across an English soldier in a cloth cap, with no rifle or equipment, and looking dazed and bewildered. He told me that fourteen Uhlans had just captured him and let him go again after removing all his kit, saying that hundreds more were coming along behind so they could not be bothered with him.

The patrol had here split up and nine had gone off to the right towards Le Haucourt, and the remaining five had taken the St Quentin road—my road! I therefore took the safer (?) road with only five on it—and went like smoke, though it looked rather hopeless. All the way it was littered with ammunition boxes, and an indescribable assortment of stuff, left by our retreating troops, or thrown overboard to lighten transports overloaded with wounded.

Meeting some civilians on the road I asked about the German cavalry and heard of a German car just ahead with five staff officers on board. This looked as if I had got right into the middle of the German army without much hope of escape. The Germans, in their bitterness against England, were said to take no prisoners, so I was not going to be captured without doing some damage. That being so, I was out to get one staff officer at least, and get away afterwards or not in the *mêlée*. I did not catch the car, but always heard of it just ahead. Quite lost by now I suddenly saw a sign post to St Quentin so abandoned the chase. Soon I fell in with two or three infantry stragglers, and then three or four cavalry, and told them to dash on into St Quentin. Just at this moment I caught sight of a patrol of Uhlans crossing the canal on my left; so I had to race for it; I don't think the troopers or infantry got home, as this patrol much outnumbered them. At last I reached St Quentin. It was a close finish and a very exciting three hours.

(About two months later I heard from Blenner Hassett that a German staff officer's car ran right into St Quentin, thinking the Germans were already in possession. Unfortunately for them the French still held the town so they were captured, saving me the trouble.)

Retirement from St Quentin.

General Headquarters, or rather the advanced portion, had already left the town by car, and I could report to nobody. A body of French troopers were trekking out of the square to the south, otherwise the town was deserted of all military units. So I rode off to the south-west, where I was told the British had gone. After a while I caught up some staff officers of one of the Vth Division Brigade Headquarters and reported my various experiences, which one of them put down and forwarded on to Divisional Headquarters.

My reconnaissance to find the rearguard had proved a complete failure. I had the consolation (?) however, on September 16th, of learning that the

The broken bridge that may have wrecked the Schlieffen Plan. Pontoise-lès-Noyon after its destruction by Lieutenants Roger West and JAC Pennycuik on August 30th, 1914. (Courtesy M Gérard de Horde.)

Lieutenant Roger Rolleston Fick West, DSO.

Field Marshal Sir John French: narrow-minded, bigoted and vindictive, the Francophobe French was a poor choice for command of the BEF in France. A nasty man in many ways, a failure in the light of history, yet he was personally brave and always paternally concerned with the welfare of his men.

Sir Horace Smith-Dorrien: a "straight, honourable gentleman" of volcanic tempera-ment; "a commander of rare and unusual coolness, intrepidity and determination" in the words of his commander-in-chief; "a good old stick" and "our man" to the rank and file. Dr John Bourne claims that the BEF were "lions led by tigers" and Horace exemplifies his claim.

General Alexander von Kluck, commander of the German First Army on the drive through France. His subordination to Karl von Bülow constrained his freedom of action and almost entire dependence on wireless restricted his information, but his "rashness" might be celebrated in German history as "initiative" had he been able to cross the Oise at Pontoise-lès-Noyon and outflank the French Fifth Army.

General Karl von Bülow, commander of the German Second Army that drove the French Fifth back from Charleroi to Guise. Though the arc of his march was shorter, he was beset by the same communications problems as his sometime-subordinate Kluck, and faced greater opposition.

General Georg von der Marwitz, Inspector General of Cavalry in the Second Reich and commander of II Cavalry Corps in 1914. His horsemen caused the BEF much anxiety through the Great Retreat. Had they been able to cross the Oise in time, they could have done possibly fatal damage to the French Fifth Army.

General Manfred von Richtofen, commander of I Cavalry Corps, whose horsemen led the attempt to outflank the French Fifth Army on August 31st. He was grand-uncle and godfather to his more famous namesake, the Red Baron.

General Charles Lanrezac, commander of the French Fifth Army, who saw the flaws in Plan XVII yet fought as directed, against his better judgement but in accordance with his duty. History has judged him harshly but hardly fairly. Roger West's destruction of Pontoise-lès-Noyon may have prevented his army from being mauled if not broken but his own fighting retreat conserved his army to fight on the Marne.

Barbara Horder in theatrical pose. One can understand why many "candidates" couldn't "leave her in peace".

Barbara Horder in 1917, when her husband-to-be, Roger West, was chief development engineer for Geoffrey de Havilland at Airco.

Roger in sailor suit at age four, with his older sister Ruth.

Kenneth and Roger West in Buckinghamshire woods, c 1895, in a watercolour by Agnes King. The image of an idyllic Victorian childhood was at odds with the often harsh reality. (Courtesy John Bucknall.)

Roger and Barbara (right), in Seattle, shortly after their marriage. (Courtesy Sally Steen.)

Roger and "Ba" in their Carmel home, 1962. (Courtesy Sally Steen.)

Roger at about age 80, still climbing in his beloved mountains of British Columbia. His short legs are evident here, his large hands less so.

Sally Steen, age 13, with cat Percy and an unidentified dog, at the residence of her uncle and aunt, Roger and Barbara West,15th Ave, Carmel, California, 1962. (Courtesy Sally Steen.)

The former West abode in 2013. (Courtesy Dierdre Leisner.)

"On their way to Utah", a watercolour by Roger West. Because of what he had endured as a child and in the war, Roger was sympathetic to the travails of others, and always conscious of nature. This painting, made on a transcontinental car trip, counterpoints the bleak beauty of the Great American Desert with the bleak reality of migrant life in the Great Depression. (Courtesy John Bucknall.)

rearguard had been withdrawn four hours prior to my starting out from St Quentin, so my inability to find it was understandable.

Farther down the road I came upon the 19th Infantry Brigade, or rather bits of it. Colonel Ward of the Middlesex was now temporary brigadier, General Drummond being out of it after Le Cateau.

Towards evening we crossed the Somme by the St Simon bridge and landed up at Olezzy.[153] It was raining dismally, and Captain Jack, the last remnant of our original staff, was lying out on some straw with a bad fever. He should have been taken to a house but he refused to go sick and leave the brigade at this crisis.[154]

Our brigade was now reduced to ludicrous proportions. Of the Argyll and Sutherlands who were bivouacking in the field I could count only fifty-seven, but was told that ninety-three in all had arrived out of the whole battalion. As for Sang and Fletcher, I didn't know where they were.

After nightfall Colonel Ward sent me out to run up and down the Somme Canal, and report conditions. At St Simon the bridge was to be guarded by a party of Cameronians who were now on their way. A little to the left was another bridge which was now being demolished. I walked along the bank in the darkness, but the bridge went up with a rending explosion just before I reached the RE pickets. The footbridge over the lock gates, however, was still intact and could not be blown up without emptying the canal, thereby defeating its own object. So I went back and told Colonel Ward and asked for a further picket to guard it.

At this point the south side of the Somme Canal is backed by a belt of meres and marshes, so I got a peasant to point me out the only path of any sort, if it could be so called, whereby the picket could retire due south if pressed. On the way back the Cameronian picket asked me to see if I could find out what had happened to their sapper officer who was to demolish their bridge, so I went and hunted him up. Colonel Ward told me to stay near the bridge so as to bring back word of an attack.

Finding everything quiet there I made a bed within calling distance on the marshes. Only the road was solid, and as I could not lie there, I pushed my way among the willow saplings growing out of the water, and found a comparatively raised position among reeds and long grasses. The water came up from below, and the rain came relentlessly down from above, and it was bitterly cold. I tried to sleep but there were constant alarms all night, though no Germans. Ducks and other things creeping and squashing through the reeds are quite enough to keep one awake at such a time.

---

[153] Today spelled Olizy.

[154] For Jack, fever is san fairy ann; he doesn't mention this episode in his *Diary*.

While West and the officers breakfast, "the men [of the Argyll & Sutherland Highlanders] had eaten nothing since 4 am 26th", but 25 hours later were "given a good meal of Tea and Bread". The contrast between this rough fare and the *salle a manger* breakfast for officers elsewhere does not necessarily undermine the famous paternalism of the British Army, but it illustrates the relatively cushy number DRs had, even in this fraught passage, compared with the PBI. Later that morning, however, the Highlanders "drew full Rations" on the train to Noyon.

To call an attractive girl "a topper" was a compliment in 1914, a gratuitously offensive sexist remark in 2014, political correctness having displaced manly gallantry.

Captain Cox's instruction, "find the rearguard, remember the lives of all these people may depend on your finding it", illustrates how essential despatch riders were in the Great Retreat. The directive might have been "rhetorical" this time, but losses when DRs failed to find their targets highlight their value. After Landrecies the entire battalion of the 2/Munster Fusiliers was cut off and lost for this very reason.

The terror that refugees show at sight or word of Germans likely is due to the current campaign of *schrecklichkeit*, but it also may be stimulated by stories of Prussian excesses in 1870.

The incident at the railway bridge is a reminder of the superiority of the Lee Enfield, the best rifle of the war, and the best bolt-action military rifle ever made. In theory less accurate than the Mauser because the latter's three-lug bolt-fitment immediately against the cartridge secures this more snugly in the breech, the SMLE's rear lug arrangement allows the bolt operating handle to be placed more conveniently to the shooter's hand; this location, together with a "cock on closing" mechanism, makes working the bolt quicker and easier, which, along with the robustness of the gun, is what matters on the battlefield. The ten- rather than five-cartridge magazine—plus one "up the spout"—exploits this quicker-firing potential, hence, in part, widespread German belief at Mons that they were facing machine-gunners rather than riflemen.

But far more importantly than anything this incident tells about a rifle is what it tells about a human being. This episode would haunt West all his life.

The route was "littered with ammunition boxes, and an indescribable assortment of stuff, left by our retreating troops"; this may describe Wully Robertson's supply dumps, or it may mean that West's contemporary notes, or his transcription of them, are a day out here. While unofficial jettisoning has been going on since Mons, it's tomorrow that GHQ will issue instructions to lighten waggons and the 3rd Division will comply, to such an extent that Kluck will decide by the roadside evidence that the BEF are in panicked flight and out of the fight. If he gets things a day wrong here West may be forgiven, for as he remarks in his Introduction "it is natural [that] notes were fewest where the action was greatest".

Failure of General Drummond's nerve has been alluded to in commentary on August 21st and is described by West in Appendix I. The diary of the Middlesex Regiment reports laconically on August 27th that the general was "sick". Colonel Ward, who takes over, was killed on October 21st, in the encounter stages of what became the First Battle of Ypres.

Drummond was not the only senior commander to suffer nervous collapse under the strain of the retreat and his responsibilities. Corelli Barnett remarks: "The British rank-and-file proved stauncher in retreat than some members of the British command" (though at least two enlisted men drowned themselves and Trooper Ben Clouting describes how even a horse went mad, "banging its head against a wall ... appalling to see").[155] French, Henry Wilson and even the cool-headed Haig were all badly rattled by the early battles. In the I Corps, which had things easy by comparison, "Many of the officers are despondent, and if we should be attacked little spirit will be found in the men for fighting",[156] while in the II Corps things were understandably worse. On the same day as Drummond's collapse—August 26th—Colonel John Vaughan, chief of staff of the Cavalry Division, also broke down, as did GHQ chief of staff Sir Archibald Murray, earning himself a disparaging nickname, Sheep Murray.[157] That same day Lieutenant-Colonels Elkington and Mainwaring, of 1/Royal Warwicks and 2/Dublin Fusiliers respectively, tried to surrender their commands to the mayor of St Quentin. (Major Tom Bridges, of 4/Royal Irish Dragoon Guards, famously roused the men with a toy drum and saved the two battalions from ignominious capture.)[158] On August 27 Colonel Frank Boileau, chief of staff of the 3rd Division, shot himself. Three days later Colonel JE Edmonds, of the 4th, also collapsed, and later in the year Colonel Delmé-Radcliffe of the RWF, referred to throughout West's account, was sent home after breakdown.[159]

---

[155] Bernard John Denore, "The Retreat from Mons" in CP Purdom, Ed, *On the Front Line: True World War I Stories*, p. 18; Richard van Emden, Ed, *Tickled to Death to Go: Memoirs of a Cavalryman in the First World War*, p. 59.

[156] Sproston, op cit, August 26.

[157] A play on the name of Sir James Wolfe-Murray, another British general but no relation (though possibly a relation to West's IC colleague H Wolfe-Murray). Sir Archibald in fact fainted, and the wonderfully-named "Fido" Childs revived him with champagne.

[158] National Archives, WO/95/1365; Jack, op cit, p. 68; Corelli Barnett, *Britain and Her Army*, p. 374; Bernard John Denore, "The Retreat from Mons", in CP Purdom (ed), *On the Front Line: True World War I Stories*, p.18; Hastings, op cit, p. 222.

[159] Hastings, op cit, p. 519; Spears, op cit, p. 222, 233. Chronic rheumatism and damp trenches probably played a part in undermining Delmé-Radcliffe's morale, but he was later relieved of his command, apparently because, "under the influence of a lady

Might Drummond have been suffering from delusion by early morning of August 26th ("a nightmare" and "perhaps the worst day of all at GHQ", as Spears describes it, when Le Cateau was being fought, and Murray's nerve was going)? He "issued the news that 40,000 French troops were moving from ARRAS on CAMBRAI against the German right flank", so perhaps disappointment and despair triggered his breakdown when these forces failed to materialise?[160] There seems to have been widespread belief that "A corps of French cavalry was to relieve us at 11:30.... Later we were told that the commander refused to come to our assistance on the plea that his horses were too tired to move any further".[161]

That Drummond could understand such a saving force to be on the move may rather be a cautionary reminder to those who, with all of a century's scholarship and perspective, judge commanders harshly. Any combatant's understanding of the war he was fighting was constrained by what he knew, which often was limited to his horizon, and West's account alone is proof that a great deal was *not* known, even by men whose horizons were broad. General d'Amade's Territorials were not bearing down on the German right flank, in the way that Drummond thought—or hoped—but tenuously supporting the British left with antiquated rifles. General Drummond likely was not out of touch with reality—on the 26th at any rate—merely inadequately informed, like everyone else.

Complacent after defeating the entire BEF, as he thinks, Kluck reports to OHL his hopes to envelop the enemy. Coming on top of all other victories this report confirms OHL's belief that "The enemy, beaten all along the line, is in full retreat ... and is not capable of offering serious resistance to the German advance." Schlieffen's plan has been one of genius, victory in the West imminent and on schedule. Independent command is restored to Kluck; but Bülow warns against gaps opening on the right wing—presciently, in light of events.[162]

Communications problems further impede the Schlieffen Plan, already drastically compromised, for the Germans have left themselves dependent on wireless and cable. Distance is "blunting the curve" of the former, while the speed of advance overwhelms the capacity of signallers to string "air" cable; this mandates the laying of "ground" cable, subject to damage by traffic and animals—and by saboteurs—and with a transmission range of only about 25 miles. First, Second and Third Armies become reliant on wireless almost completely, but the system is badly overloaded, and in addition to delays, poor

---

of position in the county, he allowed himself to deny justice to one of his own junior officers"—*Hansard*, 04 July 1917 vol 95 cc 1082-3.

[160] National Archives, WO/95/1365.

[161] Martin and Nick Shelley, *Two Wheels to War*, p. 184.

[162] Tuchman, op cit, pp. 402-03.

reception and interference from the Eiffel Tower—and dangers of security leaks—not all Corps HQs are equipped with wireless.[163] So poor are German communications that for several days Kluck imagines that the II Corps constitutes the entire BEF. Communication between First and Second Armies devolves onto von Richthofen's I Cavalry Corps, which would be much more effectively employed otherwise. Had all this cavalry been part of the trans-Oise assault on August 31st (*qv*), the Germans perhaps could have cut off the French Fifth Army; but much of Richthofen's Guard Cavalry Division will have to be left behind at Noyon because their horseshoes have been worn out delivering messages.

While the nascent Sixth Army begins to assemble under General Manoury in the Somme valley, it is attacked by elements of Kluck's First. Joffre orders Lanrezac to attack westward toward the St Quentin – Guise area in order to secure a zone for the Sixth Army to fight on—just after Sir John French unilaterally evacuated St Quentin. Again Lanrezac is placed in an invidious position, for quite apart from the operational difficulties in turning his army, BEF retirement leaves his left flank vulnerable to enemy cavalry (as he earlier had left the BEF's right flank open by his own precipitate retreat), while attacking westward is to expose his right flank to the full force of Bülow's Army. He is "much irritated against [GQG] and the British", expressing himself in "violent language".[164] His left flank will remain vulnerable after he breaks off battle and retreats, and in this matter West will play a saving role.

General French, without informing Kitchener any more than Lanrezac, orders continued retreat. At Etreux, 2/Royal Munster Fusiliers hold off an entire Second Army corps for a whole day before the surviving 240 men and four officers surrender, ammunition having given out. This stoic resistance gives the I Corps a twelve-mile lead on its pursuers, and sets the German schedule back fourteen hours.

Meanwhile the first of three battalions of Royal Marines land at Ostend, in the hope of attacking the German supply- and communication lines and cutting the armies off from their bases. They will hurriedly re-embark on the 31st, but for a short while they will frighten the Germans with the possibility that they are the vanguard of 70,000 mythical Russians with summer snow on their boots.

At home, railway hold-ups are attributed to these tens, and even in particularly heady flights of imagination, hundreds of thousands of Russians being railed from Scottish ports to troopships on the Channel.[165] The Germans pick

---

[163] Senior, op cit, pp. 317-19.

[164] Tuchman, op cit, pp. 411-12.

[165] The rumour may have originated with Highland troops wearing white spats explaining, in barely-intelligible accents, that they were from Ross-shire, but it was exploited by British intelligence.

up on the rumour and, with most of their British agents interned for more than three weeks now, are unable to verify or falsify it. German paranoia being what it has been for many years, they dare not discount it, so "Worry about a possible 70,000 Russians at their backs was to be as real a factor at the Marne as the absence of the 70,000 men they had transferred to the Eastern Front".[166]

In East Prussia Samsonov's men, despite being half-starved by this stage, resist strongly. Rennenkamf finally has been apprised of the situation and begins to move toward the rear of the Eighth Army, but with no evident urgency.

The military crisis has precipitated a political one: the French government is reconstituted.

August 28th.

In the small hours of the morning the bridge was blown up and the Cameronian picket returned. There was no food to be had, as usual, but it was too early to feel hungry. I found now that I was the only remnant of the Signal Service left for the brigade and was kept busy. (Officially, of course, neither Sang, Fletcher nor myself belonged to the Signal Service, but with the breakdown of much of the organisation we became despatch riders pure and simple.)

About 6 o'clock two more motor cycles arrived. These were the brothers Burney, mounted on their own Blackburn machines. They did not stay long with the brigade.

Soon I was sent off to Ham to find and collect any Royal Welsh Fusilier stragglers. Just north of the Somme large groups of lost men of all units were resting. I called out for Royal Welsh Fusiliers and about twenty or so detached themselves. There were no officers of any sort and the other stragglers came crowding round and asked me where they were to go. There were men of some six or more different regiments like sheep without a shepherd. I had no idea where they could rejoin their regiments and in some cases these few men were the sole survivors of their unit. I could only tell them definitely to get themselves into some sort of order under their NCOs and march on southward. They had been doing nothing else for the last four days, and fighting as well, poor devils, but they wearily pulled themselves together, and choosing their own leaders prepared to move off.

The twenty or so Fusiliers I marched up the road calling for more of the same regiment from every group we passed. In all we got together about fifty stragglers, amongst whom was a sergeant. They were a sorry-looking lot with

---

[166] Tuchman, op cit, p. 434.

their uniforms torn and partly lacking, but all but one or two had their rifles, and they were a fighting force yet. That sergeant had them into order in a minute, and I gave him instructions of the road he was to take, and how he was to wait at Berlancourt due south of Ham till the brigade arrived from Cugny to the north-east. He was abominably dirty and had not shaved for days, but he saluted sharply and with a few curt words marched his men off as if on parade.

Going back into Ham I found one of the two remaining bridges about to be blown up, oblivious of the fact that a column was just coming down to cross it. So I warned them, and then went about my next quest, which was to stop further Royal Welsh Fusiliers, the cavalry and others from coming down to Dury, as this bridge had now been blown up, and they would run into a blind alley. I dashed off to the right and went along for about a mile. Suddenly an officer jumped into the road.

"Where are you going?" he shouted.

"Dury," I said; "seen anything of the Royal Welsh Fusiliers?"

"No, but you'll see something of the Germans if you go much further."

I found I was on the St Quentin road and going straight for the German Army!

Three or four men got up from where they had been resting. These were apparently all he had of his platoon, and they moved on slowly towards Ham. After a detour I got on the right road and so to Dury. There were no signs of the Royal Welsh Fusiliers, but I was able to put a few troopers on the right road, and gave them instructions to warn others. The whole district seemed to be deserted, so I sped back along the Somme and found a railway bridge still intact, not marked on the old French map. At Ham I found one of the RE officers and told him about this, and he sent off a detachment to break it. After that I got back to Brigade Headquarters, which was just ready to move off. Breakfast was still quite off the map as everybody was now on the move to Cugny. However, I managed to ride on ahead and got a feed at a cottage just beyond Cugny, it now being about 11 o'clock.

After Cugny the brigade turned south-west again towards Villeselve and Berlancourt, and it being impossible to keep with the slow-moving column I went ahead from village to village and waited for the brigade to come up. Somewhere about Villeselve I came across Lieutenant Irwin of the Veterinary Corps leading his horse, which had developed a strain. It was fearfully hot and dusty and we endeavoured at one of the estaminets to get a drink which, however, was unobtainable due to some restriction or other. Only a few hours later, no doubt, our friends the Germans were helping themselves regardless of restrictions. It was extraordinary how some of the country people had absolutely failed to realise how things were going.

Along the stretch from Berlancourt and the junction with the Ham-Guiscard road the brigade halted as a long column from Ham was crossing us. Headquarters of the brigade (now under Colonel Ward of the Middlesex) was set up under the shade of a few scrubby trees—if such a moveable affair as a Brigade Headquarters at this time could ever be said to be set up. The headquarters horses, and for that matter all the other horses, were suffering from the continuous work. The colonel's horse had a great sore on the withers some two inches across and was tired out. The other animals were much the same, but I remember this one as we tried to fix up a pad to keep the saddle off the affected part. But it was useless trying to spare the horses in the retreat, where the men as well were suffering so badly. Both man and beast walked and worked till they dropped and were left behind.

Fletcher had again turned up on his motor cycle, such as it was, for it was beginning to show signs of wear.

Soon I was sent out by Colonel Ward to find the speed and end of the crossing column so that his brigade could join in correctly behind. At the cross-roads at Le Plessis I found the tail of the column. The troops were now going at about two and a half miles per hour, and one man who was apparently marching strongly when he passed, suddenly staggered out to the side of the road and collapsed face downwards on the grass. Two of his comrades dropped out and laid him on his back, and some Red Cross orderlies turned up and told the others to go on. I waited for a few minutes, but their efforts to revive him were unavailing, and they told me they thought he was out for good.

I calculated 5:20 PM for our brigade to be put in motion, and reported back to Colonel Ward. It worked out all right, and we joined on five hundred yards behind. The 19th Brigade was also only doing two and a half miles per hour at its best, and it was still ten kilometres to Noyon, our object. The troops, poor devils, were nearly exhausted, and were moving along with a slow swaying step by sheer will power. There was never a breath of wind, a pall of dust hung over the road and the sun beat pitilessly down. Though damnably sleepy I was not feeling so bad now and blinded on into Noyon, which seemed a fair-sized town. Anyway I managed to get a hot bath there, which was bliss, and afterwards met a Red Cross major who asked me to come in and get lunch, tea, dinner, or whatever the meal was.

After a time the troops arrived and found they had to go on still another five kilometres to Pontoise. Though almost at the last gasp they scrambled along somehow in the dark, and at last reached the bridge.

Drawn back into the pine trees was a big grey car, with its headlights shining right across the road, and lighting up the troops as they passed. Nobody questioned its right to be there until all the troops and artillery, etc, had gone over, and it was not till then that they wondered whose car it was. Whether this had been a spy car or not I do not know, but when last seen it was travelling rapidly northwards towards the Germans.

At last the brigade came to a halt, and the tired troops dropped into their billets or lay down and slept just where they were.

Here in Pontoise Fletcher and Sang turned up again. Sang had left his motor cycle in the hands of the Germans somewhere between Le Cateau and St Quentin, and had fled on foot with a Hussar officer after him, taking pot-shots at him with his revolver. However, he crawled through a hedge and got away all right into a wood where, after many adventures, he had at last managed to rejoin his brigade.

Fletcher had also had a very hot time up at Le Cateau and Solesmes, where he had come in for very heavy shelling, and a party of the Middlesex had been badly cut up by shrapnel fire. He had got a slight cut across the forehead, but otherwise no damage luckily. He was very upset over the frightful things he had seen up there—of which it is almost impossible to write.

As there was little likelihood of food in Pontoise this evening, I rode off on a foraging expedition towards Pommeraye. I tried a farm or two but had no luck as the troops were everywhere and everything was cleaned out, so I decided to return. At that moment the cycle, with a few despairing splutters, ran out of petrol. I did not know where to get any and was rather vaguely wandering in the road when a Cameron Highlander corporal and a private of the same regiment came up.

"Where ye goin' the noo?"

"Run out of petrol," I replied. "Can you tell me if I can get any more anywhere near here?"

"Wha air ye, and whaur ye come from?" was the only reply.

Somewhat impatiently I told them and added a pious hope that they should go to the Devil.

"Ai think ye're a spy," said the corporal, a slight, stupid-looking fellow. "Ye'll have to come with me."

Anybody who has tried to get any change out of an obstinate and stupid Scot must know it is useless, so I wheeled the cycle into a farm and was ushered before a certain Major Myers, to whom I presumed I would be able to show my passes and explain my business. No such luck. My captors explained that I had run out of petrol just outside their farm and it was perfectly obvious, therefore, that I was a spy. In the face of such conclusive evidence what was the major to think, and in spite of showing him my credentials and somewhat obsolete pass he too was now firmly convinced that I was a spy, and must stay there all night.

There was a big barn there with lots of straw, and to tell the truth I was very glad to get such comfortable quarters for the night. Nevertheless, since I was apparently a German spy and therefore not under the authority of the English, I took the opportunity of being quite as offensive to my superior officer as the occasion undoubtedly warranted.

The kilties, however, were now going as far as to meddle with the motor cycle, evidently with the intention of putting it out of action in case I should attempt to escape during the night. So I told them that there would be the Devil to pay in the morning if it was touched. After that they desisted and we all went up into the loft and dossed down in the straw.

I was conscious the whole time of many suspicious eyes looking at me, and stupid faces peering surreptitiously round the rafters to see that the terrible spy did not escape. I was now, of course, thoroughly enjoying myself, so took out my pocket book and made various notes for their benefit, and did little things a stage spy is always supposed to do; but I was very tired, as no doubt they were, and soon fell asleep.

On this day the Royal Welsh Fusiliers' diary records: "XIX Brigade formed rearguard to 3rd Division who moved to Noyon 32 miles finally arriving at Pontoise about 9 PM."[167]

The "brothers Burney", Alick and Cecil, had founded Burney and Blackburne in 1913, and enlisted as despatch riders in August 1914. The Blackburne (not Blackburn, as West spells it) was used by a good number of despatch riders, and appears to have given excellent service, though it was Triumph and Douglas that became the official remounts for DRs in 1915. Blackburne survived into the 1920s as a motorcycle manufacturer and into the 1930s as a supplier of highly-rated engines to the British motorcycle industry.

Alick and Cecil were attached to the Fifth Division, part of the II Corp, to which the 19th Brigade was now in reserve, and they feature in WHL Watson's seminal account, *Adventures of a Despatch Rider*.[168] A further connection: when training at Williams and Robinson, Rugby engineers, the Burneys had worked with Geoffrey de Havilland and were to base their first motorcycle engine on one of his design and manufacture, and in 1917 West will be seconded from active combat to chief of research with de Havilland's Aircraft Manufacturing Co.

Though West says little about the Burneys, what he does say suggests a system of secondment of despatch riders as circumstance demands, already evidenced by West's own secondment from the Intelligence Corps. This indicates that a supposedly luddite high command recognised the importance of motorcycle despatch riders early on, recognition that may be due in part to the important role they played in the successful Larne gun-running operation of

---

[167] National Archives, WO/95/1365.

[168] A new edition of *Adventures of a Despatch Rider*, edited and illustrated by the Shelley brothers, and which breaks the name-code DORA had imposed on its author in wartime, is forthcoming from Helion & Company: *Two Wheels to War*.

the previous April. British generals were for the very most part Unionists and would have been following events in Ulster closely.

The Royal Welsh Fusiliers were indeed "a fighting force yet", far more than they might appear at this juncture. Through the Great Retreat many units were all but wiped out while others were unscathed, and "the Royal Welsh Fusiliers lost only three wounded". But their good hard condition was part of the reason they survived so well. The man who apparently dies at Le Plessis is not the only one to die of exhaustion in the Great Retreat, many reservists being in poor shape.[169]

West seems to suspect that the "big grey car" he sees today may be the same noted parenthetically in his diary at the end of his August 13th entry: "40 HP Grey Renault". Spy mania was a feature of this phase of the war in particular, as West finds out today; he will come under suspicion again on September 1st. The brazen observation by the car's occupants would make them very cool customers, but they could indeed have been spies.

West gives no clue as to whether the "frightful things" Fletcher saw are those that inevitably emerge out of every war, or *schrecklichkeit*. His reticence reflects the more delicate sensibilities of the time, but it also may reflect his own ambivalence toward the Germans, among whom were his cousins and in whose country he had lived very happily, hence his mischievously amiable conversation with the German prisoner next morning. The dissonance was to exacerbate the psychological strain suffered by any soldier, especially one at the sharp end of conflict.

In compliance with orders from GQG, Lanrezac turns the French Fifth Army westward toward St Quentin – Guise in order to attack Bülow's Second Army, a manoeuvre that takes most of the day. Kluck learns that Lanrezac's line of attack will lead the Fifth Army obliquely toward his own line of advance, and proposes to swing left to attack the French rather than pursue the "beaten" BEF. OHL hints at agreement with this proposal, as it would help forestall French consolidation on a defensive line, or even destroy the Fifth Army. Earlier success at Liège and Namur has encouraged OHL to believe that Rupprecht can quickly break French fortifications on the other end of the front and turn a single- into a double-envelopment: Cannae on a twentieth-century scale and proof to the world of German military genius. OHL urges all units to press victory home quickly; the Schlieffen Plan is about to be vindicated. But it's now five corps short of what Schlieffen envisaged, and Rupprecht's assault—along with Kluck's left wheel—will leave it in ruins. Already a gap

---

[169] Richard Holmes, *Riding the Retreat*, p. 9; Macdonald, *Ordeal by Fire: Witnesses to the Great War*, pp. 16-17; Coward, op cit, p. 17.

is opening between the Third and Fourth Armies where two corps have been stripped for redeployment to East Prussia.

Close pursuit has been beaten off at Le Cateau, so the BEF has some respite, especially as Kluck now has bigger fish to fry. But much is not known and "The 28th was a terrible day for the Allies, a day during which the scales might have been definitely turned against them but for the iron will and faith of Joffre".[170] Lanrezac's stand against Bülow is replete with the potential for disaster and General French, in panic, issues orders for lorries and transport waggons to dump ammunition and supplies in order to hasten progress—and, in fairness to French, a "soldiers' general", to accommodate wounded and weary men.[171] In one place "eleven wagon-loads of kit were burned in huge piles by the roadside—by no means a reassuring sight".[172] Both independent British corps commanders share this view and countermand the instruction, but the lately-arrived 4th Division is under GHQ command so it can hardly but comply—greatly to the dismay of its troops, with morale in the rank and file recovering. Discovery of burned and abandoned supplies by his cavalry vanguard persuades Kluck that the BEF is a broken army in flight, and this misconception will encourage him to turn his own army's weight upon the French Fifth. (The following day, with relatively good news from GQG, GHQ sends lorries to recover the jettisoned matériel, and some is salvaged before the German vanguard forces the mission to be abandoned.[173])

Yet pause to counter the criticism of Sir John French that dominates this account: French was spiteful and small-minded; he was a bigot, a philanderer, a spendthrift, a liar, and professionally remiss more than once in his career. But he also was "warm and generous, approachable and humane. He had the wellbeing of his men at heart, and they knew it". One NCO describes his visits to billets and his ease with and obvious concerns for the ordinary soldier. French, says Sergeant Sanderson, is "a trump. Everybody simply adores him". On August 29th he stepped out of his limousine to cheer his footsore soldiers "and in a few seconds the men were crowding around with eager faces, hanging onto the words of their leader. He commiserated with them upon their losses; he understood what they had been through. In a word he appreciated them, and in the Army appreciation is a 'rare and refreshing fruit'." Lieutenant Spears describes him as "the man who never lost his head ... he would face up [to danger] and never shirk"—and while clearly this is a simplistic evaluation it reveals something about the *soldier* that French was, as

---

170   Spears, op cit, p. 263.
171   The order was sent by Wilson at 8:00 PM on August 27, "a well-meant but defeatist and unnecessary instruction"—Adrian Gilbert, op cit, p. 134,
172   Coleman, op cit, p. 47.
173   Spears, op cit, p. 247.

opposed to the *commander*. As commander-in-chief he was out of his depth; Haig's disparaging evaluation of his superior was on the mark, and exhorting the rank and file, however it was appreciated, was "not an effective use of his time."[174] Though "in many respects he was quick on the tactical uptake" French was bewildered by the strategical situation in 1914—and overwhelmed by the politics of Allied warfare. Perhaps "with the right chief of staff [he] might have been [a] good enough" commander-in-chief; but Archibald Murray—an "old woman" in Haig's opinion—was not the right chief of staff, and besides, to win a war a commander-in-chief needs to be more than merely "good enough".[175]

The Zone of the Armies is extended to include Paris, subordinating civilian authority to Gallieni, who presses all suburban inhabitants to defence construction, which West will observe on September 2nd.

In East Prussia the German right wing moves around the Russian flank, while a frontal assault pins Samsonov's centre; the ghost of Frederick the Great might have nodded in approval. The Russian Second Army starts to crumple. Rennenkamf is marching to his comrade's aid now but he's too far off to be of any help. Samsonov orders withdrawal—too late. His army is outflanked and about to be destroyed in a *kesselschlacht* ("cauldron battle").

The Serbs invade Hungary and occupy Zemun.

The Battle of Heligoland sees three German light cruisers and a destroyer sunk, with minor damage to British ships; 700 Germans and 35 British sailors are killed. The encounter will confine the *Kaiserliche Marine* to port until the Battle of Jutland and greatly boost British morale, but of far more importance than the minor naval victory that it is, this battle is cleverly disseminated as a British diversion to mask the embarkation of Russian hordes across the Channel. OHL picks up on the disinformation, making it difficult for Moltke to cheer unreservedly his armies' glorious triumphs: all the battles have been won, but not yet the war, and the German rear, if not its front, may well be open to destruction.

August 29th.

At dawn I woke up and found many of the troops already astir in the yard preparing breakfast. I put my things together and came down the ladder. In one corner of the yard, muffled up in a blanket and greatcoat, lay a captured German Hussar officer. I had a short chat with him, and he told me that he had

---

[174] Peter Hart, *Fire and Movement: The British Expeditionary Force and the Campaign of 1914*, p. 156.

[175] Richard van Emden, *The Soldier's War: The Great War Through Veterans' Eyes*, pp. 59-60; Spears, op cit, p. 312, f/n; Mallinson, op cit, pp.230, 242, 294, 321. Dr John Bourne paints a more sympathetic picture of Murray in *Stemming the Tide: Officers and Leadership in the British Expeditionary Force 1914*, pp. 51-69.

had two horses shot under him. The second had fallen on him and strained his leg so that he was caught. He was a great big fellow of fine physique, as were most of the prisoners taken at that time. He was quite inclined to be pleasant and we were well into conversation before I suddenly saw that all my friends, the Scotties, were taking enormous interest. Though no doubt none of them could understand a word of German, they would stroll across the yard and get quite close while they polished an already immaculate tin plate, and try to overhear our remarks.

My host gave me no breakfast, but took me off under a guard of a corporal and six privates to be identified at Army Headquarters. This I found to be about four hundred yards down the road in a great chateau. I was marched up the drive under escort and halted. Almost at once Ronnie Larking of King's College, Cambridge, appeared, and soon after Meldrum. Larking was highly delighted, and took the chance to compliment them on being a bright lot of Scotties. We had to wait, however, for a new *Laissez Passer* from Captain Cunnynghame, the APM,[176] who took some time to be found. Meantime my gallant escort had to stand there at attention in the court and be the butt of everybody who had time to crack a joke at their expense. After this formality was through I was released and given a really good breakfast by an Intelligence Corp man, whose name I cannot recall. (May have been 2nd Lieutenant Burney, IC.)[177]

Returning to Pontoise I found King (invaluable man) had managed to get us a billet not far from the bridge and near our Headquarters. At last—at last it was to be a day of rest. It was frightfully hot, and we all set about getting a bath. A great washing tub was lying in the kitchen and we dragged it out into the orchard. The water we drew from a little stone well in the garden wall. It came up in a bucket clear as crystal and cool as ice. I think that bathe was the most magnificent I ever had. Immediately overhead me was a laden pear-tree, and we could sit there in the cool water in the sun-flecked orchard eating luscious pears, and forget for a space the war and the long misery of that road from the north down which we had toiled.

The Headquarters Staff was now composed of Colonel Ward of the Middlesex and Captain Jack of the Cameronians. There was no Brigade Major to replace Major Johnson. He, I am sorry to say, had been hit by shrapnel outside Le Cateau and very badly wounded. He was, however, picked up and taken to a church, used as a temporary hospital. There was no time to get the wounded away, and I heard he had been left there. Later the church was set on fire by shells or otherwise, and it was presumed that he had perished

---

[176] Assistant Provost Marshal, responsible for military discipline.
[177] No Lieutenant Burney is included in West's list of the Intelligence Corps, but a Lieutenant E Burney is listed elsewhere; see WO 372/3/187888.

in the flames. (Major Johnson, as a matter of fact, fell into the hands of the Germans, and though he was reported, I believe, as missing after a long time, information came through after a year that he had died in Germany.)[178]

The troops were very badly in need of a rest, and this was the first day they could sleep and pull themselves together a bit. For my part I slept most of the day but for a short despatch or so.

After nightfall Captain Jack sent me out to reconnoitre the road to Laigle through the Bois de Carlepont. I found the road all right for vehicles in single file, but passing would be difficult due to the deep ditches on either side. Right in the heart of the woods I stopped. There was a little clearing here, and a signpost pointing the way down six dark paths leading off into the blackness of the trees. The silence was complete—the night had thrown a velvet cloak over the forest, blotting out sound and light. Then far away to the east came the muffled boom of distant guns, reminding me that away there men were fighting and killing each other, and soon these same trees might be echoing to the crack of rifles and the feet of our retreating troops.

Reaching Laigle I returned to report all clear. Sang, King and Fletcher were asleep in a kitchen at Headquarters, and I tried to get some [rest] too. About midnight, however, I was called up to take a run along the Oise and find out what bridges had been blown up. Being warned that snipers were likely to be on the far side of the canal I did not waste much time loitering, but went skidding along the towpath at some speed till I came across the first bridge to the east—the one at Varesnes as far as I can place it. This had already been broken and was lying half in and half out of the water, a twisted mass of wreckage. Farther east still I found a steel girder bridge, fully prepared for demolition, and the Royal Engineers officers only awaiting orders. Coming back again and travelling westwards I discovered another bridge broken. All the bridges on our front, therefore, were destroyed, or about to be, except our own at Pontoise and that was under orders to be broken after our departure.

Smith-Dorrien's decision to fight at Le Cateau, and Kluck's diversion toward the French Fifth Army, ease enemy pressure and mean that today the 19th Brigade and II Corps "could sleep and pull themselves together a bit". The previous day Spears notes a significant difference between the two corps, the II Corps, after its rough handling, being in lower spirits,[179] but many have remarked on how a good night's sleep works wonders for well-disciplined troops. The men are enormously reinvigorated and by several accounts morale in the ranks has by now recovered well, but not all are cheered: Sir John French

---

[178] Captain Jack reports Johnson as killed in action—op cit. p. 38.
[179] Spears, op cit, pp. 255-56.

orders the British base to be moved westward from Le Havre to St Nazaire and he continues with his plans to pull his force out of the line.

The French defence line for an all-out assault against the invader is being readied, but pursuit must be beaten off to permit consolidation, and the Fifth Army's turn to westward now complete, Lanrezac orders an attack. This, likely, is the source of "the muffled boom of distant guns" that West hears (though also today the German First Army attacks d'Amade's Territorials, toward the west). Sir John French countermands Haig's offer to support the French Fifth's attack, much to his discredit and Lanrezac's understandable wrath. D'Espèrey, on the right of the French assault, advances toward Guise, and drives Bülow's X Corps into full-tilt retreat, the first reversal on such a scale suffered by the Germans in the West; but elsewhere there is no progress and French casualties are heavy.

Though the BEF has not been pressed hard since Le Cateau, pursuit is still close and the danger of running into enemy forces remains. This danger is mutual. Today a German cavalry officer arrives at La Fère, casting no more than a doubtless-disdainful glance at the "prisoners of war" outside, who are so amazed by the effrontery they can only stare as he swaggers into the post office and writes postcards home boasting that "the British were running 'like sheep' before the glorious and victorious German armies". He learns how mistaken he has been on his emergence, and "was driven away in a cart, looking like a strange captive bird chained to its perch".[180]

This officer's delusion is widely shared. Today OHL reports: "The defeat of the English is complete. They are now completely cut off from their communications, and can no longer escape by the ports at which they disembarked."[181] German intelligence has failed to pick up on the transfer of the British base to St Nazaire, as well as on the military facts nearer hand.

Gallieni receives the first of the forces he has requested from his erstwhile protégé, Joffre, to defend Paris: a single naval brigade. It is far from enough, and to make his task harder he encounters political resistance to his orders to demolish buildings in order to give his Paris garrison a clear field of fire.

Across the world, Samoa is occupied by New Zealand forces without a drop of blood being spilt, greatly to New Zealand satisfaction. When the Tripartite Convention of 1899 had agreed that Samoa become a German colony, Premier Richard Seddon melodramatically described the place as "New Zealand's Alsace".

---

[180] Spears, op cit, p. 339.

[181] Maurice, op cit, p. 122. Both sides were caught out by porous lines. On the night of the 26th General Jack Seely had walked past a German sentry at Saint Quentin town hall, but he was able to escape in the darkness—Scott, op cit, pp. 173-74.

August 30th.

So I returned and had another try for some sleep in the early hours of the morning. Before it was yet light the brigade was called up to move off again to the south—the retreat had recommenced.

A beautiful silvery dawn found the troops out in the road buckling on their equipment, and getting ready to start. Thin wisps of mist lying in patches about the flat country disappeared in the morning sun, except in the forest to the south, where the trees rose out of a filmy white sea into the clear air above. We were evidently in for another scorching day, and the farther we went before the midday heat the better.

Fletcher's Rudge had now given out with a smashed steering-head, and Sang, as previously stated, had had to abandon his motor cycle. But near Headquarters someone unearthed a new Triumph, apparently in perfect condition but for the kick start and the gears stuck. But this did not help much as we could not repair either machine at the moment. In the midst of our difficulty a beautiful canary yellow Thorneycroft lorry suddenly turned up out of the blue and proved a friend in need. Fletcher, Sang and Churchill all got on board with their cycles and luggage and it moved off.

Up till now we had been travelling over the great plain of north-eastern France, dotted plentifully with farmhouses and single trees, with here and there tracts of low marshy land. But now the character of the country was beginning to change, and we started upon deep belts of forest, and hilly country, rising higher and higher till it drops back suddenly into the valley of the Aisne.

Leaving the Oise we turned west, and soon plunged into the mists of the Bois de Carlepont. I ran on ahead to La Bellourde and waited for the troops to come up through the woods. It was a wonderful peaceful dawn over the sleeping forest. I was just dozing off when Colonel Ward arrived on a horse and told me that the whole brigade had apparently gone astray, or at any rate the rearguard had.

Then at the end of a long aisle of trees appeared a distant horseman coming along at a hand-gallop. I rode down to meet him and found it was King, urging his tired steed to further exertions. On coming up with Colonel Ward he said that the Middlesex, who were then acting rearguard, had taken the wrong road. They had gone off to Laigle, and he had come for further instructions, as they were too far on their road to return. Colonel Ward told him they were to meet at Carlepont, and King's horse being almost exhausted I rode off to scour the country and find them. They had not gone far beyond Laigle when I caught them, and in trying to direct them to Carlepont I found I had left all my maps at the Pontoise billet, so dashed back there to get them.

The British retirement leaves the French Vth Army in the air. German cavalry try to enter the gap via the Oise bridges. Destruction of the last Oise bridge.

I found the village quite deserted. The inhabitants were not up yet, and all troops had gone. I searched the billet but had no luck, so decided to return; but happening to go on to the bridge I found it still intact. It was a suspension bridge and the charges intended to cut the strap had failed, while a fire lit in the roadway to burn it down had gone out without damage.

It seemed a pity to leave this bridge intact when all the others were down, so I went off at full speed to report to Colonel Ward and if possible get it blown up. There would probably not be much time to lose as we had now left Pontoise two or three hours and the Germans might take possession any time. I am sure that road from Pontoise to Carlepont was never travelled faster. I roared up the slope in the village and found Colonel Ward at the cross-roads and offered to go back and break it, given the necessary para-phernalia. He did not believe it possible at first, and said "Don't be a fool and commit suicide". However, after a little argument he allowed me to run onto the 59th Coy RE about a mile farther south and get explosives.

They were trekking slowly along the road with all their transport at a little village Le Four à Verre when I came up with them. I here met Major G Walker (later General) and told him that the demolition of the Pontoise bridge had failed, and said it might just be possible for me to get there before the Germans did. But I would need a supply of gun cotton, primers, fuses and detonators. He gave immediate orders for this. Then I told him that with my rusty knowledge of demolitions I would much like to have an expert engi-neer along with me if he could spare one. He hesitated, evidently thinking as Colonel Ward had done that this would probably be suicide, so did not give an order, but called for a volunteer. From among the group of officers Lieutenant JAC Pennycuick stepped forward, and said he would go with me on the carrier of my motorcycle.[182]

So we heaved my baggage hurriedly onto a waggon and strapped on a 14-lb tin of gun cotton, fuses and primers to the back. Pennycuick put the detonators carefully in his breast pocket, lest they go off with the jolting of the ride; then after borrowing a clip or two of cartridges, he scrambled up on the pile of stuff and we fled north.

We were riding I thought straight into the German army, and the hints of our impending suicide did not add to my peace of mind. Afterwards I think far the most dangerous part of the trip was the ride, as we were in a hurry, and the road was full of troops, gun limbers and horses! I could fully sympathise with Pennycuick as I know of nothing more terrifying than sitting on the back of a

---

[182] West mis-spells the name as *Pennycuik*.

motorcycle behind an unknown rider at desperate speed through traffic. I felt his hands grip on my shoulders in anguish at some of the narrower escapes, but with a pocketful of temperamental detonators he could only sit still and take it.

After a time we broke clear of the troops and away into the forest travelling fast. The back tyre bumped ominously now and then with the increased weight, but there was no time for extra air. So we fled on praying that it should not puncture, and expecting that the Germans had by now entered Pontoise. At last we dashed through Mont-a-Lagache, and drew up behind a house at the entrance to Pontoise. Some of the inhabitants were now up and about, as it was, I suppose, 6:30 or 7am. *"Est-ce-qu' il-y-a des Allemands dans le ville*?" we asked. *"Non, pas encore, mon Capitaine."* We were neither of us captains but we let that pass and unpacked the gun-cotton and primers and pointed the machine for home before walking out to the bridge. It was all quite still, and there may not have been any Germans for miles, but it would not do to waste time. After examination we decided to blow up one of the suspension pillars, as we had not enough gun-cotton to smash both, and a second attempt to break the strap might meet with no more success than the first.

I swarmed up to the top of the pillar and Pennycuick threw up the gun-cotton slabs. By the merest luck the slab fitted tightly without tamping between the steel blocks over which the straps passed. When they had been fixed Pennycuick scrambled up with the detonators and fuse, the former definitely not being suitable for throwing, and cast an experienced eye over my efforts. Having fixed the fuse and detonator he climbed down again. Lighting it up I slid down after him, and we ran for a neighbouring house where we waited for it to go off. After a bit there was a feeble bang. The primer must have been wet or something, and I daresay my efforts at arrangement had not been very expert.

We ran out into the street cursing the thing, and this time Pennycuick swarmed up and fixed the thing again with another detonator and fuse. There was a sudden burst of rifle fire somewhere behind the wood beyond the river, where some stragglers of ours had probably butted into an advancing German patrol, but it may have been a long way on such a still morning. However, there was not much time to waste, and anyway the fuse was now fizzling again at the top of the pillar, and Pennycuick was sliding down to get away.

But at this moment a paralytic old dame arrived at the head of the bridge. She had heard the pop and thought it was all over, so had come out to see what the bridge looked like when broken. Her fastest sprint would, I daresay, only have reached two miles an hour, so there was nothing for it but to push her into the toll house beside the bridge and run. With unerring instinct we were lucky enough to enter an estaminet and got a couple of ciders. We were just drinking to the success of the demolition when a tremendous crash announced that this time it had gone off. We ran out and found the straps had been thrown clear of the pillar, and the whole roadway had slid sideways into the river, forty feet below. One of the steel straps had whipped back in breaking and gone slap through the roof of the toll house. I do not know what happened to the old dame. Quite pleased with our morning's work we ran to the cycle and made a bee-line for the horizon.

Somewhere beyond Carlepont we came up with Colonel Ward, and later the general of the 5th (?) Division, and reported the result of our efforts. The general laughed and said, "Now that's a funny thing, that was the very bridge we wanted to use for our advance!"[183]

Soon after we passed the yellow Thorneycroft with Fletcher, Sang and Churchill on board, and then the long-threatened disaster to the back tyre occurred and it flattened out with a sigh.

Back to the Aisne.

After Carlepont we travelled due south till the road dipped into a gully, a tributary of the Aisne. Here we made a halt for half an hour and while we waited some of our cavalry arrived and a battery of "Cow" guns (60-pounders) dinted and ripped by shrapnel in some northern scrap. The drivers led their horses down to drink, followed soon after by a party of troopers with the same intent. A slight mix-up occurred, and the troopers uttered oaths and imprecations for which they are justly famous. How refreshing was this torrent of abuse. Two days before everyone was in a state of nightmare stupor from weariness and exhaustion, and here, after one day's rest, were men capable of playing their part with vigour and word-perfect once more!

About 6 o'clock in the evening we reached Attichy-sur-Aisne and crossed the bridge. It was brilliant and hot, and below us the water was full of troops, swimming and washing the dust out of their eyes and skins. I was longing for a bathe, but we moved right on and after a kilometre turned into the main Soissons-Compiegne road, and so to Couloisy.

Brigade Headquarters set up in a little house at the entrance to the village, and Captain Jack asked me to take him urgently back to Divisional Headquarters at Attichy, on the carrier of my old Premier. I think I must have effectually cured him of any desire for carrier-riding as we went at a suicidal

---

183 If West is right in his recollection, this would be General Sir Charles Fergusson, not renowned for jollity, but a stern disciplinarian. Though a Unionist, he was opposed to the stance taken by Hubert Gough in the "Curragh Incident", holding that "revolution is the danger, not Ulster and Home Rule", and that a soldier's job was to obey the orders of his King, whatever his own politics, and stand against revolution, not help foment it.

pace. On the way back we had a narrow shave between a car and a gun. I could almost feel his finger nails as he gripped my shoulders, right through my uniform and Sam Browne belt. But we missed them by about a quarter of an inch each side! My mistake, but of course I made out I always did that sort of thing. Later I heard he told King he had ridden pillion with that "crazy Lieutenant West. It was Hell! Does he always ride like that?"

After a little argument with Churchill, we got a billet opposite Brigade Headquarters in an old cottage. We were quite a happy family here—Sang, Fletcher, King and myself. Each for himself we foraged round the houses, and then pooled our finds. Sang acted as cook, and though crockery and cutlery were sadly lacking we got a quite passable meal off tin lids with our pocket-knives, a fork or so, and one valuable spoon.

The cottage consisted only of a tiny mud-floored kitchen with a bed-closet attached. It belonged to a very old woman who sat, huddled and indifferent, in one corner, never uttering a sound. About 10 o'clock she got up and shuffled out into the night and did not return. We were sorry for the old lady, but she did not seem to understand a word we said in any language, so it was no good urging her to stay.

My leather bag had mysteriously been slashed right across, as I entered Couloisy, and I sat up that evening laboriously stitching it together so that it should not fail me on the morrow and scatter my few precious belongings on the road. Having lost my haversack at Pontoise with all my maps, I managed to raise a horse-cloth from Yates and with two old puttee tapes sewed up a quite passable haversack as well. After a while we all fell asleep huddled in a blanket on a chair or stretched out on the unsympathetic hard mud floor, but the continual lack of sleep for the last week made mere discomfort of no consequence.

"At dawn the Sapper officer responsible for blowing up the bridge remarked that his orders were 'to blow it up at dawn, and he didn't care if the rest of the Army was on the other side'. So he fired the charge, but the effect was only partial"—as West discovers when he returns to Pontoise to retrieve his maps.[184] The sapper's anxiety to blow up the bridge, even at the risk of isolating residual British forces—and the gunfight West hears as he prepares to demolish the bridge indicates that stragglers remain north of the Oise—and the evident alacrity with which the sapper abandons his task when the explosives fail, indicate general nervousness at proximity of the enemy. This nervousness counterpoints the courage of West's undertaking, hours later, to return to this bridge and destroy it.

---

[184] Dunn, op cit, p. 37.

"It seemed a pity to leave this bridge intact ..."—indeed! The understatement camouflages the importance of Pontoise-lès-Noyon and renders explicable West's later reputation as "the man who saved Paris". Today OHL orders: "The First Army has wheeled round towards the Oise and will advance on the 31st by Compiègne and Noyon to exploit the success of the Second Army". Though the Second Army had been chastened at Guise, and was reluctant to pursue Lanrezac, could Kluck's First take the French Fifth Army in the flank, while it was retreating, the consequences could have been calamitous. The bridge just beyond Noyon, however, Kluck will find destroyed, forcing his army to search for crossings miles downstream.[185] (Further analysis of the results of West's actions follows in "The Man Who Saved Paris".)

The diary of the Argyll & Sutherland Highlanders describes Pontoise-lès-Noyon as a "Swing Bridge", which is incorrect: apart from West's description, contemporary photographs clearly show a partly-collapsed pier and sagging suspension cables. But the same diary reflects the importance of this bridge: earlier, the regiment had told off "6 NCOs and 24 men to guard [it]".[186]

It becomes evident later in West's account that "the smashed steering head" of Fletcher's Rudge does not mean a broken frame, but likely damaged steering-head bearings, which prove repairable. West's subsequent explanation, "everything was badly chewed up [but] I managed to fake it so as to be steerable anyway", suggests that the cups-and-cones of the bearing assembly had become notched from poor lubrication, faulty adjustment and/or hard treatment, and he is able to reposition the bearing components to shift the notches from the straight-ahead position—a "bodge" that a good engineer would easily come up with. A measure of the hard treatment motorcycles as well as men have suffered is West's considering his month-old mount an "old" Premier.

The despatch rider served not merely in communications, but in various other roles such as personnel carrier. West's belief that he "effectually cured [Captain Jack] of any desire for carrier-riding" may be correct, but the occasional *need* for such a mode of transport remained. Poor Jack again was condemned to ride pillion on a motorcycle: on September 5th he was forced to "proceed uncomfortably on the luggage-carrier of a despatch-rider's motor bicycle to Headquarters 5th Division at Brie-Compte-Robert, five miles away," and more rides follow, "clinging to the despatch-rider. This is a really terrible means of conveyance on the French cobbled roads".[187] Discomfort was the least of any rider's concerns: French *pavé* was both difficult and dangerous to ride on a motorcycle, but far more senior officers than Jack also took such

---

[185] Kluck, op cit, pp. 83, 86. See also West's Map IV.
[186] Plate 1; National Archives, WO/95/1365.
[187] Jack, op cit, pp. 47, 59.

unlikely lifts. "I have a vivid recollection of this distinguished officer [General Hunter-Weston] ... careering past me on the flapper's perch of a motor bicycle, and of thinking how such a means of progression was possible only for a British [as opposed to French or German] General."[188]

The "canary yellow" Thorneycroft lorry is a reminder that the BEF, while relatively speaking the most mechanised in the world, was such by dint of the volunteer spirit, and a pre-existing arrangement for requisitioning civilian and commercial vehicles.[189]

Sir John French advises Joffre that the BEF will not be fit to offer battle for ten days, and orders a retreat for tomorrow, without liaising with Lanrezac, who meanwhile breaks off his attack on Bülow and retires. French informs Kitchener of his intention to pull back behind the Seine, in an eight-day march west of Paris to place maximum distance between the BEF and the Germans—despite acknowledging that French success at Guise has relieved pressure on his own army. This proposal "recalls vividly the extraordinary point of view held seriously in some quarters, a legacy of the South African War, that the British Army could withdraw and refit as and when it liked.... Even to entertain such an idea was to show a complete misunderstanding of the merciless and ruthless foe we were now opposed to".[190]

Besides, "French success at Guise" is far from unqualified. With Bülow's Army still menacing his right flank, Lanrezac has no choice but resume retreat across the Oise, using bridges that he will destroy behind him, and then hurry by forced march toward the Aisne, to put that natural defence also between him and pursuit. In fact Bülow makes no attempt to pursue, reporting to Kluck that his army is too disrupted and exhausted to follow. As Smith-Dorrien has done at Le Cateau, so Lanrezac has put in an effective performance at Guise; but what seals his fate is that though Joffre has ordered resumption of the Fifth Army's retreat, its commander has anticipated the order, thus making his later "Limoging" easier. It will take Johnny French longer to "Stellenbosch" Horace.[191]

---

[188] Dunn, op cit, p. 50.

[189] The army possessed about 80 vehicles but under the terms of this subsidisation scheme it was able to add the best part of a thousand lorries and about 250 cars to its complement on the outbreak of hostilities. The "canary yellow" colour of this lorry attests to the haste of mobilisation and consequent lack of time to over-paint civilian livery.

[190] Spears, op cit, p. 246.

[191] Limoges is a town in the heart of France, far behind the lines. Commanders dismissed by Joffre were, officially, sent there, to while away the war, as failed British commanders in the South African War had been sent to Stellenbosch. "*Limogé*" was not a literal, geographical term, but it carried the same connotations of failure and disgrace as "Stellenbosched"; not as bad as a court-martial, but not much better for such a proud man as Charles Lanrezac.
Horace Smith-Dorrien saved the II Corps, if not the entire BEF, by standing to

For the moment the danger is less to Lanrezac's career than to his army—and indeed the Western Allies and the Entente cause: the Fifth Army's two flanks are in the air now. This and the next day may prove to be among the most critical of the entire war: "For two dreadful days all seemed lost".[192] For if the Fifth Army can be smashed now, the BEF and the nascent Sixth Army can be screened off, and the Fourth, Third, Second and First taken in enfilade while pinned by the several German forces opposing them. Joffre's plan to consolidate his armies along the Paris-Verdun line and counter-attack from there can never be realised if his Fifth is annihilated.

The direction of Lanrezac's retreat from Guise has persuaded Kluck that he can roll up the French armies by turning southeast-ward, swinging north of Paris rather than to the west to surround it; this move will also close the twenty-mile gap that has opened between him and the Second Army, and comply with Bülow's request to do precisely this. He discounts the threat from the French Sixth Army, despite having made contact with Manoury's marshalling forces, while discovery of the BEF's jettisoned stores and ammunition—a consequence of the 4th Division's compliance with GHQ order of the 28th—has convinced him that the BEF is in full flight, so he leaves a single reserve corps to secure his right flank.

Yet consider: had events turned in his favour Kluck's "impetuousness" would be lauded as *initiative*. Besides, lacking the two divisions stripped by Moltke to send east to the Eighth Army, or reinforcement from the left wing to replace his losses in combat and through investing his lines of communication, he now has too few men to carry out Schlieffen's original plan. The strategic point of surrounding Paris was to outflank the enemy and Schlieffen had foreseen the French as deploying farther west than they actually did in 1914. The effort to adapt Schlieffen's theory to the reality Kluck encounters is perfectly in line with *Großer Generalstab* doctrine, and what Moltke the Elder had proclaimed back in 1870: Paris might be the direction taken, but the military objective must be the enemy's field armies, without which the capital cannot withstand. OHL, aware of troop shortages and anxious to close up gaps, aware too of the opportunity presented by an open Fifth Army flank, approves Kluck's action.

That action proved German undoing. "The German General Staff had absorbed the principle that the first object in war is the destruction of the enemy's main forces in the field, and that this achieved all else follows." In

---

fight at Le Cateau rather than retreat as commanded; at Second Ypres he will choose not to stand as commanded but—as prudently as Lanrezac after Guise—to retreat, leaving himself open to unfair dismissal as Lanrezac did. Each general's commander had privately endorsed his subordinate's actions, but each sacrificed his subordinate to "national interest"—or petty vindictiveness and vanity.

[192] Jack Seely, *Warrior: The Amazing Story of a Real War Horse*, pp. 67, 69.

August 1914 "The fallacy in this reasoning lay in the assumptions that the British Army had been defeated so decisively as to be incapable of interference, that Paris had only a moral and not a military value, and that Manoury could be safely neglected".[193]

This analysis seems incontrovertible—but it is the complacent post-war judgement of a triumphant British general who would have been sweating bullets in August 1914. The Schlieffen Plan was no less a gamble than the Manstein Plan in 1940, and Kluck's roll of the iron dice might have won the war; for had the bridge at Pontoise been open to him, he could have defeated Lanrezac, while screening off Manoury and the BEF, and then rolled up the whole French line. Further analysis will follow.

OHL today moves from Coblenz to Luxembourg to be closer to the front and alleviate problems with wireless communications, but these remain: on September 4th, almost on the eve of the Battle of the Marne, a message from the First Army to OHL takes sixteen hours to get through.[194]

Gallieni warns the new government to leave Paris before raiding German cavalry can cut the railway lines to Bordeaux (a measure of how mobile is the war at this point, how rampant the Germans, and how effective cavalry). Joffre learns of the disastrous defeat at Tannenberg—but also of the detachment of two German corps from the Western Front to East Prussia, which gives him hope.

The Times carries the "Amiens despatch", reporting on "a retreating and broken [British] army", something that causes outrage but serves as a spur to enlisting too, putting an end to the "patriotic reticence", as Asquith puts it, to acknowledge the potential calamity confronting the country.[195] In the field, however, already-resurgent British morale is boosted further when the gap between the I and II Corps of the BEF, separated since August 25th, is closed south of the Oise, greatly easing the burden of work on despatch riders, staff officers and commanders.

In East Prussia, with his army destroyed and racked with shame and sorrow at having failed his sacred Czar, Samsonov shoots himself. The Battle of Tannenberg is the most decisive victory of the whole war; it will take 60 trains to transport the 500 captured Russian guns, and other spoil of battle, back to Germany. In Berlin civilians and politicians are "already beginning to make plans for the victory booty [and] the erection of vassal states";[196] but for all their victories the generals are uneasy. They might have taken up to

---

[193] Maurice, op cit, pp. 135-36.
[194] Hastings, op cit, p. 314.
[195] Tuchman, op cit, p. 432.
[196] Hastings, op cit, pp. 247-48.

100,000 prisoners but where, worries Falkenhayn, are the captured guns that a truly significant French defeat must yield? His pessimism affects "Gloomy Julius" Moltke, aware of the Schlieffen Plan's shortcomings and of his own departures from it, and of the risks attendant to Kluck's turn.

August 31st.

Up at about 4 o'clock and slightly feverish after an all too short night's rest. Near the banks of the Aisne was our yellow lorry, up to its axles in the mire, and there seemed little chance of ever extricating it. Here I met Lieutenant Sproule again—the RAMC officer attached to the Royal Welsh Fusiliers who had come to see me at Quiévrain in Belgium, and who had advised two or three days' rest for a poisoned foot! We had had it! All the troops had left or were leaving, and Sproule, who was endeavouring to get the lorry out, gave it up and followed their example.

It was now 10:30am, and Fletcher's bike was no longer in commission, though Sang's could still be ridden. And now our lorry, too, had failed us though the drivers were still toiling to pull it out of its muddy grave. So we took our machines into a deserted garage at La Motte, and I started to work on Fletcher's steering head. Though everything was badly chewed up I managed to fake it so as to be steerable anyway. It meant leaving somebody or our kits behind if all the bikes could not be made to work, neither of which we wished to do.

Happening to look out into the road while at work we saw a man in blue overalls steering an erratic course over the bridge on a push-bike. He caught sight of the drivers in the field, waved feebly, and collapsed. We ran out to pick him up, and the lorry drivers brought a stretcher and laid him on the roadside. We thought him dead at first, but after a bit he came to and explained he was English. He had been captured, he said, at Ham on the Somme, but disguising himself as a French artisan had escaped on a push-bike. In his flight, although he had received one bullet and two lance wounds, he had somehow managed to get away and ride forty kilometres to catch us!

Soon after the drivers were rewarded for their efforts, and with a screaming engine and wildly-revolving wheels the lorry climbed out of its grave. Pitching and lurching about in the muddy field it at last reached hard ground and safety.

I had just started to work on Sang's bike when there were reports of Germans coming up, and we and the lorry were the last of the whole crowd. Sang had meanwhile lunched at the one little hotel at La Motte, so we ate ours in haste. Some push-cyclists came in from the west and reported that the Germans were already in Compiègne. They went off to the south, and we did not wait long in following them. Now that the lorry was in working order again, Sang put his bike, the wounded man, and himself on board, and Fletcher and I riding we all set off.

We bore away to the south-west and after a time plunged into the beautiful forest of Compiègne. It was a lovely day, and when we thought we had put a safe distance between ourselves and the enemy, Fletcher and I left our machines and strolled into the forest for a little sleep, pending the arrival of the lorry which, having no maps, would have got lost. We lay for a while in the idly-shifting patches of sunlight looking up into a roof of green, with a wonderful blue sky shining through. It was a grand respite after the stress of the previous days, and we let the peace of the forest sooth our jarred nerves and spirits.

When the lorry arrived we directed it further and gave it about a quarter of an hour's start. Then getting on our machines we went on after it and expected soon to come up with our rearguard. But at a road junction we suddenly found one of the drivers, very hot and out of breath. He had run back to catch us in case we should take the wrong turning, and told us they had driven into a ditch about two miles on. We turned off in the direction indicated and soon came upon the lorry, hopelessly stuck in a very deep ditch. The wretched wounded man had luckily not slipped off. The rest of us were all right as we had bikes, or could walk anyway, but we could not very well leave him there, nor take him along as we were. So I sped back five kilometres to a farm we had passed on the outskirts of the forest. The farmer was very obliging and harnessed up a horse and cart and started off for the scene of the breakdown. But before we got there somebody (I think Fletcher) had by a most fortunate accident discovered a Red Cross horse waggon lost and wandering in the forest. This suited the case so admirably that we thanked the farmer very much for his trouble and sent him back.

We had an idea (afterwards proved quite erroneous) that we would be able get back and pick up this lorry later, so we only partially dismantled it and hid most of its valuable freight such as a barrel of petrol, etc, in the forest. But we should have burnt the lorry, freight and all. As it was, I am afraid a perfectly good lorry fell into the hands of the enemy.

We pushed Sang off on his motor bike, and the drivers disconsolately got off and walked, each making a bundle of his more essential belongings and carrying it on a stick over his shoulder. They had no rifles.

Soon we came up with the tail end of our cavalry, and here and there a trooper was resting his tired horse in the shade. We overtook some of our infantry, a portion of the Royal Welsh Fusiliers marching along and singing—actually singing—as they went. The Royal Welsh Fusiliers always were a musical crowd (and I found out later the more it rained the louder they sang!) But how different was this spirit from a few days before. They were still very much alive in spite of all their hammering and marching. They crossed us and went on to the south-west, while we went after the main body of the brigade. At last we found them and reported that we were still alive.

Acting on instructions from Captain Jack, Fletcher and I fell back to hustle on stragglers, both men and horses. The end of our column was always brought up by a sad, straggling line of men, lame and footsore, stumbling onwards, interspersed with wretched horses, gaunt, wounded and dying, yet limping along, compelled by that gregarious instinct which forbade them to be left behind. Captain Jack thought that such horses, given rest and food, would become quite fit again. So we had to do our best to get these miserable scarecrows along, and those that stopped were to be shot. There could be no mercy for man or beast.

At the tail of the line was riding Major Vandelour of the Cameronians, also keeping tired stragglers on the move. We found two of the Cameronians beside the road trying to cook their breakfast, dinner or tea, or whatever meal it was, ideas of time being lacking. One was removing his boots to ease his tired feet and both were dead weary and practically refused to come along when told. Suddenly the ever-resourceful Major Vandelour arrived. Far away down a long ride in the forest a few horsemen came into view. We got our glasses and saw that they were some of our troopers trotting in a bunch through the trees.

"Here come the Germans," said the major. "They don't take prisoners. They'll have their long lances into you fellows if you don't hurry."

The effect was magical. The fellow with his boots off pushed them on again without doing up the laces, stumbled up to Fletcher and myself and asked us to take him along. The other one stuck his cooking into various pockets and followed suit. They clambered on the back, and we roared away through the forest. We caught up their comrades some way ahead and deposited them with severe reproofs on their criminal behaviour. They were very repentant, but they were absolutely exhausted, and it is doubtful if they kept up long with their unit.

We dropped back again and fell in with a sad little cavalcade hurrying along, with a dying comrade held up on his horse by two troopers riding shoulder to shoulder on each side. Three or four others were riding with this group, and one of them told us that this man had been very badly hit, but they hoped to come up with an ambulance in time to save him. Fletcher rushed on to stop an ambulance further ahead and get them to wait. Some time after he returned and said that all the ambulances were full, and the horses too tired ever to catch up again once they stopped. I do not know where the troopers had got to by now, nor whether they ever managed to bring their man to safety before it was too late.

We were now quite alone, and far behind. In a clearing we came upon two loose horses, quite fit and not at all tired out. We had a sort of idea that we were to advance shortly, so we decided to chase them off the road into the forest. The one Fletcher selected disappeared rapidly among the trees and he got back to his machine, but mine was a more mulish brute and refused to leave the clearing. At last I persuaded him to enter the thicket, and was chasing him farther in when suddenly there came a shout from Fletcher in the road, followed by several rifle shots behind us. I rushed back for the road but the roots and saplings of the thicket were apparently wilfully obstructive, tripping me up and seizing my stocking cap off my head. I turned and snatched it when a few more shots rang out, and I heard Fletcher's bike start up and get away. I was now near the road and he yelled to me to hurry up as he sped off into the forest. I needed no urging and leapt on the bike and fled, with the stand down and kicking up the dust. I don't know how many of our friends were behind as I never looked to see.

We reached Verberrie after dark, and found it full of troops—mostly the Seaforths, the Middlesex and the Royal Welsh Fusiliers. This took me off my map sheet, and one apparently was expected to get to unheard of places by mere instinct.

The "spy mania" was getting rather bad. Captain Claude Raoul Duval, our French Liaison Officer, was coming back from headquarters when he was suddenly pounced upon by one of the Middlesex officers, who took him for a spy. Captain Duval said nothing, but went off quietly enough under escort to be identified. On his return he hunted out the Middlesex officer in a great rage, demanding satisfaction for the insult given him (a French officer) in being marched as a prisoner through a French town. Captain Jack, who had now arrived, tried to act as peacemaker, but Duval demanded a duel, and gave in his name and that of the Middlesex officer to Captain Jack so that they might decide it in the morning. But Captain Jack tactfully forgot the names and all about it!

Soon afterwards, however, an apparently genuine spy arrived. He was dressed as a little fat French tourist, and rode into Verberrie on a motor cycle, and started asking all manner of questions. Looking closely at his motor cycle in the dark I found it was an English Rudge Multi, with a London number, LA or LE or something on the plate, which had evidently belonged to one of our despatch riders. I therefore removed his high tension wire to prevent him going off before I could make enquiries. This was not necessary as some of the Middlesex had already had their suspicions aroused, and were now taking him into custody. I do not know who he was, and never saw or heard of him again.

Our rapid retreat had been too much for the mapping department. Captain Jack said he was going off to St Seuveur, and disappeared in a car, and now nobody had any maps, or any idea where that was. Finally, as it was impossible to find headquarters, I put myself at the disposal of Colonel Delmé-Radcliffe of the Royal Welsh Fusiliers, at the level crossing. The battalion was holding a line just inside the forest, running due east from the level crossing.

After dark, Colonel Delmé-Radcliffe sent me out to keep up communications with various pickets and outposts in the forest. The woods were said to be full of Germans, and all the men were very jumpy. It was not advisable therefore to ride with lights, and on several occasions I stopped just in time to prevent a sentry slaying me with his long bayonet.

It is very hard to find one's way along these woodland tracks in the dark, and stopping now and then one hears the forest full of noises and occasional panicky shots. The undergrowth cracks and rustles and a horseman comes out onto the path and stands dimly in the dark listening. German or English? Suddenly a heavy volley rings out somewhere in the forest, but one does not know in which direction.

Get back to the level crossing. Here one of our cavalry pickets and a patrol of Death's Head Hussars have just come charging through our lines, all mixed up, and fighting as they ride. Our machine guns and rifles at the crossing let drive indiscriminately at the whole lot as they pass. It is impossible to tell friend from foe in the dark. Almost by a miracle only one of our picket's horses was grazed, while three Hussars were killed. The accoutrements of one who had fallen near the crossing was brought in. In the lining of his fur cap were one or two photos of the members of his mess and a girl. Lieutenant Fitzroy of the Royal Welsh Fusiliers got the cap, I think, with its beautiful silver crest. The other two Hussars were not found until dawn.

That he would have taken a nap, "pending the arrival of the lorry which, having no maps, would have got lost" seems a rather cavalier attitude for a man of such pronounced sense of duty as West; part of a despatch rider's responsibilities was convoy management, so if there had been a fear of the lorry getting lost it was his job to ensure that it didn't. But for once West's command of the English language slips to the point of allowing ambiguity to insinuate: the danger of getting lost without maps is meant in the future conditional sense, were he and his chum not there to guide the lorry, and such is the pressure on DRs that any opportunity for sleep was not to be passed up.

Stashing the petrol and other freight and leaving the immoveable lorry suggests that the troops believed a stand against the Germans was imminent, rather than almost a week away, and indeed soon West is to say that "We had a sort of idea that we were to advance shortly."

The incident with Captain Duval and his "insulter" is also recounted by Captain James Jack, an actor in the drama. According to Jack, he gave Duval the name of "Lieutenant Smith" as his insulter—Duval having threatened to shoot Jack if he didn't find out the name! "This ends the unfortunate incident," Jack concludes, adding that Duval's "death at Verdun cancelled the risk of this duel".[197]

Being slain by a sentry with a "long bayonet" was an all-but-commonplace hazard for despatch riders. The DR was caught between giving his position away to German snipers if he rode with lights on, and risking being bayoneted or shot by his own side if he travelled in darkness. The latter danger was heightened by nervous sentries tending to challenge from a long way off, their challenge often not being heard over distance and the sound of the DR's engine. This happened to West on September 7th, when he failed to hear a challenge over the noise of a particularly loud engine.

Today's account makes clear how porous were the lines during the Retreat, and the encounters in the forest were clearly fraught. Kluck has sent General Georg von der Marwitz's II and General Manfred von Richthofen's I Cavalry Corps across the Oise at Bailly-Thourotte,[198] the former in pursuit of the BEF, the latter to cut off the French Fifth Army. The diary of 2/Royal Welsh Fusiliers gives greater detail on the clash between British pickets and German Hussars:

> One of our Cavalry patrols was driven in by German Cavalry Detachments trying to capture them. Our cavalry patrol galloped through our line. A picket of A company opened fire on the German cavalry, it being nearly dark by then, and the Germans made away very quickly. I am not certain how many we accounted for, but I know we captured one wounded German cavalryman, who said he belonged to the 8th German Hussars.[199]

The incident also illustrates the panicky nature of real war, which could and often did lead to casualties from friendly fire, even when professional soldiers like those of the BEF are involved. Captain Dunn gives a more comprehensive description of this fracas.[200]

In London Kitchener receives John French's proposal to retreat west of the Seine and is horrified by the political and military ramifications of abandoning the French and opening a gap in the Allied line that the Germans could

---

[197] Jack, op. cit, p. 44.

[198] The two cavalry corps were attached to, respectively, the First and Second Armies. (Richthofen was great-uncle and godfather to the Red Baron.)

[199] National Archives, WO/95/1365.

[200] Dunn, op cit, pp. 40-41.

exploit. He departs for France to buck French up. The government doubles its previous order for 162,000 shrapnel shells.[201]

Joffre learns of Lanrezac's qualified success at Guise, which improves the prospect of consolidating his armies in order to launch an assault on the Germans. He issues orders to the Fifth and Sixth Armies to stand their ground on the Marne—but this will only be possible if the Fifth can reach that river safely, and if the BEF stands alongside it to close the gap with Manoury's Sixth, and Sir John French refuses to commit to this proposal.

While Allied commanders argue, the long-suffering *poilous* of the French Fifth Army stumble southward from Guise, as Richthofen's cavalry race to cut off its retreat and exploit the potential for complete success if this can be achieved. Forced marching sees the Fifth Army safe across the Aisne that night, but had West not blown up the bridge at Pontoise what might the outcome have been? Bailly-Thourotte is several miles southwest of Pontoise and in a direction directly across the line of German pursuit, so adding a significant distance and even more significant time, which was so critical, especially given the state of cavalry horses. Horseshoes are worn thin as the poor beasts they're nailed to, which are "at best inadequately fed"; Moltke reports, "we've hardly a horse in the army which can go faster than a walk". Though "it was a close run thing", the Fifth Army escapes to fight another day.[202]

[September 1st.] [203]

It was now somewhere round about midnight and inky black in the forest. The advancing enemy patrols were butting into our pickets all along the line, and there was frequent firing in various parts of the forest, some with a target and some no doubt pure panic.

The Royal Welsh Fusiliers' headquarters was in a little house beside the level crossing. There was nothing doing at the moment so I went in and lay down for a bit. The floor space was limited, but there were the colonel, Major Williams, Captain Powell, Captain Owen and three or four others, so it was a close pack. We were really too tired to sleep, and only fell into occasional fitful dozes. The continual night work and lack of sleep was beginning to tell. None of us had shaved for ages and stubbly growths, black, tawny or grizzled, according to individual taste, covered gaunt and haggard faces. For

---

[201] Martin Gilbert, op cit, p. 64.

[202] Kluck, op cit, pp. 85-86; Hastings, op cit, p. 305; Senior, op cit, pp. 166, 186.

[203] Riding round the clock, West again misses dating his account: Néry was fought on 1 September, and what follows from this point to what is noted as "September 2nd" takes place on that day.

my part I was beginning to be conscious of a dull fever, and a great desire for sleep which would not come.

At 2am a motor cyclist arrived at the level crossing with a blazing light. He had a message to take through to the Middlesex at a little village called Saintines. This, it appeared, was away on the right. He had no map and neither had I. But I knew the way through the forest to La Mabonnerie, and Saintines, I heard, was just beyond, so I came out to pilot him. He, poor devil, had probably been up for nights on end, too, and "had got the wind up proper." It was not a good thing to ride with a light in the forest and advertise one's whereabouts so plainly, but he was scared to put his out. This made it impossible for me to see where I was going, as his following light cast my shadow ahead and blotted out the road.

We got through, however, without being fired at, but as we reached the top of the rise in the village the blackness beyond was picked out by little jets of flame, and a fusillade of rifle fire was let loose upon us by six German Hussars in the road. Some of the Middlesex who were holding the village fired back for a bit and then turned and fled for their lives; we turned off into a convenient yard on the left, as the Hussars charged down the road. I could find no officers at all and the Middlesex picket seemed to be without any so I went down and collected some of the refugees out of the orchards and brought them back to the road. The Hussars had now gone and everything was peaceful again.

Soon we fell in with Captain Jack and later Colonel Ward and Major Ross of the Middlesex. The motor cyclist delivered his message and I mine, which was to enquire upon what place the Royal Welsh Fusiliers were to retire at dawn. In the end I find that Fe la Boussiere is the place. No map to hand, and nobody else seems to have one, but I get a rough idea from Major Ross and an inhabitant.

Off I went again to the level crossing and reported this to Colonel Delmé-Radcliffe, and was sent out to order in the pickets for him. The Royal Welsh Fusiliers, under Colonel Delmé-Radcliffe, seemed to be the only battalion that night with any organisation and not completely panic-stricken.

So we retired on Verberrie, which was full of the Seaforths. As far as I knew it I gave the direction of Fe la Boussiere, when suddenly heavy firing was heard from that farm itself far in our rear! Heaven only knew what has happened.

The stand of L Battery at Néry.

Some of the Royal Welsh Fusiliers are out on the right of Verberrie holding the banked road towards Saintines, and behind the houses are numerous transports, horse and mechanical, besides a few Belgian refugee carts. A party of the enemy comes out of the forest, and advances over the fields.

A panic ensues among the transports, and they all fly westwards towards Verberrie. Some of the infantry take part at first, but a handful remains and opens fire.

With difficulty I prevented my machine being smashed by an enormous waggon in flight, and then went back along the road with a few privates who had fled in the first panic, but rallied almost at once. We joined these holding the road, but the enemy had had enough, as there was no cover for them in the open field, and they were hurrying for shelter to the forest.

Heavy gun-fire is still in progress in our rear. The position is confused and full of anxiety and may be critical. There must be a complete breakthrough behind us.

The battalion broke off the fight at the forest and bore away to the west. We straggled up the steep hill mixed with the Seaforths and other units. The troops appeared somewhat shaken but small parties of a French unit appeared. These were sturdily-built men of the French *Chasseurs Alpins*, clad in dark blue, with a Glengarry of the same colour and stockings. They were quite fresh and stood beside the road in knots, offering cigarettes, and cracking jokes with our men as they passed. Many of the horse transport waggons were left at the foot of the hill, and went up in relays with two teams of horses, as the wretched beasts were now too weak to pull their loads alone.

There was no room to ride, and I had to push the Premier most of the way, but at last we all came out on top of the plateau. Here I heard there had been a further fight on the level crossing while I was away at Saintines. In the morning mist cyclists were seen approaching, but it could not be ascertained in the dim light whether they were French or German. At about thirty paces they were seen to be German. Machine guns and rifle fire opened upon them and caused terrible havoc in their ranks. I ran back to a barricade about two hundred yards from the level crossing. This was now manned by the *Chasseurs Alpins* who gallantly held on some two hours after we left, and prevented the Germans from leaving the forest. Through field glasses I could see two cyclists lying in the road with smashed machines right on the level crossing itself.

Returning I ran back onto the plateau, and at the top of the hill met Lieutenant Sawyer with Lieutenant Spier on his carrier, both of the Intelligence Corps. They came bumping along up the road from the east. We could now get more news of what all this gun-fire meant in our right rear, and it did not sound cheerful. They said they had just escaped out of Néry. Our cavalry had apparently been surprised in their billets by short range machine-gun fire and hopelessly outnumbered. They had suffered heavily; Spier had left his bicycle down there and Sawyer had somehow managed to bring him out of the village. (This actually was the famous fight put up by L Battery at Néry, ending in victory to the last gun left in action in the orchard.)

At this point the 19ᵗʰ Brigade suddenly pulled itself out of the general confusion at the edge of the plateau. In good order they marched off to Néry, where I heard they assisted in completely "scuppering" the Germans who had broken through, and also captured five German guns and many prisoners.

Somehow I lost them and arrived at Ferme la Fay, due north of Néry. Between Ferme la Fay and the edge of the plateau German shrapnel was hard at it, spraying a large turnip field. There was not a soul in this field, but except for the large flat surface of the cap the British khaki was so invisible that the Germans never seemed to be sure where our troops were.[204] From the gully to the west of the farm, I could see two of their guns firing from among the houses of Saintines. They were too long a shot for a rifle. A battery of horse artillery was limbering up behind la Fay, prior to retiring, but the Germans did not know it, and soon they went galloping off across the stubble to the next position. The range was lengthened and two pieces of shrapnel came cutting down into the roots quite close to me. So I, too, limbered up and departed.

The 19ᵗʰ Brigade had gone beyond my ken, so I came back over the field tracks, and finding the 4ᵗʰ Division staff under General Snow somewhere near Raray reported there. The 19ᵗʰ Brigade, it appeared, was still at or about Néry, but with no map that conveyed nothing. After a fruitless cruise I returned to Raray. Here they had already arrived by some route, bringing with them about a hundred German prisoners and wounded. This troop, for some reason or other, was solemnly marched round the four streets of Raray, which here form a square. The end of the procession was brought up by a decrepit old Victoria, in which lay a German on a heap of straw. He was unconscious, and his white, drawn face and stertorous breathing told that he was badly wounded. I think it was really intended to bring these prisoners up to headquarters or somewhere, but their faces seemed to display that they were under the impression that they were being shown off prior to being killed and eaten.

The brigade now came to a halt round about Raray, and I lay down on a hay cock for a minute among the Cameronians. Suddenly I was startled to

---

[204] West has summarised the advantages and disadvantages of the 1914 uniform. A sniping officer points out that "the British were much easier to see than the Germans. This was not because khaki was a bad colour to blend with backgrounds, but because the tops of the British caps were … so much larger than the German. The flat-topped caps which so many of the British at one time wore were simply an advertisement of their presence...." H Hesketh-Pritchard, *Sniping in France*, pp. 141-42. No wonder savvy soldiers threw the wire cap-stiffeners away.

hear: "I don't know if you know, Sir, but the troops have left here about two hours ago." Wake to find I am quite alone in the field but for a Cameronian private, and have slept about four hours—absolute, unconscious sleep.

The brigade was now approaching Rully, a few miles further south, and I rode on ahead of the troops and entered a big square fortified farm to get breakfast. All the women-folk had fled, but a man and a little boy still remained beating an old white horse to further efforts, drawing water for the thirsty cavalry. The boy came round with me and managed to find six eggs, and these I took into the deserted farmhouse, lit a fire in the kitchen and cooked them. They made an omelette of most gratifying magnitude. An officer of the Royal Field Artillery came in when I had almost demolished it and we got into conversation. He evidently took me for a spy, or anyway a doubtful character, as nobody seemed to have heard of the 19th Brigade at that time. I left under a cloud.

We trekked in slowly to Chamicy, just north of Rully, and here Sang turned up, so we had another breakfast in a little cottage. The owner and his wife were still there. He was a man of villainous aspect with a great healed-up gash across his temple. With pride he told us that he had been in the Moroccan War and had received this wound for France.[205]

Sang was now on foot again. He carried his belongings in a sack over his back like a tramp. In fact we all looked like rogues and vagabonds. After our second breakfast Sang took me up a path to the east, about a quarter of a mile, to see some captured German guns and limbers. (I have seen no reference to these guns in any history. Guns were certainly captured at Néry, but this was some miles further south. These may have been just the limbers brought down from Néry and finally abandoned again at Chamicy, but it is not clear. The guns had been taken away, but the limbers remained, though the shells had mostly been thrown into a pond nearby.)

Leaving Rully we came down onto the fine wide road from Senlis. Motor cyclists, cars and ambulances were flying up and down in clouds of dust. We crossed over and made for Fresnoy-le-Luat.

The character of our march had now changed. During the first few days the country people stayed and awaited the arrival of the English. They loaded us with all manner of kindnesses, fed us out of their small means for nothing, and gave up their rooms to give us some place to sleep for a few hours; then when the retreat recommenced they would stand at their doorways and weep hopelessly, while some more practical would pack up what they could on any sort of vehicle and leave their homes to follow south. In the evening,

---

[205] This probably would have been the Second Franco-Moroccan War of 1911-12, which led to the Second Moroccan Crisis. The man must have been disabled, or he would have been receiving more wounds for France.

looking back over the line of our retreat, we would as likely as not see the village hidden in a dense pall of smoke where the barbarians had set it on fire. But now terror of the German hordes had outstripped their advance and the inhabitants had left before we arrived. The villages we entered were as villages of the dead, desolate and still. Such a village was Fresnoy-le-Luat. There was nothing to be obtained anywhere. All the shops were shut and deserted. The old church clock, not yet run down, chimed the hour down the abandoned streets, and added the last touch of dreary desolation.

Here I came across King wandering disconsolately looking for provisions. Together we broke into a shop but found nothing. Our horse transport had gone astray and we had no food for the brigade. King, after much foraging, found some butter and some Caporal cigarettes.[206] My only success was one tin of sardines. After a time the brigade and staff arrived—or what remained of it—and fixed themselves up in a cottage. Across the way was a large house where somebody said was some petrol for the motor cycles. Not only was there petrol, but also a car. There were three wounded to be driven to Beaulieu Farm, where we heard there was a dressing station. After much fiddling about we got the thing to go. Fletcher arrived and I asked him to look after my bicycle while I took the wounded along. I had never driven a car more than a hundred yards in my life, but we got going. I soon found that the car had only one gear, top, and the clutch slipped like anything, and before we got to Dury it gave out on the rise. We were getting sniped at long range from the direction of Rully, but I had my hands too full to notice it. It was no good, so we turned around and went back. The sun was now going down.

Fresnoy lies right down in the hollow, and after the experiences of Néry it was decided to move out of the village as it would probably prove another death trap.

From Fresnoy-le-Luat a muddy track takes one steeply up onto the three-cornered plateau of Rozieres. By this route the brigade arrived on the top and settled into bivouac with the headquarters in a gravel pit to the right of the road. We were all tired out and hungry, but our transport had not arrived and there was no food to be had. However, on the hill top I fell in with Wynne Edwards, Pritchard and three others of the Royal Welsh Fusiliers, and we pooled our resources, a hunk of bread, my tin of sardines, and a rum ration in some tea without milk or sugar of course. We ate with our "indispensables" (the Regular Army knife with marline spike attached).

---

[206] Caporal were French army issue, though clearly not exclusively so. They were less harsh than the Soldat brand but nothing close to Turkish or good quality Virginian tobacco. They "were not an efficient substitute for 'Woodbines'"—Dunn, op cit, p. 47—and Woodbine was one of the cheapest British brands.

After a bit we had to go round to kick out the fires made by the Tommies on the very edge of the hill, as they showed up our position. The men pleaded almost in tears to be allowed to cook what they had got first. We explained that the officers had no food or fires either. Try to sleep near some haystacks beside headquarters, bitterly cold and miserable.

"The advancing enemy patrols were butting into our pickets all along the line…" All today the 4th (Guards) and 6th Infantry Brigades fight a rearguard action against elements of two German corps, withdrawing successfully in the evening.[207]

The "Action at Néry" is another extraordinary encounter that helps "make the Retreat into an epic and the Advance a triumphant ballad", in the words of another despatch rider.[208] Despite their advantages of superior force, surprise and high ground, and the initial gains that all these advantages endowed, the Germans were beaten at Néry. Motorcycle despatch riders speedily fetched help from the 4th and Cavalry Divisions as well as from other batteries.[209] German casualties totalled 162, British 133, of which the heaviest loss was incurred by L Battery: 23 killed and 31 wounded, in addition to 150 of its 228 horses. While British losses were numerically fewer, proportionately they were greater, but this does not invalidate the victory: apart from the fact that the Germans fled the field, abandoning two-thirds of their guns and others later at Ermenonville Wood, General von Garnier's 4th Cavalry Division (of Marwitz's II Cavalry Corps) was "finished"; consequently it "could play no significant part in the decisive battle that lay ahead" and many Germans who fled were disoriented, and subsequently killed or captured by Lanrezac's men.[210] Though some were put out of action, no British guns were lost, and three men of L Battery were awarded the VC.

That "The Battle of the Marne was won at Néry", as the memorial there claims, seems an inflated claim, though one not without merit. "Néry was destined to be the 'horseshoe nail' which in the course of a very few days would puncture the balloon of von Kluck's plans and aspirations and decide the final outcome of the Battle of the Marne."[211] Devastation of Garnier's cavalry meant that concentration of Manoury's Sixth Army could proceed without hostile observation, and so give Kluck a nasty surprise on the Ourc a few days later. But any possibility of German victory already had been compromised at

---

[207] Kluck, op cit, p. 87.

[208] Watson, op cit, p. 199.

[209] Macdonald, *1914*, pp. 255-56.

[210] Martin Gilbert, op cit, p. 65; Macdonald, *1914*, p. 260.

[211] Macdonald, *1914*, p. 257.

Pontoise-lès-Noyon, by a humble second lieutenant in the Intelligence Corps, as will be examined.

The diary of the Middlesex Regimental describes the 19th Brigade's part in the Néry action:

> Attack was carried out on village of NÉRY—D, ½C, A Coys to S & SE of village, B and ½C to N of village—on the attack on S of village getting close the enemy's gunners fled and the Batt rushed in and captured about 30 of them and eight guns [not five, as West claims; twelve guns in total were eventually captured]. These guns were at once disabled—the attack via N of village was continued to a large farm 1½ miles E of the village, there an ambulance was captured with some 15 ambulance corps and 2 med officers—of these all were brought away except 1 med officer and 2 orderlies left to attend the enemy's wounded who were left behind.
>
> On the attack reaching NÉRY it was found that Cavalry Bde had suffered very heavily—the enemy's guns having come into action on them at an estimated range of 500 [yards] & nearly all horses of 1 Rgt and 1 Batt RHA had been killed.

About half of the dozen guns captured were hauled away, the rest sabotaged and abandoned as there were no horses to pull them. West's estimate of "about a hundred German prisoners and wounded" is endorsed by the diary of the Royal Welsh Fusiliers, which records "12 guns and 100 prisoners accounted for."[212]

That there seems to be "no reference to these guns [that West observes at Chamicy] in any history" is a reminder that important discoveries have been made since West wrote his account—and that there remains much detail on the Great War still to be unearthed.

Meanwhile, to the east of Néry, the I Corps fights a ragged battle at Villers-Cotterêts, an often-chaotic, hand-to-hand running fight, with evidence that the Germans are doped-up on Dutch courage (drunkenness has been tolerated since at least as far back as Louvain, accepted by some officers as a necessary evil and even encouraged). The Guards brigade suffers 300 casualties, the CO of the Irish Guards being among the fallen.[213]

In this action at Villers-Cotterêts West's IC colleague Lieutenant FH Bevan is wounded and captured by a German lancer in a narrow roadway. Raising "[his] right hand in token of surrender" Bevan finds himself knocked off his motorcycle and comes to with a lance-wound in his right wrist. The following

---

[212] National Archives, WO/95/1365.

[213] Mallinson, op cit, p. 398; Hastings, op cit pp. 191, 255-56.

day it is told that "one of our motor cyclists ... had been found dead with lance holes in his hands and his body partially burned".[214] Could this be the origin of the infamous Crucified Canadian myth that would emerge?

"Lieutenant Spier" is long-since better known as General Sir Edward Louis Spears; born Spiers, he later changed his name by deed poll. In 1914 he was merely "the most important subaltern in the world", serving as liaison officer between the BEF and the French Fifth Army, and usually travelling by staff limousine, not by bicycle. West is mistaken in accrediting him to the Intelligence Corps; Spears was in the Hussars, though intelligence certainly was his concern. When Lanrezac precipitately and indefensibly retreated on August 23rd, leaving the BEF flank exposed, it was Spears who warned Sir John French of the British peril. As West may have saved the French Fifth Army a week later, Spears may have saved the BEF on that day.[215] Later he courageously hectored Lanrezac to counter-attack: "*Mon Géneral*, if by your action the British Army is annihilated, England will never pardon France, and France will not be able to afford to pardon you." His book, *Liaison 1914*, has classic status.[216]

"In the evening, looking back over the line of our retreat, we would as likely as not see the village hidden in a dense pall of smoke where the barbarians had set it on fire"—from a Germanophile like West this word, *barbarian*, says a lot about how already the war has polarised and embittered the best of people.

Kitchener arrives in Paris in the uniform of Field Marshal to meet John French—an ostentatious display of seniority, as the resentful French sees it—and the Minister of War persuades the Commander-in-Chief to conform to Joffre's plans, retiring or advancing in conformity with the French Fifth and Sixth Armies.

Kluck realises that the "chance of dealing a decisive blow against the British Army was now no longer to be hoped for", and focuses his attention on the French Fifth.[217] After clashes between the French rearguard and Kluck's vanguard, blood-stained German plans to turn toward the southeast are found by the French, confirming what reconnaissance has indicated, though official acknowledgement of this move and its significance must wait until the captured orders reach GQG tonight.

---

[214] AD Harvey, "Taken in the First Few Weeks: Five First-Hand Accounts of British Prisoners of War", p. 56; Coleman, op cit, p. 85.

[215] John Terraine claims that "The British Army was saved by the skin of its teeth, more by the efforts of Spears, a subaltern, than by any other single man".

[216] Long out of print, it was republished by Pen & Sword in 2014.

[217] Kluck, op cit, p. 91.

Since Le Cateau the BEF has shaken off pursuit—but not entirely, as last night's skirmishes in the forest and the attack at Néry show. This is very much a war of movement; enemy cavalry constitute a menace and infiltration continues. On 29th August a careless officer was captured and carried into captivity like a trussed bird of prey; today another German officer and his staff are cut off and captured, but this time "remorsefully shot, as it would have been impossible to bring them away under the heavy fire".[218] Gallantry has become something that modern warfare cannot afford.

Joffre's General Order No 4 calls for continued French retirement toward the Seine in order to draw the Germans "between the horns of Paris and Verdun", and to allow the Fifth Army to disengage fully so that it can be readied for attack. Gallieni warns that without reinforcement the Paris garrison cannot withstand a German assault and calls for three more corps. Joffre subordinates Manouri to Gallieni, thereby effectively incorporating the Sixth Army, fallen back to just north of the city, into the garrison, and adding a division of Zouaves and an incomplete corps that has been badly battered in the Battle of the Ardennes. The decision to move the government to Bordeaux on the morrow leaves Paris as a fortified camp for Gallieni to defend, rather than the open city it pitifully will be declared in 1940.[219]

In Germany there is euphoria at news of "victories in both east and west. It represents a divine judgement, as it were, branding our antagonists as the criminal originators of this fearful war".[220]

In Africa, the first units of Indian Expeditionary Force C disembark at Mombasa to put manners on Lettow-Vorbeck.

September 2nd.

Up before dawn and away. No breakfast in prospect, and everyone has eaten his last morsel of food the previous night. Suddenly, however, Captain Yates arrives with the horse transport. An enormous fire is made in a hollow and hot tea served round—the situation is saved. Nothing ever tasted better, and by the time the sun came up we were new men and moving south on Baron. The road such as it was became a mere track, and finally lost itself altogether. Motor-cycling, therefore, became an unmitigated joy till we reached the hamlet of Baron, where anyway there was some sort of road. From Baron we moved south through the Bois de Montlognon, and so to Montagny, a pretty little village surrounded by many orchards.

---

[218] Watson, op cit, p. 66.

[219] Tuchman, op cit, p. 449.

[220] Hastings, op cit, p. 257.

Major Ross of the Middlesex was now acting as right-hand man to Colonel Ward the [acting] brigadier, and he sent me on with a message to Dammartin. There was only one map with the whole brigade, and that was not in my possession. However, I obtained access to it to get a rough idea and went off south through Raperie to Eve. In Eve the road was blocked with the usual collection of troops, transports and guns, and in trying to stop suddenly the exhaust wire broke. I hit a GS waggon and damaged the poor old Premier considerably. I gave the message to a cyclist orderly and told him to go right on to Dammartin with it. The bicycle was pushed into a yard and a trooper assisted me to fake up an exhaust wire of sorts. How the machine had stood up to its gruelling treatment till then was a marvel.

Reports now came through of heavy fighting on the hill above Eve in the direction of Raperie. After a time I got going again in a rather rickety state and rode back to Raperie. Here I found Captain Jack and reported. The brigade was now extended east and west across the road, taking cover in the luxuriant clover and beet. There was a fairly lively scrap in progress, but nothing really serious at the moment, and the reports of heavy fighting were evidently exaggerated.

I obtained leave to run to Dammartin or farther for repairs. Just beyond Dammartin I suddenly came on a kilometre stone bearing the legend "Paris 35 Kilometres"! This gave me furiously to think. We had retreated almost without a halt for the last ten days and the continual withdrawal had become almost a matter of unquestioned routine. But we had never lost the feeling that after all it was all part of a preconceived plan. With this idea in our heads we went on and on to the south, ever buoyed up with the belief that the Germans were doomed in the end, whatever misfortunes we suffered in the meanwhile. This kilometre stone was an eye-opener. I had no idea we were anywhere near Paris—and still retreating!

I rode on towards Gonesse, the bumpiness of the *pavé* adding to my depression. Here and there the road was taken up and barricades extended three-quarters of the way across the track alternately from either side, so that vehicles had to steer a zigzag course. But the barricades were not manned, and for the main road to Paris it was peculiarly deserted. Somewhere between Villeneuve and Le Mesnil Amelot I came upon a deserted car which had collided with a tree. It could only just have occurred as petrol was still pouring out of the tank into the road. I wondered where everybody was as the whole country seemed deserted. But I ran on and finding the *pavé* too rough took to the path. After a mile I caught up two French Army cyclists on the footway. I could not stop suddenly with my broken exhaust-valve lifter, and tipped them both into the ditch. Pulling up about fifty yards beyond I came back to apologise, expecting to find them rather annoyed at their drastic dispersal; but they seemed to be only too pleased, and assured me they did not care a bit, and were glad to have caused any amusement. That was a great thing about the French, they were always cheery and polite, no matter what occurred.

Soon after I came to another barricade, and then I knew what had happened to everyone. For miles on either side field fortifications were being thrown up with feverish haste. Soldiers and civilians, women and girls, were there in thousands digging, filling sandbags, bringing wood, iron and wire, while others were cooking out in the open for the toilers. The capital was threatened, and those who could not protect her with arms had turned out to do so with work. Three huge refugee waggons from the north were drawn up just behind the barricade. The horses had been taken out and were dragging sleds of faggots across the fields for revetments. The parents had left their children playing in the straw, and were working somewhere among the thousands of others. They had reached the defences of Paris and had turned at last to take their share in the coming fight. Nobody troubles me for my pass, so I went through, and came to Roissy and at last to Gonesse. The town was full of French soldiers in their long blue coats and baggy red trousers. It is an extraordinary uniform, and I often wonder how it came to be evolved. It could never be considered smart or soldierly, and by comparison with many of the French cavalry uniforms was not even picturesque. What is more, its mere colour makes it quite impractical for modern warfare.

Few British troops had passed that way and the people all came out to see this uncouth, unshaven apparition in dirty, torn khaki. I went into an estaminet for a meal. It was full of *pious pious* in an atmosphere of tobacco and wine, like a superheated London fog. The soldiers rose from the benches and gathered round, and argued among themselves as to who should have the privilege of standing me the first drink, and entreated me to stay and share their meal. I was too hungry to care about the distinctions of rank, and would indeed have been a boor to refuse. A burly French sergeant acted as host and ordered toasts to the King, *la France*, Belgium and Russia. It was the first substantial meal for a long time, and thanking them very much I went out with the sergeant as guide to find the mechanic.

Hardly had we got into the street than a ragged fusillade broke out somewhere to the north, and soon the drone of an aeroplane became audible. Everybody came running out and looked up into the sky. A Taube had appeared flying at about two thousand feet or more over the town, and this was the signal for all arms to go off simultaneously. Every sort of weapon was requisitioned from a shot-gun to a pistol, and one man had even climbed out on the roof to get a bit closer, and was popping off into the sky with a revolver. The whole thing was absurd and amusing, everybody having quite lost their heads in their enthusiasm to "strafe" the Boche *le cochon*. I must admit I borrowed a rifle too, from the burly French sergeant, and had a few shots. But in spite of all our efforts the machine sailed on like a great hawk southwards towards Paris. Scarcely had it passed when another appeared, and the same pantomime started all over again, with the same results. (We afterward heard these two machines dropped bombs on Paris, doing their best apparently to hit Notre Dame.) The mechanic at Roissy patched up the exhaust wire to the best of his ability, but the carrier and the rest of the cycle rather defeated him. So I started back hoping to get an opportunity of having this put right later. But as the exhaust wire lengthened and became useless, I decided to run to Paris and get it properly mended.

On the way I caught up a party of about ten British soldiers. One with a Scotch cap was apparently mad, and was jabbering about having shot six aeroplanes that morning, and being commended by the general, or some such jargon. They were all dirty, dust-grimed and tired out. I stopped to find out who they were and what they were doing, but they did not seem to know, and they may have been deserters.

The advance of the Sixth French Army on the Germans' right.

After a long and bumpy ride I at last reached the outskirts of Paris, and here met the head of an extraordinary procession. This was the French Reserves hurrying out of Paris to the north. Composed mostly of African troops, they presented a picturesque and motley crowd in their brilliant-coloured uniforms. But the most peculiar feature was their transport—every known form of vehicle had been requisitioned to hurry them out in support of the troops. Victorias; decrepit old taxis grinding along on bottom gear, magnificently-upholstered private cars; tumbrils and waggons; pony traps; and even coster carts—all had been pressed into the service. No one could say that they formed an imposing array, yet this was the Sixth French Army rushing up to the River Ourcq, and which three days later was to take von Kluck's army in the flank and cause his ultimate overthrow on the banks of the Marne.

I could only make my way with difficulty as the road was thronged with people, some of them looking on, others standing about in knots and talking excitedly. But after a time I reached a guarded barricade which was the entrance to Paris. Here I was held up by the military, but a little parleying and my uniform (or what remnants remained thereof) took me through. One can get very grimy on a motor cycle in an hour, but I had now been at it a fortnight or so, and the luxury of a wash had been rare, and a shave rarer. So that I must have presented a very poor appearance as a specimen of the British Army officer.

Not far down on the right I came upon a second-rate cafe and entered with a sigh of relief at the prospect of a good meal. But a slow, dull feverishness, either from want of sleep or the inflammation from my poisoned foot, prevented me from doing it the justice it deserved, though there was real milk, and real butter which we had never seen for over a fortnight. As I was beginning to feel a little better a man came in and asked me in fluent English how I was. Seeing what an uncouth state I was in he suggested that I should come back to his house and take the chance of getting cleaned up a bit. An excellent idea, and I had the most gratifying hot bath I ever remember, but it was beastly getting back to one's tired clothes again. After that he gave me a good meal, and meanwhile had my bicycle taken over to his works and repaired. His foreman, who apparently understood the work, made a first class job of it.

My benefactor's name, I found, was Mr A Cottray, of 10 Rue L'Ecluse, Paris 17e, also trading as L Barbellion, of 79 New Bond Street, London W, his card also bearing the name L Mulquin. It was now getting time to return since my motor cycle was in running order, so I thanked him very much for his assistance and said good-bye. It was soon quite dark and the acetylene lamp was working none too well, so that at Roissy I ran into a roadside pond, motor cycle and all. The magneto became tired at this and refused to fire. It must now have been 11 or 12 at night, and I could not see what was to be done to the machine, so pushed it wearily up the cobbled street till I found a lighted house. This proved to be the headquarters of a French Medical Unit. The officers were very kind and cordial and did everything possible for me. They had the cycle brought into the house to dry off, an orderly was told off to look after me, and one of the men gave up his camp-bed and slept on the floor in the corner. But I was by now frightfully tired and feverish and scarcely slept a wink. Looking back on it all now I cannot understand why I did not get someone to look to my poisoned foot and have it bandaged up, being in the headquarters of a Medical Unit; but we had all become merged in a sort of torpor, from lack of sleep, and were not up to thinking for ourselves.

Deterioration of the road in the vicinity of Baron serves to remind the modern reader that roads of a hundred years ago were often primitive, especially in rural areas—and France then was predominantly agricultural, and most of its population rustic. If it seems stretched to say that a road could "lose itself altogether" one should bear in mind the experience of an English motorcyclist who, just a few years before this episode, "lost altogether" the London-Bristol road, somewhere in the Marlborough Downs.[221]

The "exhaust wire" referred to was a Bowden cable that "lifted" the exhaust valve off its seat, interrupting the combustion cycle and thereby stopping the engine, so that this acted as a brake on the rear wheel. Actual brakes

---

[221] Carragher, *San Fairy Ann*, p. 102.

at the time were primitive and quite pitiful, a stirrup-type acting on the front wheel-rim and a block bearing on the rear drive-pulley; a dead engine was a far more dependable and effective brake, so a broken "exhaust wire" was a potentially serious breakdown. It would not stop the bike, but it could prevent it from being stopped as we see here and later on.

That the French "were always cheery and polite, no matter what occurred" is both a corrective to the stereotyped view of that nation as superior and snobbish and a highlight to the unnecessary and costly problems caused by the touchiness of John French and Charles Lanrezac. How many lives might have been saved, British and French, if these vain, stubborn men had been "cheery and polite" toward each other, and as generously helpful as M Cottray?

As West describes here, more than taxis make up the fabled fleet of "taxis of the Marne"—"tumbrils and waggons", even. It was only by calling on all resources that Gallieni was to save Paris; a portent of the future, for ultimately it was only by such resource to "total war" that Germany was beaten.

Kluck's men are "done up" after marching 100 miles in four days, requiring "abnormal stimulants"—alcohol—to keep them going. Both the stimulants and the need for them disgust the German generals, and alcohol may well contribute to today's atrocity at Senlis, when the mayor and six civilians are murdered,[222] obviously only hours after West passed through. Was the garage proprietor he met there among the victims?

Evidence of French consolidation is reaching OHL and tonight Moltke's General Order modifies his earlier instructions to Kluck, mandating him to follow Bülow in echelon, thereby securing the right flank of the right wing; but Kluck decides to press on in an effort to roll up French forces from the west, leaving the 4th Cavalry Division, weakened and fragile after its beating at Néry, to help the IV Reserve Corps guard the flank. As late as this he still believes: "In co-operation with the Second Army it might be possible to damage the French western flank very considerably. The First Army by its deep formation was in a position both to cover the flank and rear of such an attack and also to hold in check the garrison of Paris and the British."[223]

With Kluck's guns in imminent range of the capital, the French government at last heeds Gallieni's warning and leaves Paris for Bordeaux, many in tears of humiliation on Sedan Day. The Norwegian ambassador offers to mediate with the victorious Germans when they enter the capital. Mindful of the fate of the medieval library of Louvain, the American ambassador resolves to save the museums and monuments of Paris from *Kultur* by placing them under the protection of the American flag, "in the custody of humanity at large", thereby

---

[222] Tuchman, op cit, pp. 445-46.
[223] Kluck, op cit, p. 91.

earning the enduring admiration of Gallieni.[224] If the *taubes* West sees today really did intend to bomb Notre Dame—and after Louvain this is certainly possible—such protection is sorely needed. In Brussels the new German governor officially imposes *schrecklichkeit*: "punishment for hostile acts falls not only on the guilty, but on the innocent as well", a resolution later praised by Hitler.[225]

To the east the last remnants of the Russian Second Army are fully mopped up and Ludendorff turns his attention northward toward Rennenkamf's First Army, standing on the defensive—and now the Germans have numerical superiority, thanks to the two corps Moltke has sent from the Western Front (where very soon they will be needed far more than in East Prussia).

September 3rd.

Next morning about 6 o'clock I got away back to Dammartin to find the brigade. The magneto had dried out, apparently, as it gave no more trouble at the moment. On the way a column of cavalry crossed the road going south-east, and with it Second Lieutenant WG Gabain of the IC now driving a baby Peugeot which he had found in some abandoned chateau on the retreat. In the town not an Englishman was to be found, and the place was full of French troops.

When I had left Eve the day before just outside Dammartin the Germans were close upon the town, but now everything was quite peaceful. The *poilous* had pulled tables out into the sun in the cobbled streets and were playing cards and singing, as if there were no enemy within a hundred miles. The whole scene struck me as a vivid contrast from the order and discipline of the British Army. (Yet these happy-go-luck, apparently ill-disciplined, French troops proved their worth a few days later in the brilliant victory of the Marne.)

Running towards Eve I heard of a squadron of German cavalry which had been seen in one of the woods close by. A large body of French cavalry was turning out to clean them up. On enquiry they told me there were no English in the district any more, but that the *Quartier General* back in Dammartin might tell me where they were, but they were not very illuminating either. They said that the British units had mostly retired south and south-east, and they (the French) had come out on the British left flank. Rumours were current that the new bridge across the Marne at Lagny recently opened had been blown up, so the only thing to be done

---

[224] Tuchman, op cit, p. 454.

[225] David Bilton, *The Germans in Flanders 1914-1915*, p. 132.

was to return to Paris and find out from the *État Major* how to rejoin.[226]
I reached Paris at dusk, and ran round trying to find the GQG, but without
success. Everywhere people hailed me in English, and I seemed to have
many compatriots in Paris. I decided to put my cycle up and stay for the night
somewhere as it was now getting late.

It was soon evident to me that I must have run so fast in the retreat as
to be the first Englishman in Paris of the whole army! Anyway, I have never
been so popular and it was most embarrassing. Everybody crowded round
me and asked me how things were going. The little *midinettes* wanted to
kiss me on both cheeks, and competed for the honour of being seen on the
boulevards with a British officer, even though my clothes were grimed with
dust and mud, and I had not washed since the day before. With difficulty I
got away at last, and dropped into an hotel with no luggage but my cap, my
Sam Browne belt, and my revolver, but it was a clean hotel and a real bed!

The BEF and Fifth Army, the latter reported by Bülow as "decisively beaten",
cross the Marne, leaving many bridges intact for use in the assault being
prepared by Joffre but of course leaving them open to the Germans to follow;
Kluck's vanguard reaches the river toward evening and secures every bridge
available. Kluck resolves to pursue, ignoring instructions to protect Bülow's
army in echelon, and the ubiquitous problems in communication leave OHL
ignorant of his insubordination. Further problems stem from the pace, some
25 miles today, which outdistances Kluck's supplies and artillery and exhausts
his men, but an officer dismisses complaints: "Sweat saves bloodshed".
Meanwhile, Rupprecht renews his expensive and futile assault on the French
fortress line, soaking up troops that Kluck and Bülow need if the Schlieffen
Plan is to have any hope of succeeding now.[227]

The Germans have come within 25 miles of Paris, with cavalry patrols in
Ecouen, eight miles distant; but aerial reconnaissance confirms to GQG what
the orders captured two days ago have given away: Kluck has turned toward
the southeast, exposing his right flank. But the Sixth Army is not yet fully
mustered, and composed largely of reserve and colonial divisions, and any
possibility of a successful attack requires changes in command along the entire
French line.[228] Lanrezac, who yesterday was heard muttering, "*Nous sommes
foutus*", is replaced by his subordinate Franchet d'Espèrey, who issues a brutal

---

[226] *État Major*: staff headquarters.

[227] Macdonald, *1914*, p. 247; Tuchman, op cit, p. 462.

[228] Fifty-eight French generals were dismissed by 6 September; see Hew Strachan, *The First
World War: A New Illustrated History*, p. 56.

command: "March or drop dead".[229] But Allied success equally is contingent on the cooperation of the BEF, and John French is still in full flight, BEF bases now fully relocated to St Nazaire on the Atlantic coast.

The French cavalry that "had come out on the British left flank" likely would have been from Manoury's Sixth Army, and West's vagueness here is reflective of the fluidity of the situation and the rapidity of change as one side sought victory within the narrow time-confines, and the other struggled for survival. The need for French cavalry, however, is an indictment of the BEF's uncoordinated retreat, which has left a gap in the Allied line; the Fifth Army also had to send cavalry to help fill this.

A "brilliant victory" is seldom attributed to the Battle of the Marne— "critical" yes; "historic" certainly. But in some sectors the Germans had better intelligence on local conditions than the native French did: Foch divided his forces to attack von Hausen's Third Army around the Marais St Gond, but Hausen was aware that this "marsh" could be crossed after the uncommonly-hot summer, so he attacked the French centre and drove Foch back. But by this time the German First and Second Armies' lines were attenuated and their men exhausted, and the battle-front, extending for about 150 miles, from Paris to Verdun, was simply too long for either side to force an issue.

Yet in confirming failure of the Schlieffen, or Moltke, Plan, the Battle of the Marne forced the Germans to fight a protracted war on two fronts and so ensured the eventual success of greater numerical and logistical odds. To this extent it was indeed the battle that won the war. Barbara Tuchman's bleak evaluation prompts another consideration: "For France, for the Allies, in the long run for the world, the tragedy of the Marne was that it fell short of the victory it might have been"; but it seems doubtful that the superb German army, in its full strength, could have been decisively defeated at this early stage.[230] The war in the West could only have been won quickly by a successful outflanking of the Allies, and it is arguable that the last chance to do this was lost on August 30th. Though out-flanking remains the mutual aim in the "Race to the Sea" that is to follow, already the war has degenerated into a series of frontal assaults, with technology favouring the defence.

In the event the Germans were able to disengage from the Marne with relatively light losses, retreat to the high ground above the Aisne, dig in and defy the Allies to dislodge them for four more years.

---

[229] Peter Young, "The Great Retreat", p. 204; *"Nous somme foutus"*: "We're fucked"; pardon my French.

[230] Tuchman, op cit, p. 484. For more consideration of lost opportunities see Hastings, op cit, pp. 340-55.

September 4th.

Next morning I was up rather late and went to the garage for my bicycle. Here I got into conversation with a very genial fellow, by name Charles Sachs, who spoke English well. He was just taking out his big 60-HP Fiat car, which being chain drive had not been requisitioned like all the others. Hearing I wanted to find the *État Major* he at once offered to take me there in his car. This was quartered in the *Hôtel des Invalides*, and on enquiry we were told to return at 12:30 as I suppose the necessary reports were not at the moment to hand. In the meantime Charles Sachs took me round Paris in his car. It was a beautiful day, and it being my first visit to Paris I was immensely impressed. On returning to the *Hôtel des Invalides* we were not kept long—in fact I was surprised at the promptness with which they told us the positions of the units without asking us for our credentials; and indeed I doubt if I had any to show had they done so.

Paris was extraordinarily calm. It was perhaps somewhat empty, but everybody seemed at peace with the world and the general situation at the Front. When it is remembered that the Front was now as far from the centre of Paris as Harrow is from London, it is the more to be wondered at. The people were imbued with a tremendous confidence in their generals. "It is all part of the scheme." "Joffre knows what he is doing." One heard remarks like these on every side. Along the Seine were a few sightseers looking unconcernedly at the marks of the bombs dropped the day before by the German Taubes. Meanwhile Senlis, a short run from Paris by car (45 kilometres), was being pounded and smashed by the German artillery. Only at a little garage that I entered did I find any preparation for flight. The proprietor was packing off his wife and belongings while he himself was going to stay and look after the place.

Charles Sachs now insisted on my coming back and lunching with him at his house, prior to starting, arguing that I must lunch somewhere. I was glad to accept, and was introduced to his wife and family. We had an excellent meal, and much champagne to celebrate the occasion, and when I left on my motor cycle I regret to say my speed was great, but my factor of safety small!

After a beautiful ride along the broad Seine valley I reached Lagny and shortly afterwards Chanteloup, and here at last joined the 19th Brigade. The headquarters were down a leafy lane, in a little farmhouse. It was a peaceful enough spot and some of the Welsh Fusiliers' officers were lying out on the grass, basking in the hot sun. Charles Sachs had very kindly supplied me with a great sheaf of newspapers of all dates for the last three weeks, and these were greedily devoured. We none of us had any idea what had happened in other theatres, and were none too clear as to our own. The papers, as usual, grasped at tiny needles of victory in the present haystack of defeat. The general impression, therefore, was that everything was going rather well. (We had not at that time realised that the papers rarely tried to tell the truth, and even when they did they had a genius for getting their facts wrong.)

I reported to headquarters, and then with King set about billeting ourselves in the house. But at about 11 o'clock at night, when we were preparing for peaceful slumber, the brigade was ordered to move. When we got out the battalions were all ready and waiting to flit, and about midnight, I suppose, we all moved off. I was sent on to Ferrières to find if the road was clear for some cyclists with a despatch.

The rejection of M Sachs' chain-driven Fiat is an interesting detail on requisitioning policy, and on the "taxis" of the Marne, which brought 6,000 troops into action against Kluck's right flank. That this powerful 60-HP car would be passed up because it was driven by chain rather than shaft is surprising when one considers that a "Marne Taxi" in the *Musée de l'Armée* is a twin-cylinder 8-HP Renault.

Given his comfortable family background and university education, part of it in Germany, and his fluency in French, it seems surprising that West has never been to Paris before. Even more surprising, given the extent of spy mania at the time, is "the promptness with which [the *État Major*] told us the positions of the units without asking us for our credentials". Perhaps this reflects the urgency of the position just then.

Very telling is the observation: "We none of us had any idea what had happened in other theatres, and were none too clear as to our own". In war the knowledge of most participants is restricted to the compass of their gaze, and in the Great War, given problems of communication, the knowledge of even officers might not be much greater: General Henry Horne, commander of the I Corps artillery, remarks in a letter to his wife that "one knows little of what goes on elsewhere".[231] This intrinsic limitation is something armchair generals of today ought to bear in mind before they condemn generals in the field a hundred years ago.

That "The papers, as usual, grasped at tiny needles of victory in the present haystack of defeat", suggests that *The Times* of August 30th, with its "Amiens Despatch", is not among the newspapers M Sachs supplies his guest, but more significant is West's *post facto* observation "that the papers rarely tried to tell the truth". After the Great War a new scepticism entered the world; "Never such innocence again," as Philip Larkin concludes "MCMXIV."

Kluck defends to OHL his refusal to march in echelon to Bülow, citing his successful crossing of the Marne as evidence for the soundness of his actions,

---

[231] Mallinson, op cit, p. 390.

and refusing to wait a requested two days for Bülow's army to catch up for fear of losing the initiative to the enemy; the Germans are right up against Schlieffen's forty-day deadline to win the war in the west and no delays can be tolerated. But now there are too few troops to deliver a knockout blow. Though they have yet to endure defeat, the Germans have suffered over a quarter of a million casualties. Moltke has critically weakened the right flank by detaching those two corps for East Prussia, and the Kaiser, excited by Rupprecht's potential to break through, refuses to allow reinforcements to be transferred from the left wing. Likely, though, the Belgians' sabotage of their railway network would have delayed such troop transfers beyond the point of doing any good, whereas Joffre has been able to shuffle troops in huge numbers and short order all along his front, thanks to shorter interior lines and suitable railway lines: "between 27 August and 2 September an average of thirty-two trains travelled westwards every twenty-four hours".[232]

The Fifth Army is now sufficiently clear of pursuit to be considered disengaged, and available for offensive action. Nevertheless, the "extraordinary calm" of Parisians is not shared by the generals in whom the people have "tremendous confidence"—apart, of course, from Joffre, who remains as imperturbable as ever. Overall, French morale is subdued, with GQG being moved back 30 miles to Châtillon-sur-Seine.

OHL fails to pick up immediately on the Fifth Army's consolidation into the French line but Moltke remains nervous: "We must not deceive ourselves. We have had success but not victory". He realises that "Prompt reinforcements are urgently needed",[233] but incorporation of their reserves into their front line—which has given the Germans the numbers that, together with superior matériel and strategy, have made them unstoppable so far—means that they now have no forces from which to fill their depleted ranks,[234] unlike the French and the BEF; the latter receives 20,000 reinforcements today, along with much-needed matériel. As evidence accumulates that the French are concentrating, OHL recognises that the right wing has failed in its enveloping attack, and that the First and Second Armies will have to withstand an assault from Paris. Moltke orders the right wing to halt and move to the defensive; the Schlieffen Plan has been abandoned.

At 9:00 AM Gallieni, on receipt of aerial reconnaissance reports, orders Manoury to ready the Sixth Army for a flank attack—but Joffre refuses to

---

[232] Strachan, op cit, pp. 57, 56.

[233] Tuchman, op cit, p. 467.

[234] The Reich could have greatly increased the strength of its armies had it not been suspicious of the urban proletariat's bringing dangerous socialist thinking into the ranks. According to one estimate, "about half its elegible young men [were] untouched by the [pre-war] draft" as a result—Jack Beatty, *The Lost History of 1914: How the Great War was not Inevitable*, p. 12.

endorse this. At an Anglo-French conference at Bray in the afternoon d'Es-pèrey determines to restore cordiality to relations with his opposite number in the BEF—but Sir John French is absent. The Francophile Wilson is persuaded that the BEF should conform to an attack along with the Fifth and Sixth Armies, to be launched on September 6th, and he promises to do his best to persuade the commander-in-chief. However Murray, the chief of staff, orders a continuation of the march away from the Marne. That night Joffre endorses the plan of attack; no one knows what Johnny French will do.

Meanwhile the Belgians open the dykes to impede a German attack on Antwerp, flooding the lowlands behind the coastal dunes for the next four years.

From Scotland Karl Lody warns Berlin that "great masses of Russian soldiers have passed through Edinburgh on their way to London and France"; he reports an estimated 60,000.[235] Coming on top of everything else this cannot have improved morale at OHL.

In the Declaration of London Allied politicians resolve that none will make a separate peace with Germany.

September 5th.

Dawn found the brigade still distributed roughly in the district of Ferrières and Jossigny. But by about 6 o'clock in the morning we had strung out into a well-ordered column and were tramping away into the woods. All that day the troops marched through the forest south to Grisy. It was not so hot now in the shade of the trees, but the roads were as dusty as ever for motor-cycling.

Arrived at Grisy, King and I tried to get a billet in a large white house from which, however, we were ejected in favour of the Royal Welsh Fusiliers. Finally we got a small room with a bed bearing one spring and one plain mattress. We tossed for them and I won the bed and King the spring mattress so we were both fairly comfortable. During the day I raced about on the Premier, running various messages. At the Pontcarré cross-roads I found a party of reinforcements. They were sitting in the shade completely done up, having marched apparently 40 kilometres due south after their retreating unit. The day before they had passed through the level crossing just north by train and then had to walk all the way back again. Gave them what food I had in my haversack—not much—but they had water, which is the chief thing. On my way down to Grisy every level crossing was defended with machine guns as if the Germans were in sight already, whereas they could not have been within 30 miles. "Are they coming?" they asked at one crossing in the

---

[235] As a spy Lody was a pathetic amateur; facing the firing squad, his courage evoked the admiration of the men who shot him.

forest. I tried to explain that there weren't any Germans for miles as I had
just come through. But they were frankly incredulous.

There is little in West's account to portend the imminent events, and the
confusion he comes upon at Pontcarré crossroads seems a poor portent.
Reinforcements who arrived fresh only yesterday are already "completely
done up" after being railed to the wrong place and marching 40 kilometres
in pursuit of the main body of the BEF—still retreating southward while the
French muster to attack northward. French railway management had put
trains at the disposal of the BEF, at a cost to their own mobilisation; how effective was management of these trains? Was this episode an instance of the fog
of war, blurred command, poor Anglo-French liaison and lack of hard intelligence in a fluid situation creating extra problems? Or simple incompetence?

At 3:00 AM plans to attack on the 6th are finally conveyed to Sir John French—
but he refuses to commit. Early in the afternoon Joffre motors 115 miles to
meet him and tells him that the attack will go ahead in any event; that the
"lives of all French people, the soil of France, the future of Europe" depend
on its success; that cooperation of the BEF is critical; and that "the honour
of England is at stake!" Emotionally, French agrees that "we will do all we
possibly can". Though the BEF is ten miles too far south to conform with
the Fifth-Sixth Army line—and, from what West observes, partially frag-
mented—Joffre confirms the order to attack on the morrow: "no failure will
be tolerated".[236]

Meanwhile, at 7:00 AM Kluck has been warned again of danger on his
flank, and Moltke's order to stand on the defensive, but he persists in his
southeast-ward pursuit of the Fifth Army, which by now has fully consolidated
into the French defensive line and is beyond the point of being cut off. Kluck's
actions no longer can be covered by the leeway given to field commanders in
Großer Generalstab doctrine. Colonel Richard Hentsch is despatched from
OHL to find the First Army commander and personally order him to desist
and retire to the north bank of the Marne. To his chagrin and disgust, Kluck
learns that troops he could and should have had to reinforce the critical right
wing are dying in Rupprecht's deadlocked assault on the French fortress line.

He learns also that his flank defence has repelled attack by a sizeable
French force, confirmation of the danger Hentsch warns against. This attack,
by elements of Manoury's Sixth Army along the River Ourcq, is the opening
movement of the Battle of the Marne. Four days from Schlieffen's deadline
for victory in the west troops of Kluck's vanguard are in Claye, ten miles from
Paris; but his First Army's railhead is still 40 miles behind, and given all the

---

[236] Tuchman, op cit, pp. 482-83.

logistical problems that entails, the commander of the German First Army orders his exhausted men to retreat.

September 6th.

The First Advance.

Started off in the morning, the whole brigade retracing their steps north along the Pontcarré road. It was a beautiful morning and everybody was feeling rested and "full of beans." At first I tried riding with the brigade, but the dust was appalling, so I saw Churchill and said I would go on about a mile and wait, and then go on again. Captain Claude Raoul Duval still as cheery as ever. The forest of Armainvilliers apparently belonged to his family. There were plenty of pheasants and rabbits about, and during the waits for the brigade to come up I strolled out into the woods, but could not manage to get the proper sights up. It was most enjoyable in the forest and amazingly peaceful after the previous fortnight. Towards midday we reached the northern limit of the forest and at Villeneuve St Denis, Sang, who was now riding the Premier, broke down with a smashed chain. We had rather a job putting it right again with no proper tools but it went at last. All this time I don't quite know where Fletcher was as there were only two bicycles between us three.

Here we have another reminder of that long-forgotten road hazard—"the dust was appalling"—and another illustration of the rapid rate of wastage of motorcycles in the Great War, especially during the war of movement, when recovery of a broken-down machine often was not possible due to proximity of the enemy. Breakage of the Premier's chain, only a few weeks and probably less than a thousand miles old, is due to lack of maintenance through the fraught retreat, when there was little time and often no spares or even oil to lubricate a drive-chain, but the dust played a part too, infiltrating between the rollers and bushings of the chain and acting as an abrasive. This vulnerability is part of the reason the Army stipulated belt final-drive for motorcycles in early 1915; belt might be more "primitive", but it also was more suitable to conditions, and easier to repair in the field if it did break.[237]

The "amazingly peaceful" quality of the forest camouflages the fact that German and French armies are marching toward battle. Indeed, battle already has been joined, since Manoury's attack along the River Ourcq yesterday afternoon, and today the Sixth Army advances more than two miles against Kluck's forces. The BEF, because of Johnny French's dithering, will make a

---

[237] Carragher, *San Fairy Ann*, pp. 76-78; passim.

tardy entrance into the fight. They begin the march northward only in the late morning while the French are fighting hard.

Thanks more to circumstances and luck than to planning, the Marne is timed just about right, with the French Sixth Army fully mustered and in place and the Fifth securely pulled back into a coherent defensive line, and the German First and Second Armies at the limit of their endurance and their supply- and communications-lines. The French have a further advantage in being able to select favourable ground on which to fight. Yet the battle's outcome is by no means a foregone conclusion, and it cannot be delayed any longer. That the BEF is behind the action on the first day does not help matters, forcing Joffre to deploy cavalry to fill the gap and enraging Desperate Frankie, facing the whole of Kluck's army with greatly inferior numbers. However, the belated entry of the BEF into the fray greatly alarms Kluck, who has written the British off.

September 7th.

The battle of the Marne.

Advanced to La Haute Maison. Here we fell in with the first German resistance since turning about, and perhaps the scrap is worthy of a short description. Turning to the right we left the screen of woods marked "B" and came out at the corner of a big cornfield marked "A," the corn being cut and in cocks. Here occurred a scene such as one would see on manoeuvres with blank cartridges only. The infantry, I think the Middlesex, deployed along the road "C" and advanced in open order across the field "A."[238] Meanwhile a column was trekking along to the village by the poplar road to the right, apparently oblivious of the fact that they were ahead of the advance guard. Some German battery, probably on the Signy-Signet road, caught sight of them through the gap between the woods at "D" and opened fire. The ranging was bad, and the tail of the column was already screened by the wood and entering the village before the shells found the road. They then turned the guns on to the village and shells started bursting in the houses. General Gordon, I think it was, rode out after the column to find out what on earth they were doing. Meanwhile a certain amount of rifle fire opened from the woods "E." The amusing part about it was that the infantry seemed to be the only people behaving sensibly. All the rest of us were standing about in conspicuous positions, or riding about like umpires at manoeuvres, where no such things as ball cartridges or live shells were known. Nobody seemed to be any the worse for it, and I don't think there were any casualties.

---

[238] West is referring to a map that is not in his IWM folder.

That night we retired slightly and bivouacked on the site of an old German bivouac. The chief indication of it having been German was the litter of wine bottles of all shapes and sizes![239] There was not much straw here, but King and I managed to collect some on a bank and try to get a little sleep with his horse tethered close by.

We had little rest and about midnight I was called up to take a message to Divisional Headquarters a few miles back, and get orders for the morrow. I was now riding Fletcher's Rudge, an abominable machine, which made a fearful noise. Fletcher was on foot and trying to raise a horse if possible. Due to the beat of the engine I never heard a sentry close to the camp, and he was so excited that he nearly succeeded in shooting me!

It was, indeed, the Middlesex Regiment that was shelled by the German battery. The Regiment's diary reports:

> ... advanced along road between SIGNY & SIGNETS going N till high ground overlooking R MARNE was reached. Here Batt[ery] deployed to hold this high ground & immediately after deployment heavy shell fire was opened by enemy on road we had advanced along. This fire caught Batt[ery] first line transport which was following Battalion and was effective and well aimed till [illegible word] could be got away—9 horses were killed but all transport was saved with exception of 1 water cart which was riddled by shrapnel so discarded as useless.

Subsequently "2 batteries came into action and enemy was more or less silenced."[240]

The fact that West sees so very little of one of the most important battles of the war—at least on this day; he will see more—illustrates again the short radius of any soldier's horizon, even that of so mobile a soldier as a despatch rider. Here a skirmish, almost comical and harmless in its effect, is all he sees of a battle described in the German Official History as "the worst day in the war so far for troops". With victory slipping away Moltke reproaches himself: "I must answer for this horror".[241]

Yet it's anybody's game still. Kluck's men move toward the west and north as he turns his front to face and fight Manoury in an impressive display of generalship. This manoeuvre widens the gap with Bülow's Second Army but Kluck's counterattack threatens to turn the Sixth Army's left flank and open

---

[239] Further evidence that German troops have been fuelling themselves on Dutch courage.

[240] The National Archives, document WO/95/1365.

[241] Martin Gilbert, op cit, p. 73.

the road to Paris. Manoury is saved by Gallieni's famous despatch of 6,000 men from the Paris Garrison to Nanteuil in "the taxis of the Marne". Even with this thrust parried the Germans remain formidable, and the advantage of shorter interior lines has—locally—gone over to Kluck.

While the French have been fighting hard, the British have had a rather cushy time. Today they march some fourteen miles against little opposition but driving rain, but by evening the BEF has crossed the Grand Morin and entering the gap that has opened between the German First and Second Armies. The threat of the right wing being split worries both Kluck and Bülow. Marwitz's cavalry contests the British passage, but there is little actual fighting and Haig, seven miles short of his objective, complains to his diary at the slow pace of advance. Several rivers cut the terrain from east to west, in deep channels and steep-sided valleys, and it is vital that the Germans be kept moving in order to prevent their digging in, which eventually they will do on the heights overlooking the Aisne. That they are allowed to do so endorses Haig's criticism and is an Allied failure that will help the Germans gain good defensive positions and protract the war. An officer in the ASC remarks: "The Germans, we were told, were in desperate plight this day, and if we could have pressed on, many thousands of exhausted men and much munitions of war might have fallen into our hands".[242]

Industrialist Walter Rathenau, in charge of the *Kriegsroffstoffableitung* (War Raw Materials Department) at the Ministry of War, sends a memo to Bethmann Hollweg urging "the necessity for controlling France in order to defeat England, and reiterates the importance of German supremacy in central Europe".[243] The strategy designed to deliver that supremacy is about to meet the critical test.

Moltke's famous uncle, "Moltke the Elder", once pronounced strategy to be "a system of expedients"; but the Moltke on the spot in 1914 is too close to nervous collapse to be able to think of expedients. His stripping of two corps from the right wing of the German invasion has made Schlieffen's planned defeat of the Allies in the west impossible. A bolder, more imaginative commander might still win the war by transferring troops toward his *left* wing now, reinforcing the assault that Rupprecht has been driving for days, leaving Bülow and Kluck to contain the Allied forces north of Paris and rolling the French line up from the *east* over the broken fortress line. Fortunately, Moltke displays no signs of such boldness, initiative or imagination.

---

[242] Herbert A Stewart, *From Mons to Loos*, pp. 83-84.

[243] James Joll, "The 1914 Debate Continues: Fritz Fischer and his Critics", p. 38. Rathenau became Foreign Minister in the Weimar Republic and was assassinated by right-wing extremists the after signing the Treaty of Rapallo with the Soviet Union.

Hindenburg and Ludendorff, however, are well familiar with Moltke the Elder's pronouncements, and they move toward driving the last of the Russian hordes from East Prussia when they deploy their now numerically-superior forces against Rennenkamf's First Army.

Rennenkamf, with his Germanic name and Germanic ancestry and a moustache like a fox's brush, is distrusted by many Russians. In days to come much will be made of his failure to come to Samsonov's assistance at Tannenberg; but while he and Samsonov may have had their differences, the blows they allegedly came to on a Mukden railway station platform seem to have no deeper basis in fact than gossipy Max Hoffman's claim. Samsonov was beaten by a better army, better organisation, better supplies, better communications, better leadership; Rennenkamf is to be beaten by all these too, plus superior numbers, but not to the extent that Samsonov was. The Germanic sympathies attributed to him have no more to do with his eventual failure to overcome his German enemy than does his Germanic moustache. His name may be translated as "running fight", an apt enough rendering of his escape from abject defeat at the Masurian Lakes.

September 8th.

In the dusk before sunrise we were all up and ready to move. The brigade headquarters was on the Signy-Signet road, just where it leaves the woods. The infantry deployed on either side in the beet fields, and when all in position moved silently in open order. The road here goes straight as a ruler to the Marne, which it hits off at a little hamlet called Sammeron. (See rough sketch.)[244]

From La Haute Maison a view can be obtained right over the Jouarre Ridge, intervening, and on to the wooded hills beyond the Marne. The road, however, lies in dead ground in the Signy-Signet's dip until the summit of the Jouarre Ridge. From the hills to the north of the Marne, therefore, any column coming out of La Haute Maison is clearly visible as it advances down the hill, but is lost sight of again till it reaches the Jouarre Ridge. There are no large woods, villages or houses along the length of this road. Signy-Signet lies a quarter of a mile to the left, and Jouarre some way away to the right in the woods. Such then was the country through which we marched out in the morning of September 8th to the battle which we know now was the turning point of the whole war.

The main body of the 19th Brigade came down from La Haute Maison in column, an infantry advance guard being thrown out ahead, about a hundred or so strong. Major Heywood, who was now Brigade Major, sent

---

[244] Again, this is missing from West's IWM folder.

me on to see if I could find out what was going on beyond the Marne. Riding on ahead I dismounted just over the crest of the Jouarre Ridge, and walking on down the hill climbed a haystack about forty yards from some orchards. From here I could see the German columns trekking out up the hills beyond, transport and men, more transport and men, in knots, followed always by a hanging cloud of dust in the still hot air. Did a rapid sketch of roads being used and walked back to the machine. As I reached the crest some of our infantry appeared over the top and were immediately fired upon from the orchards—now about three hundred yards away—so that the Germans had evidently let me off, thinking it was not worth giving their position away for one man.

Returning to Brigade Headquarters I reported, and so forward again to the advance guard, this time accompanied by Sang. We left our cycles on the crest and walked down to the infantry. The slight fire from the orchards had ceased. Suddenly down in the valley a squadron of German cavalry burst from a little spinney at about 300 yards range and made for La Ferte-Sous-Jouarre. A somewhat indiscriminate spluttering fire was opened by our infantry. I think it must have been rather ineffective as I only remember one riderless horse. The target was immense and the Tommies were all laughing and ragging one another about the bad shooting. These must have been some of the crack corps of *Jäger-du-Pferde*, as they were dressed in dark green-grey.

Soon some volume of rifle fire was opened from the woods beyond the Marne, and the air was full of little hissing noises. The men all took cover in the standing tobacco crops, but not having been under rifle fire (the report of which was inaudible before) I did not realise they were firing at me in the road, till a Tommy with a broad grin on his face mildly suggested from the ditch: "Isn't it about time you took cover, Sir? They're firing at you, you know." Anyhow it was very bad shooting, but I got behind a convenient hay-stack. Here I knocked up against Sang again, and we crossed the road together. He, I believe, stayed with his cycle, but that was the last I saw of him alive.

Just now (for some reason quite unknown) the brigade and regimental transport appeared over the rise, headed by a water-cart. Then the trouble began. Over came a shell and landed on the box-seat of the water-cart, removing driver and anyone else aboard. The horses bolted for the Marne, with the remains of the heavy vehicle tottering behind them down the hill, and some long-legged fellow—I think Lieutenant Brodie of the Middlesex—flying after to stop them.

After that Hell broke loose. The air became full of shrapnel, concentrated more especially down the road. Everybody scattered to the fields, and shells started falling, bursting in the ground, in the air, and all over the place. I met

Churchill wandering aimlessly like myself in the field; also, I think, King and the general. There was a little coppice on the left of the road and we took what we thought was cover there.

Some of the 66th Battery Royal Field Artillery galloped up and came into action just to our left, but right on the crest. The German gunners found them almost at once, and the coppice became highly unhealthy. In a little hollow among the trees some of us collected for cover. Just in front was a lance corporal of the Royal Field Artillery and some other gunner working a Barr and Stroud range finder. I strolled out to have a look at it when a shell arrived in the middle of us with a crash. The Royal Field Artillery man went down with a smashed knee, and the Barr and Stroud also suffered, but neither the other man nor myself were touched. I managed to get the wounded man under the bank, but one might just as well have been outside for all the cover it afforded. Soon another man was hit in the chest with a shrapnel ball, and was helped over into the hollow. We got in as close as we could to the bank.

I was immensely struck with the coolness of the Royal Field Artillery officers. In the short lulls between shells one could hear them calmly giving their orders. "Correct three degrees right at 4300," etc. Then the voice would be lost in the crashing of our guns or the scream of arriving shells. Apparently, as one of them told me, they could not really spot the German guns in the woods opposite at all, but it put spirit into the infantry to hear our shells coming over.

The 88th Battery Royal Field Artillery had now swung into action on the right of the road, but screened behind the ridge, *not on it*, and were pounding away briskly. The 66th had lost some men now, and the order was given to cease fire, as they could not do much, and only drew fire by their efforts. The German shelling slackened down a bit on our sector after that, and I started back on foot to get an ambulance for our wounded. Over the crest I found the Argyll and Sutherland Highlanders forming up into diamond or "blob" formation, and soon after they advanced like a swarm of ants. I imagined the German gunners tearing their hair, trying to get the range of them. There were about twenty men to the group.

My bicycle which I had left by the road had disappeared, but I found Sang's Premier, smashed here and there by shrapnel and covered with blood. Since they were still shelling the road at intervals, I got away on it as quickly as possible, and found my cycle at the bottom of the hill. Had a slight altercation with the thief who had somewhat lost his head.

Here I learned from Sproule that Sang had been hit in the head by shrapnel—a deep wound, but he hoped not serious. Rode back to the crest and fetched away the man with the smashed knee on the back of the cycle. Saw Fletcher for a moment on the side of the road. He told me Sang had come out of the scrap on the back of the Rudge, with blood streaming over his face, but still had a cheery word, and waved to him as he passed. (Sang died October 26th, 1914, in hospital.)[245]

The brigade was now in order again, and headquarters were set up beside a haystack, just outside Signy-Signet. Fletcher and I went into the village and got some sort of breakfast. There was a great gathering of long-legged, scraggy fowls up at this end of the village. They had apparently not been fed for weeks. I discovered later a little shed full of the most delicious cream cheeses, flat discs, hidden behind piles of straw. Someone discovered about 700 eggs also hidden from the Boches, before the villagers fled, and someone else made a further discovery of wine, so we did ourselves fairly well. That night we lay out near the haystack in the field. The hot weather was beginning to break, and it rained on and off till dawn.

"Isn't it about time you took cover, Sir? They're firing at you, you know." The modern reader rather doubts that such were the exact words spoken by Tommy Atkins in such a situation that West describes, but West occasionally seems to be having a droll old time recounting his exploits—and one can never dismiss the stiff upper lip factor even in the "other ranks". The incident illustrates how militarily naive West was, yet it was citizen-soldier despatch riders like him who, in effecting communications through the Great Retreat, enabled command and control to hold the BEF together.

Again, reflecting in equal measure West's military naiveté and Old Contemptible *sang froid*, the diary of Royal Welsh Fusiliers equates his "Hell broke loose" to "Advanced Guard heavily shelled on reaching SIGNY SIGNETS.... Fairly heavy rifle fire". The diary of the Argyll & Sutherland Highlanders reports "hostile rifle fire and Machine Gun fire from N bank [of the Marne]" with one man wounded.[246]

Similarly, West's emphasis that the RFA was "screened behind the ridge, *not on it*", betrays a neophyte impressed by a rudimentary artillery tactic of locating guns on a reverse slope, where they are hidden from enemy view yet have a clear field of fire across a protective crest, from which a Forward Observation Officer corrects the gunners' aim, by voice or semaphore or—increasingly as the war went on and ranges increased, and targeting became more sophisticated—by telegraph.

That a general should be "wandering" about a battlefield is a reminder that far from having a cushy war, generals often shared the same risks as their men, especially in the first year. Almost 80 British generals were killed in action or died of wounds, nine at the Battle of Loos alone. After this they were very properly told off to direct from behind rather than lead from in front, though

---

[245] As already noted, Sang died on October 2nd.

[246] National Archives, WO/95/1365.

a few still insisted: "Galloper Jack" Seely led a cavalry charge on March 29th, 1918.

West's mention of "diamond" and "blob" formations, so often associated in recent years with the "Learning Curve" climbed by the BEF during and after the Somme battles, is a reminder that such formations, and the tactics employed in later years of the war, were all familiar to the Old Army. The Learning Curve was in large part, as Dr Peter Simkins puts it, a "reskilling" of the New Armies following the necessary "deskilling" of the early years, when there was neither the time, resources nor skilled instructors available to teach sophisticated infantry tactics. (Yet "bad shooting" and the amusement it provokes gives further cause to question the supposedly universal excellence of the Old Army.)

The outcome of the Battle of the Marne remains uncertain as Kluck's and Manoury's forces jostle northeast of Paris. Meanwhile the German Fourth Army falls on Foch's Ninth (prompting the famous words, "My centre is giving way, my right is in retreat, situation excellent. I attack"), forcing the hard-pressed d'Espèrey to lend reinforcements from the Fifth Army.

But success of the Schlieffen Plan has been predicated on a knockout blow delivered in the first round, and this has called for all reserves to be incorporated into the front line. Their impressive successes have cost the Germans about a quarter of a million casualties and, unlike the British and the French, they have no reserves to call upon to fill their depleted ranks and plug the gaps between their armies. Bülow is battered by d'Espèrey's assaults and forced to tighten his right wing. This improves his position but widens the gap between the Second and First Armies to about twenty miles, and all but total communications failure means that he and Kluck effectively are fighting separate, uncoordinated battles. At OHL a fearful Moltke despatches Colonel Hentsch again on what today would be called a fact-finding mission.

With the outcome in doubt the British save the day, riding into the breach between the First and Second Armies to win the Battle of the Marne—except that such is their leisurely pace that the BEF has barely reached the river. Deserter Private Thomas Highgate is shot by firing squad in front of two companies by order of Smith-Dorrien, *pour encourager les autres*, the first of 346 British and Empire soldiers to be executed through the war.[247]

---

[247] About 3,000 were sentenced to death, out of some 20,000 who were tried for offences that could have carried the death penalty. Almost 90 percent of death sentences were commuted.

September 9th.

Up at sunrise after a fairly peaceful night and moved down into the farm at Signy-Signet. Fletcher and I got busy in diminishing the number of eggs, in a looted saucepan in the yard, when the Germans livened things up by shelling the farm with small shrapnel. However, we went out and prevented our eggs getting hard in the intervals. Of course one is really pretty safe from shrapnel in a house, but about nine o'clock the headquarters moved out, went up to the right of the road, and set up under the trees. The Rudge had been hit the day before and was a bit disorganised, so I had to stay and put it right behind the farmyard wall.

The day turned out hot and fine, and I was sent off with a Tommy on the carrier to try and find four GS waggons that had gone astray at Aulnay. We went into the chateau and met M le Comte de Charnace, who gave us of his little all for lunch. He had been completely cleaned out of food by the Germans. Some officers had been staying there and had made the most filthy and indescribable mess of the place. He and his old housekeeper had held on during the German occupation, while his family had fled. He was delighted at the return of the English. It was extraordinary to see the owner of a large chateau and beautiful grounds reduced to wondering where his next meal was coming from.

Left the Tommy at Aulnoy to wait for the waggons, and returned to Signy-Signet. Colonel Delmé-Radcliffe reports at headquarters to the effect that the Royal Welsh Fusiliers are down in La Ferte-sous-Jouarre under heavy machine-gun and rifle fire, along the streets, and probably cannot be extricated till nightfall. After dusk we move off to Jouarre on the hills above the river. I rode on ahead and prospected the road through the woods. Got stuck on the hill, and found I was too "done in" to get the bike started again, so had to wait for the Argyll and Sutherlands who came up ahead of the brigade to give me a push off. We got into "bivvy" about eleven or twelve midnight, just west of Jouarre.

About one o'clock Churchill came along with a despatch for Divisional Headquarters, which were the other side of a valley east of Jouarre. It was pitch dark and the roads were none too good. I ran on for a long time through the woods, and coming out into a big gap stopped to get my bearings. Here I stood on the edge of the Marne Valley, the hillside dropping steeply away below. It was as silent as death, and I felt as if I were the only creature left alive in a desolate world. Across the Marne a silent red blaze marked a burning village. The glare shone across the river and showed up the red trunks of the pines in a flickering uncertain light. Now and then a stick would crack startlingly somewhere behind in the forest. The whole world seemed unreal and ghostly, and perhaps I was a bit light-headed from want of sleep, but I rushed to the bicycle in a meaningless panic and made off into the forest. After a while a steep stony track was reached leading straight down into a ravine towards Tartarelle. It was a mere mule track with a gradient of about 1 in 3 or 4, but I managed to get to the bottom without mishap and ran out at last onto the main road to La Ferte-sous-Jouarre.

Here I was held up by a sentry. I was told in a whisper to "Go quietly, for God's sake; the RE are building a bridge just below." I made my way up a track to the left—there appeared to be no roads in the direction I wanted. At last I got to a hamlet of a few dirty little houses. I didn't know a bit where I was in the woods, but a lantern was swung across the road and I stopped to enquire.

"*Où est Chateau Tartarelle?*" I shouted.

"*Venez par ici! Venez par ici!*"; and in the lantern light I saw that I was talking to an uncouth Apache in shirt sleeves. I followed him thinking he was going to show me the way, but he seized me by the sleeve and murmuring "*Espions! Espions!*" led me down some steps into a filthy cellar below a hovel. On the right was a dead body stretched on the ground, and on the left, lying on a shelf covered with straw, lay a dirty, ragged man bound hand and foot, and moaning weakly to himself, with one of his wrists swathed below the cords in dirty bandages. These two unfortunate creatures my guide informed me with much pride were two spies whom *he* had caught, and he showed me a note from some officer commending his astuteness. One of these had killed himself, and the other had tried to by cutting an artery in his wrist, but they were keeping him alive to shoot him in the morning.

I told him what I thought of him, in no uncertain terms, and at last got some directions out of him regarding the position of Tartarelle. More tracks and some marshes, and soon was lost again, but at last I discovered the chateau in the forest, and delivered my message. I was given a reply to the effect that the 19th Brigade was to cross the bridge at dawn—no other troops were to cross before the 19th.

The "delight" of M le Comte de Charnace at "the return of the English" is no sort of propaganda on West's part, and not merely because by the time he wrote his diary up for submission to the Imperial War Museum there was no need for any such: *schrecklichkeit* was a fact of German warfare, and M le Comte got off lightly. So many accounts describe bestial behaviour by the Germans that one is tempted to wonder if these might not be motivated by malice, especially when one thinks of other testimonies to the excellent order of German trenches, and the decency of many German captors. Undoubtedly malice was a factor in some accounts, and soldiers of every army are capable of shameful behaviour; French colonial troops befouled and vandalised even French civilian property and carried out atrocities.[248]

But the Germans and the Austrians—and, notoriously, their Ottoman allies—were the only forces with a *policy* of civilian terrorisation. This is beyond question: they widely proclaimed it. Besides, West, especially given his German ancestry, cannot be doubted. He is a frank and truthful person, an instinctually-decent man with absolutely no personal animus against his enemy, as he reveals when he tells the "uncouth Apache" what he thought of the latter's treatment of alleged spies. Moreover, even if many humane Germans deplored *schrecklichkeit* one can see how in the pace of their advance it could have been difficult for such men to impose discipline. West's observation of empty wine bottles on September 10th is only one of countless such observations, and evidence of German generals' acceptance of the need for "abnormal stimulants" to keep their troops going—and perhaps dull their sensibilities to atrocities.

The burning village across the Marne is as likely to have been the incidental victim of shellfire as of *schrecklichkeit*; what is far more significant is West's horrified reaction to it. His flight in "meaningless panic" may portend anguishing psychological dissonance, a harbinger of the "neurasthenia" that will invalid him out of the battlefield in 1915.

Finally the BEF makes a contribution to the Battle of the Marne, pushing almost unopposed into the gap between the First and Second Armies that now is some thirty miles wide, threatening to cut Kluck off. However, Kluck retains a numerical advantage over Manoury, and moves to envelop the Sixth Army's north flank. By afternoon this has been turned and it looks as though local advantage has swung back to the Germans, with the road to Paris again open toward the west, the gamble about to pay off on the fortieth day of Schlieffen's timetable, the day by which the German Armies must be victorious in the west if they are to win the war.

Bethmann Hollweg sends a memo to his deputy, Clemens Delbrück, State Secretary of the Interior, mandating that any peace settlement must ensure "the security of the German Empire in the West and in the East for the foreseeable future. To this end, France must be so weakened that she cannot rise again as a Great Power, Russia must be pushed as far as possible from the German frontier, and her rule over non-Russian subject peoples must be broken."[249]

Clearly, however, communications at OHL have broken down, and not merely with the armies in the field; for even as Bethmann is instructing

---

[248] Hastings, op cit, p. 319; see also West's experiences with "Turcos" later on.

[249] Cited in Joll, op cit, p. 37.

Delbrück, Colonel Hentsch is back in his staff car looking for Kluck, and this afternoon, in "the most dramatic manifestation of delegated authority in military history",[250] he reappears at First Army HQ, conveying OHL's directive to retreat to the Aisne, whose heights offer a defensible position. The risk of the BEF isolating the First Army, and turning the right wing of the Second, is too great, given the force's freedom of action in the gap between the two armies, and retreat will allow this gap to be closed. To the threat of division of the two armies and subsequent defeat "in detail" is the fear at OHL of 70,000 rumoured Russians disembarking on the Channel coast and taking those armies in the rear. Karl Lody's recent report from Edinburgh makes this fear seem plausible, and so paranoid are the Germans that rumour will raise the number to close to a million fierce whiskered Russians sharpening their teeth and preparing to devour them.[251]

Kluck complies with Hentsch's order, with surprisingly good grace,[252] and he and Bülow commence to retreat, forcing the Third Army to conform. British aerial observers report the Germans falling back along the whole front, but in good order, and a formidable fighting force still. Remarkably, however, the Germans leave most Marne bridges open to their pursuers. The French left them intact earlier, but that was, truthfully at last, part of *"un mouvement stratégique pour attaquer le mieux"*. The Germans' failure to destroy those bridges may be due to the rapidity of implementing change in strategy, and the confusion that can cause, but the broken glass of thousands of wine bottles that litter the roads hint that the use of "abnormal stimulants" may have turned against the invaders. AJ Sproston, another despatch rider, notes this day that "a rear-guard of [German] cyclists had been left to destroy this bridge [at Charly-sur-Marne]; they, however, got intoxicated with drink looted from the town and were surprised and captured in a drunken condition by some of our infantry".[253]

One German officer attempts to justify tolerance of apparently widespread drunkenness: "It is the delirium of victory which sustains our men,

[250] Hastings, op cit, p. 329.

[251] Martin Gilbert, op cit, p. 63. The French milked the rumour for all it was worth: in April 1916 "French papers ... were full of reports of the Russians landing in France"; but by this stage the Germans would not have been worried and and the "reports" would have been designed to assuage native fears over the onslaughts on Verdun. See Felicity Jane Laws (ed), *War on Two Wheels: A Diary of Overseas Service*, p.66

[252] Not all German officers were as phlegmatic. Kapitan von Egan-Krieger, of Second Army HQ, lamented: "If the pessimistic Hentsch had crashed into a tree ... somewhere on his journey of 8 September, or if he had been shot by a French straggler, we would have had a ceasefire two weeks later and thereafter would have received a peace in which we could have asked for everything"; cited in Ian Morris, *War: What is it Good For: The Role of Conflict in Civilisation, from Primates to Robots*, 246.

[253] Sproston, op cit, September 9, 1914.

and in order that their bodies be as intoxicated as their souls, they drink to excess, but this drunkenness helps to keep them going.... If there were too much severity, the army would not march. Abnormal stimulants are necessary to make abnormal fatigue endurable."[254] Alcohol also, notoriously, makes atrocities more palatable and far more likely.

[September 10ᵗʰ.][255]

The outflanking of von Kluck across the Marne.

At about three o'clock I got back to Jouarre, but could not hit off the bivouac in the dark. It was not till just before it was quite light that I managed to find it, and the brigade was moved off at once for the bridge.

Starting to the west we descended steeply into the valley of the Marne. Here I met Wynne Edwards of the Royal Welsh Fusiliers. He told me that Captain Thompson, also of the RWF, had been killed the morning before, at the end of the bridge. They had stayed all night in a house close by, and the next morning Thompson walked out into the square by the big red brick building. "There are no damn Germans here any more," he said. At that moment he was shot in the stomach by a sniper from the houses across the river. Two of his men crawled out and fetched him in, and one of these in returning for a second time for his kit got shot in the wrist. They could not bring Thompson out, and he died that night in the house.[256]

At the bottom of the hill I met the brothers Bernheim, interpreters to the Royal Welsh Fusiliers, and they helped me onto the bridge. The Rudge after its frightful treatment was impossible. It would not start, and was so stiffened up with dust and mud that it would hardly push, and when it fell over (which it frequently did), I no longer had strength to raise it without assistance. At the pontoon bridge I could go no further, and finding a spot between some barrels and bridging material tried to sleep for a couple of hours. Waking up at intervals I found the long column still crossing—infantry, cavalry, guns and transport. The heavy transport and the guns went across at a gallop to get up impetus for the stiff bank beyond. The horses would tread delicately and dubiously at first, but once properly on the bridge the drivers would let them have it and they would charge across with a thunder of hoofs, and up the other side. Pulled myself together at last and had a look

---

[254] Macdonald, *1914*, p. 248.

[255] Not for the first time, West's riding round the clock prevents his noting the change of day.

[256] This appears to have been 2/Lt Edward James Collingwood-Thompson. Frank Richards claims that he "lived about half an hour" but he lingered on for a day. His rescuers were awarded the *Medaille Militaire*, and the one who was wounded also the DCM. Richards, op cit, pp. 26-27.

round. Half hoped somebody had borrowed the bike, but nobody had been so stupid, and it was still standing there.

The original masonry bridge over the Marne had been completely demolished. It had consisted of two arches with a pier in the middle of the river. This pier had been shattered and a large mass of masonry still holding together was lying in mid-stream. The two arches had quite vanished. The engineers, whether English, French or German, had made a very good job of it, in fact the most thorough demolition I have seen. The new bridge consisted of about five pontoon rafts and one big barge incorporated in its structure, the whole "chessed" and "ribboned" in the regulation way. This was a wonderful piece of work on the part of the Royal Engineers, under the circumstances. What I had seen and heard of La Ferte-sous-Jouarre, it appeared to be mostly machine guns and shells and no place for me, and the next I heard of it was that the Royal Engineers had built a bridge there.

Still just about dead-beat, I got some infantry to help me push the cycle across the bridge. They must have been pretty weary too, for that matter, but I never knew them not ready and willing to lend a hand cheerfully whenever required. At the far end of the bridge was a German waggon with, I think, "8th" or "18th Jaeger Bn" painted on it. It was lying upside down in the road, and the wheels had been removed. Beside it were standing an old woman and a girl, some of the very few who had remained in the town, and were dealing out cups of hot coffee to the troops passing on to the hills. It was good stuff, that coffee, and I wish them luck wherever they are now.

On the hill we were directed by men covering each corner and crossing. At the top I ran onto the plateau and soon came upon the 19th Brigade Headquarters in an orchard opposite a big farm. Here I met Churchill who, in spite of the fact that men of the Royal Welsh Fusiliers and I think the Argyll and Sutherlands were present, started cursing me for falling out. I was furious with him and saw General Gordon shortly afterwards and pointed out to him what had occurred. He being a dour old Scotchman told me to "go away and get some sleep." Did so on some straw under an apple tree, but it rained slightly from ten o'clock till lunch.

Fletcher woke me up, accompanied, I think, by either Wynne Edwards or Williams, or one of the Royal Welsh Fusiliers' officers. Colonel Delmé-Radcliffe, seeing Fletcher and I were on a loose end, and only got our meals somehow and sometimes, had kindly asked us to join their mess. We went up into a large loft running over a big barn and got a thoroughly good meal for a change.

Almost immediately afterwards the brigade moved off northwards. It is a real advance at last. There is a wonderful elation in the air, after the atmosphere of continuous defeat of the last few weeks. The Middlesex were doing advance guard, Major Ross being at the head, and I got permission from

Brigade Major Haywood to be up with Major Ross and run any messages back for him to Brigade Headquarters—always about half a mile behind or more.

The country rolls away to the north in steep undulations, with here and there a small stone village and a few woods and copses. The road wound its way like a long white ribbon over the green landscape bathed in the warm September sunshine. Fletcher came up occasionally, and together we did a sort of advance-advance guard. Fletcher was now riding my original Premier, rather a good old 'bus.[257]

All the afternoon the brigade marched along this road without much incident. The fields on either side were strewn with wine bottles of all sorts, some half full, and the great majority empty. This and the thin enamelled telegraph wires were characteristic of the track of the German armies throughout the advance. The telegraph wire referred to was at first thought to be lines laid to road mines, and it was very diligently cut by all of us who had the means of so doing. This fine black wire is apparently never taken up again like our heavily-insulated stuff, it not being worth the trouble as so much more can be carried.

Picked up a letter on the road from a German soldier writing home. It was dated some time on our retreat and he said that they had been very short of food, so we were not the only sufferers in that respect.

Soon afterwards the brigade took to the fields, and the poor old bicycle had to follow. Thence on up a very steep hill into a little stone village. Out on the other side we got a view right across the north-west. On a big poplar-lined road some 6000 yards away we descried a long column marching to the north-east, transport and men in knots, and now and again a section of men resting a moment on the bank of the road. Major Ross sent me back to report and I met Captain Jack. We hoped that some guns might roll up shortly so that we could get onto them. These were apparently the tail end of the German columns in retreat. Later we thought they might have been French who had got too far ahead. Anyway, the guns never arrived in time so nothing happened.

Towards evening we arrived at Catigny, a little hamlet on a hill. Brigade Headquarters were set up in the one big farm, and when all were settled I went out and fed with the Royal Welsh Fusiliers in the big open barn. "Tiger" Phillips and Major Williams arrived with two German rifles and various equipment. Apparently they were having a bath in one room of a small farm when the lady of the house came rushing in and said there were two Germans in the other room having a meal. Of course they dressed pretty quickly and went next door to make their acquaintance, but found them

---

[257] "Bus": slang at the time for a motorcycle—or any self-powered vehicle.

both lying dead, having been killed by the Turcos, who had been introduced first. The Germans were not at the moment armed and the affair was really nothing short of murder.

Slept in a straw stack again that night. Rather cold, and a bit showery, but so long as there is plenty of straw one is all right.

The death of Captain—or Lieutenant—Thompson is the tragic outcome of the sort of behaviour James Jack deplores: "Although one cannot keep up meticulous regard for one's safety all the time, few things annoy me more than men running unwarranted risks".[258] Thompson's reckless venturing onto the bridge again questions the view of the Old Contemptibles as a body of universally flawless professional men.

His inability to lift his motorcycle makes it clear that, after weeks of almost unbroken and very strenuous activity, West is utterly exhausted, and one of his feet is infected and very painful and debilitating.

The condition of the Rudge may be accounted for by dust getting into the bearings. In those days frame- and wheel bearings were unsealed, and wheel bearings in particular suffered from dust clogging. Normally copious oiling, through a hole in the centre of the hub, washed the races clean from the inside out, as well as lubricating them, but such maintenance could not be given through the Great Retreat, so the bearings partially—sometimes fully—seized up in an abrasive paste of greasy dust. Steering-head bearings tended not to be so badly affected, as they were above the level of the worst dust, but even slight stiffness in the steering will affect machine control, and along with West's exhaustion may explain his frequent falls.

The altercation with Churchill is not West's first—see entry for August 30th—and tomorrow night Churchill will rouse West from sleep to deliver what seems to be an unnecessary message in the foulest weather and in darkness. Is Churchill, an Old Army man, resentful of this "wart" West, and his commission? Later in the war such non-career officers will be disparagingly dismissed as "temporary gentlemen".

The "fine black wire" laid by the Germans is disposable, insulation being a thin coat of enamel. It was sometimes used to "clothesline" British despatch riders on the advance to the Aisne.

The "Turcos" West describes were likely Spahis, indigenous Algerians recruited into the French army as light cavalry. Their uniform was vividly colourful, red white and blue with a bright yellow turban. As no shots were reported, they likely murdered the Germans with their sabres rather than their Lebel carbines, speculation that seems justified by West's own subsequent encounter with a Turco tomorrow.

---

[258] Jack, op cit, p. 99.

The Germans have pulled back all along the line, to the widespread anger and disbelief of officers and men who have been invincible up to now and have, as they imagine, had victory in their grasp. The scapegoating of Moltke for failure of the Schlieffen Plan, perhaps even the *Dolchstoßlegende*, can be traced to today. Twenty years later Ludendorff will claim: "The army was not defeated on the Marne in 1914. It was the victor."[259] Joffre's post-mortem is more nuanced and ironic: "I don't know who won the Battle of the Marne, but if it had been lost, I know who would have lost it."[260]

Yet if they have been repulsed in the West, in East Prussia the Germans now are rampant, driving the Russians hard and hoping for another great victory. Rennenkamf, however, maintains order and defends his vulnerable southern flank: there will be no *kesselschlacht* here.

[September 11th.][261]

We were now getting into touch with the French Sixth Army on our left, though we had previously seen some of their cavalry now and again. This morning a battery of French 75's passed through the hamlet going north. They struck me as being the most ramshackle and unimposing little guns. We moved on afterwards and shortly we passed a big chateau standing close off the road, and flying the Red Cross. In it were about forty wounded Germans, and one or two English ex-prisoners, also wounded and left behind. Two German Red Cross orderlies had been detailed off to look after them until the arrival of the English. The drive was strewn with kit of various kinds, and being short of many things such as water-bottles, etc, I borrowed and decked myself out in German spoil. A peculiar thing about this and most subsequent German kit we found was that there were always liberal supplies of face cream in glass bottles, whether for the feet or in order to beautify the looks of the unshaven Boche I do not know!

One of the Third Army staff had come up on a horse, and I made some attempt to examine the prisoners with him. Later, having a wondrous thirst, I descended into the chateau cellars, a German Red Cross orderly as my guide, and tried to find something drinkable. It had, however, been quite cleaned out by the Germans. At last we found a full bottle and held it against the light from the window to be sure. It looked pretty good and we poured it out liberally into two tin mugs in the dim cellar. "*Prosit*," we said, and took a big draught, to find it was—salad oil!

---

[259] *Dolchstoßlegende*: propaganda that the army, victorious in the field, was "stabbed in the back" by Jews and Marxists, and only thereby was Germany defeated.

[260] Hastings, op cit, p. 342.

[261] Again, West's days run into each other.

The orderly was quite a pleasant-spoken fellow, and in the course of conversation he admitted that he thought the Germans must in the end be beaten with "*Die ganze Welt*" against them.

In the drive was standing a very fine big Mercedes, and the German driver sitting in it. The car was apparently in perfect order, and when asked why he had not escaped the occupant said that he was Alsatian, and had no spite against the French, and did not want to fight for the Germans. The general for whom he had been driving was expecting him at some point farther north, but much to the delight of the burly ex-chauffeur he must have had to walk.

All that day we picked up German stragglers and deserters. Most of the men appeared to be very pleased that they were out of it. One Uhlan officer, however, was as morose as possible, and would not have a word to say to anybody. They all looked healthy and of good physique, with the exception of the Uhlan, who was rather a poor specimen. There were not many officers taken, and in the absence of any actual statistics I should say about one officer to 50 or 60 men.

About midday we came across a German, wounded in the arm, sitting miserably beside the road, under the guard of a Tommy. On the opposite bank sat a Turco, eating his lunch with a villainous-looking knife, and glaring hungrily at the prisoner. At last his feelings got the better of him, and smiling sweetly he got up and nudged the Tommy, pointed to the German and then himself, and made horrible gestures with his knife to get the Tommy to let him cut the prisoner's throat. Leave was not granted, however. These Turcos are good fighters, but awful savages.

Most of the day I kept with the Royal Welsh Fusiliers, and towards the evening it turned out wet, and later very wet. The roads became terrible, being for the most part only earth. However, we pushed on to a little village on a high hill, called Maritzy St Geneviève, and here called a halt. King arranged for the Brigade Headquarters in a big farmhouse, and I tried to get a wash and a shave—the first for ages—in a bucket in a cow stall. I then went out and joined Colonel Delmé-Radcliffe, who was seeing his men into a big straw barn. Though racked with rheumatism he stayed there in the drenching rain, as muggy and bitterly cold as only these late summer days can be, till all his men were settled in, before he went to find his own billet.

On returning to the farm I found King had arranged the attic for us. There were yards of curtains and a few mattresses, so we were quite comfortable. The Royal Welsh Fusiliers had commandeered two of the farm rooms for mess, and we soon had a roaring fire going, and started drying ourselves. Old Wynne Edwards, Holmes, Stable and others were in the best of form and wanted to start a sing-song, but we suddenly remembered the general the other side of the wall.

In the little room upstairs was lying a wounded French trooper. He had been shot through the leg and had been there, the farmer told us, for three days without any attendance, save that which the farm people could give him. When our Red Cross came and fetched him away he was in a state of delirium and could give no account of himself.

Shortly after dropping asleep that night I was roused by Churchill on a perfectly ludicrous errand. He wanted me to take by motor cycle a message with which a push-cyclist orderly had already started. The whole distance was only a couple of miles. It was then about midnight, raining, and the roads impossible. It was about a quarter of an hour before the cycle even started, and then at the bottom of the hill I skidded in the darkness, and stopped the engine. I had knocked off one of the pedals on an errant pig on the 7th, so that from then on it could only be started by running with it. How to run with a heavy machine in six inches of mire is a problem so far unsolved. This meant that I finally had to push it up the other side. I took two hours reaching the place, losing myself once on the way, and of course the cyclist had long since been and departed. They had no idea at the time of the limitations of the motor cycle. Over short distances like that it is a pure waste of time, and on some roads pure waste of a machine except in the hands of the most skilled.

The Battle of the Marne is effectively over—though sporadic fighting continues here and there—German victory in the war now unlikely, yet not impossible. Hard fighting and heavy casualties will mark the Battle of the Aisne, presaging the next four awful years.

In Galicia the Russians drive the Austrians back, but in East Prussia the threat of German envelopment from the south is now too dire to leave Rennenkamf with any choice but withdraw into Russian territory. This he accomplishes. The success of his fighting retreat may be compared, though not in detail, to Lanrezac's; but unlike Lanrezac, there is to be no belated acknowledgement of his achievement. The German Eighth Army has pulled off the greatest victory in the Great War, destroying one enemy army and defeating another, clearing the sacred soil of Germany from the sacrilege of foreign feet; a truly splendid accomplishment. Rennenkamf will be dismissed and even accused of treason—though never charged—but unlike Samsonov he will live with the shame and his not-very-sensible moustache until murdered by the Bolsheviks in 1918.

Nevertheless, the orderly West meets today is not the only one to realise that with "*die ganze Welt*" against them it will be hard for the Germans to win; Moltke is coming to the same conclusion, and to help ensure their defeat, in London the War Office issues orders for the raising of a second New Army of six divisions.

September 12th.

About 8:30 the brigade moved off, and we tried to start the cycles too, but Fletcher's had burned out a valve. We got it going by twelve o'clock and started down the hill after the brigade. The so-called road had vanished under well over a foot of sticky mud pitted all over with horse tracks. Somehow or other we reached the bottom without mishap, but we had to keep the engine going to drive it *downhill* through the mire. At the bottom, however, the Rudge again stuck. I rode Fletcher's cycle through all right, and then we both pushed the Rudge and tried to persuade it to start until we were tired. The back mud-guard was jammed full of mud, and the wheels would not go round!

The Premier had scraped the foot-boards on one side clean off, skidding in the slime, but it still had its kick start and was going strong, so I said I would try and ride it back to Maritzy, and see what I could do. I do not know how many times it stopped with the back wheel spinning in the morass, nor how many times it fell over, but I arrived at last with the machine flattened out both sides, no vestige of foot-boards, kick start or any projection, and the lamp all crumpled up. Walked back to Fletcher with the Rudge, and found him disconsolately damning it.

By the merest fluke, one GS waggon which had also found the road too much for the horses was returning, and we helped the drivers put the Rudge on board and take it to Maritzy. They were already badly overloaded, and it was a wicked pull for the horses who could scarcely keep their feet in the slime. With many frantic lashings, and intervals for rest, the poor brutes dragged the heavy waggon to the top of the hill.

Our bikes were frankly finished beyond any roadside repair. In the village we met Captain Carter of the ASC with his supply train of motor lorries. He was just starting to go back to Coulommiers, it being then twelve midday.[262] Both bicycles, after some struggle, were lifted onto a lorry and we climbed in too. Fletcher found he had lost £3, his last, I think, at the farm, but I still had some £5 in my belt so we were quite happy financially as yet. Some Uhlans were seen in the woods close by, but the lorries were under way and I was too weary to care if it snowed Uhlans.

Soon we were joined by three Argyll and Sutherland stragglers. We told them we weren't going their way, but it was all the same to them. Our little lot now consisted of nine men, some of them wounded, Fletcher and myself, two great vats of petrol, and two motor cycles besides various oddments, so we were pretty cramped. I managed to wedge down between the vats somehow and fell into a fitful sleep to the accompaniments of jolts and

---

[262] West's timeline is contradictory here—he only set off after the brigade at mid-day.

pitchings of the lorry and vats, monstrous blasphemies from the Argyll and Sutherlands, and groanings from the poor wounded fellows. Fletcher told me it was the worst night (for we went on all that afternoon till far into the night without a stop) that he had ever spent. Towards evening we passed through what I suppose must have been the battlefield of the Chateau Thierry scene of operations on the Marne, anyway the country was strewn with dead Germans. At one place where two were lying close to the road the Argyll and Sutherland stragglers shouted to the driver to stop, and they ran out and robbed them of sword-knots or bayonets or something, and came back proudly with their trophies. We ran on and I don't know quite where we went as I was lying at the bottom of the lorry. After dark it came on to rain in buckets, but luckily the big hood over us kept us fairly dry. I don't know how long we travelled thus as I was dozing on and off the whole time, but some time during the night the lorry stopped, as it had lost the rest of the column.

Coming toward autumn and the end of the glorious summer of 1914, the weather takes a particular toll of motorcycles. Mud is all but synonymous with the Great War and mudguard clogging was the most consistent of all despatch riders' complaints, right to the end. Some abbreviated or even dispensed with mudguards, or substituted high-level flexible ones made from old tyres.[263]

We are on the eve of the Battle of the Aisne. If the Marne denied the Germans the rapid victory they needed to win the war, their successful defence at the Aisne denies victory to the Allies, and condemns Europe to years of war. Haig's complaints about tardiness are vindicated, for the Germans have been allowed to fall back to a dominating position and dig in before they can be dislodged.

September 13th.

The next thing I remember was that it was dawn and the lorries had drawn up outside a farm in the bright morning sun. Fletcher and I got down and Captain Carter kindly asked us to come and join him at breakfast, which we did. I had a very big appetite but Fletcher had none, having been quite upset with the smell of dead horses en route.

After breakfast we started away again and reached Coulomniers about ten o'clock. On all this ride the constant stench of dead horses was never out of our nostrils. In some places they were burying them or covering them with lime, and once or twice we saw people trying to burn them, but for the most part they just lay about in the fields and became impossible and impassable.

---

[263] Carragher, *San Fairy Ann*, pp. 78-79.

There were no workshops open at Coulommiers and we wandered round all morning till a garage across the bridge opened. The town had not been touched much by the actual fighting, but it was pretty thoroughly looted. The shops suffered particularly, and what the Boche couldn't use, such as women's clothes and shoes, he had dragged out and thrown about the streets in the mud. I was still lamentably lacking in footwear, having but one pair of boots, my spare consisting of one boot and one carpet slipper which Sang had got me somewhere at Quievrain during the first day's scrap on the Mons-Condé Canal, but I couldn't raise anything here.

After lunch I was walking down towards the bridge when who should I meet but Ivor McClure. I was looking so like a tramp, not having shaved for about a week or washed for some days, that he scarcely recognised me. He was as cheerful as usual, and I was awfully pleased to meet him. It seemed about three years ago that he had left me that night at Baldock.[264] He had just arrived with the 6th Division detraining at Coulommiers and had been appointed Lance Corporal Despatch Rider.[265]

The garage over the bridge was now opened, but there were no work people there. However, we got the machine shop running and I started to work on the Rudge. It was pretty badly messed up, but I had almost finished it before it became too dark to see. Slept at the Hotel de la Bourse. The Germans had been there, and of course the place was deserted and filthy, but we collected blankets and slept in a real bed that night as comfortable as kings. (Members of the General Headquarters IC slept there afterwards and said they had never been so uncomfortable in their lives, so comfort must be purely relative!)

Today the Battle of the Aisne opens. The Germans have reached the ridge of the Chemin des Dames and dug in. For the next month they will successfully repel costly assaults. What stands to them, again, is the realistic attitude that they have brought to the war. In addition to high ground, they have the advantage of having learned from the Russo-Japanese War the value of entrenchment, which featured in their soldiers' training when French emphasis on *cran* turned entrenching into a shameful admission of failure. Indeed, the Germans' belief that a strong defence could not be dislodged reinforced their commitment to a powerful, rapid thrust into France before the French could establish such a defence. The Germans have 36 battalions of field engineers,

---

[264] See entry for August 9th.

[265] Because of regulations at the time, DRs had to be NCOs, as it was forbidden for a private soldier to approach an officer directly, and despatches all had to be delivered in person to their recipients, invariably officers. Thanks to his breakdown in Baldock, West ended up with a commission, rather than as an NCO.

ten more than the French,[266] and until Ludendorff's breakout in March 1918 they will take professional pride in building impressive and often impregnable trenches, while the Allies will make do with ramshackle constructions. The difference will be rooted as much in politics and national psychology as in geomorphology: the semi-permanence of the German defences is a manifestation of successful invasion; if the French were to emulate, it could imply a tacit acceptance of enemy occupation.

In London, in recognition of the long slog ahead, the War Office authorises the raising of a third New Army of six divisions.

September 14th.

> Up to an early breakfast and finished off the Rudge. Fletcher goes off alone, and I started work on the Premier. This poor old bus completely flattened out both sides so machine two footrests on the rickety lathe. In the afternoon, going down to the station to get materials, I suddenly met CEF Bevir on a horse. He had also arrived with the 6th Division. (CEF Bevir killed later. Known as "Squirrel".) Extraordinary how he had followed me around—Rugby, Cambridge and BEF. At the station were crowds of wounded and about 50 prisoners. I could not finish the Premier in darkness and there were no light to be had, so slept that night at the house of a kindly old couple just beyond the Hotel de la Bourse, which had been shut and barricaded.

"Your Majesty, we have lost the war." Moltke apologises to the Kaiser and is replaced as Chief of the German General Staff by Erich von Falkenhayn, the Prussian Minister for War, as hawkish as his name and a far more able man, energetic, aggressive and driven. Yet arguably his nerve also will buckle in a few weeks at Ypres, when the BEF was put to the very pin of its collar and breakthrough could have been achieved with further pressure. For the moment he joins in the blame game: "Schlieffen's notes are at an end and therefore also Moltke's wits." The new Chief, unlike some, does not reserve his criticism to detail failures of the Schlieffen Plan, or even to the army: "If we did not have the Navy we would have two more army corps and would not have lost the Marne battle."[267] His words are addressed to Tirpitz but the barb might be directed at Wilhelm's extravagant and destructive naval policy (destructive in that it helped drive Britain into his enemies' camp), a straw in the wind that will see the Kaiser blown to the sidelines by Ludendorff after Falkenhayn, in his turn, is dismissed.

---

[266] John Keegan, *The First World War*, pp. 122-23.

[267] Hastings, op cit, p. 338; Beatty, op cit, p. 11. Beatty claims "Three battleships could have paid for five new army corps", and these might have altered the outcome of the Marne.

Handicapped by heavy rain and with woodland foliage constraining visibility further, the BEF fights uphill against strong and often well-concealed German positions. The small, vicious, largely uncoordinated and mostly futile local actions are harbingers of dismal things to come.

September 15th.

> Finish off the Premier by 4:00 PM. Report at somebody's headquarters so that they should not think I had quite deserted, and then go and buy a few things before starting. Suddenly met du Vignaux of the 19th Brigade in the square with his Peugeot. He was complaining bitterly that he had never been given any time to keep his car in order, and it had now let him down badly, entailing a journey to Paris and a lot of trouble.[268] We started away to rejoin our unit together. The roads were in an awful state. After a time we again arrived on the Marne, at La Ferte-sous-Jouarre, and so to the right up the valley, as we could not cross there. It was a lovely sunny evening and a delightful pleasant run beside the river. After dark we stopped at a roadside farm for a meal, and there we parted company; du Vignaux drove on, but my tyre went flat and the lamp would not work, so I lost him. Late at night I reached Chateau Thierry and stayed there at the station. It was raining heavily, but I found a spot to sleep in the boiler house and everything was dry by the morning.

In South Africa, a short-lived Boer rebellion erupts. It will eventually be defeated along with German forces in *Südwestafrika*, into which the rebels retreat.

September 16th.

> Started off in the morning for Fère-en-Tardenois, and there met Fletcher, Captain Cox and Dunnington Jefferson, and drew £4 to help me on my way. Captain Cox was amazed to see me. "I thought you had got scuppered outside St Quentin," he said. "Why the rearguard had been withdrawn four hours before you were ever sent out to find them." Fletcher told me that the 19th Brigade were not very worried really about our disappearance, and were at that time just above Venizel, in the woods. However, I went straight on to find them. The country from here to the Aisne is a fairly level plateau, for 17 or 18 kilometres, and the road is good and straight. Just after leaving the town one bears to the right over the railway bridge and comes out by the flying ground. In comparison with some of the others this must have been a

---

[268] See entry for August 23rd.

very good aerodrome, as there was plenty of room, and no hedges or ditches to trap the unwary. It was a fine sunny day again and the machines were pretty busy coming and going. They were mostly painted with broad Union Jacks on the under planes and a small Union Jack in the tail somewhere, but there were a few ringed machines either French or English.[269]

About half way there I stopped to enquire the way from some cavalry who were just returning from Braisne. They were having a pretty thin time down there, they said. Shortly afterwards an English aeroplane did a forced landing in a field, the engine having stopped. Unfortunately it charged into a corn cock and smashed the undercarriage. It had a tubular steel undercarriage, and was a tractor (BE2C?) type of machine.[270] Like an eagle another suddenly appeared out of the sky and did a pancake landing not far off. The pilot and observer of the second got out and came across to discover what was the matter. But two Royal Flying Corps mechanics had already arrived on a P&M motor cycle and were getting to work on it, so the sound aeroplane went off. The whole thing struck me as being done with amazing despatch. Hardly had the damaged machine grounded before the people were on the spot to repair it.[271]

The beginning of trench warfare, and stalemate for four years.

The edge of the plateau was fringed with little white puffs of shrapnel thrown by the Germans from the other side of the River Aisne. Unfortunately I would have to run through this as the brigade was in a wood down over the crest. I rode on as far as the little stone village of Acy, which stands on the very edge of the plateau. Here I had to ask again, but nobody seemed to know much. In this spot I found the remnants of a battery which had been badly cut up by shell fire. Huge HE Jack Johnsons had fallen into the village and whole houses had been completely demolished with one shell.[272] An

---

[269] They must have been French, for the RFC and RNAS only adopted the roundel in December 1914.

[270] The Blériot Experimental, model 2, was made by the Royal Aircraft Factory through most of the war; the 2C was typical of the early years, having a 70HP Renault V8 engine that gave it a top speed of about 70 mph and a ceiling of 10,000 ft. Eventually armed with a Lewis gun, it was a good fighter but was withdrawn from combat long before the end, development of the aeroplane, unlike that of the motorcycle, being rapid and radical through the war.

[271] The RFC, RNAS and RAF all used P&Ms, motorcycles made by Phelon & Moore, for both their mobile mechanics and their despatch riders. P&M became Panther, whose last model, the 120 of 1966, looked recognisably the descendent of the Great War machines. But if by 1966 Panther was almost a byword for backwardness, fifty years earlier the P&M was a fine machine indeed.

[272] HE: high explosive; a "Jack Johnson" was a 150mm HE shell, which burst in a huge black cloud. It was named after the eponymous black boxer.

old white-haired priest was walking disconsolately in the narrow street, his little church had been hit, and his flock had fled. A wounded horse hobbled painfully down the stone-paved alley—otherwise, except for the remnants of the battery, the village was deserted. There was an absolutely continuous roll of guns of all calibres, but at the moment nothing was coming very near.

The 19th Brigade, I heard, were just away to the left down the hill. Skirting the edge of the hills I at last came to the road, which cut steeply away across the side of the valley towards Venizel. Halfway down was a huge shell-hole partially overlapping the road, just below was another in the field, and farther down more and more. Skidding in the mud at the bottom I tried to hang myself on a signal wire right across the road. What transport were supposed to do with this wire I don't know. I suppose they just cut it before proceeding, anyway it wasn't there later.[273] On and down into a wood, and soon came across the Royal Welsh Fusiliers who were bivouacking there. Pritchard, I think it was, conducted me to the headquarters.

These were right on the bluff, overlooking Venizel, but screened by a hedge. Just behind was a hazel or privet thicket and paths had been cut like a maze through this, so that one could walk along the crest of the hill without being seen. A couple of ground sheets had been put up as a sort of shelter for the general to sleep under and it was very much an al fresco headquarters. Reported there to General Gordon, and lunched with the Royal Welsh Fusiliers.

Huge artillery battle in progress and constant shelling. The Boches continued to plaster the ridge behind us with big lyddite, but nothing came near us, except one that fell short near some horses in the wood, but it did no damage. One howitzer in particular used to send over a messenger now and then. The old shell would come wandering out of the distance, whistling, and whistling slowly as it came, and finally pass overhead and descend with a tremendous crash some way further up the hill. We had already dubbed him "Whistling Willie" or "Little Willie," but he was a nasty big beast when he went off. This must have been about 8.4-inch stuff. Our guns were firing away all they knew and limbers were tearing backwards and forwards through our woods all day, but we had nothing big with which to reply to the heavy German stuff. The biggest we had in our neighbourhood was a battery of 5-inch field howitzers, just below Brigade Headquarters, and these were very active occasionally.

---

[273] This may have been fallen British "air" cable, which had been strung on trees, but the Germans seem to have strung their cable, light and thin, with enamelled insulation, and designed to be disposable, across the roads of their retreat, deliberately to "clothesline" despatch riders. See West's account of September 9th; Max Burns and Ken Messenger, *The Winged Wheel Patch: A History of the Canadian Military Motorcycle and Rider*, p. 23; *Motor Cycling*, 5 October 1915, p. 554.

Out on the hills above Bucy-le-Long one could just see the remains of a battery, limbers and all. They had come into action there, but had immediately got under heavy German fire. Nobody could get the guns away so there they had to stay. One of the limbers was struck and blown up; I did not see it myself but I heard that it spun round a bright point of flame and vanished. The one or two limbers and a few horses and men I had seen at Acy were, I think, all that survived of that battery, but perhaps they belonged to another lot.

We had gained the passage of the Aisne here, and had pushed right on about four kilometres to hold the edge of the plateau above Bucy-le-Long. The Argyll and Sutherlands advanced through Bucy so the German gunners took a dislike to it, and we watched Bucy-le-Long become Bucy-le-Flat—as Wynne Edwards said—in record time.

Just below us at the head of the bridge was a large white house. This was now being used as the 5th Division Headquarters. It was really very advanced and exposed being geographically actually a few hundred yards ahead of the Brigade Headquarters.

The weather had now broken and that night it rained in torrents. I got away into some bushes with Fletcher, who had arrived from General Headquarters, and we tried to fix ourselves comfortably, but it was hopeless to attempt to keep dry as there was very little straw to be had and no real shelter.

Today Bülow breaks off his assault on the Soissons-Reims front, the last residual action of the Battle of the Marne. Sir John French, in a prescient letter to King George, says: "I think the battle of the Aisne is very typical of what battles in the future are most likely to resemble. Siege operations will enter largely into the tactical problems—the spade will be as great a necessity as the rifle."[274] But for a long time the British will have little or "nothing big with which to reply to the heavy German stuff".

September 17th.

Woke up saturated and generally miserable. Still raining and everything turned into a sea of mud. It rains like Hell all day and every time it tries to clear up the gunners take advantage of it to fire a bit harder, and down it comes again. The Royal Welsh Fusiliers had erected rather a fine shelter in the woods thatched with straw, a triangular affair on three lopped-off trees. Stay there most of the day and mess there. However the rain comes through

---

[274] Hastings, op cit, p. 354.

everything and we all get soaked. The big gun sends over a messenger now and again. Ask Colonel Delmé-Radcliffe regarding joining the Royal Engineers.

In the evening Fletcher and I constructed a double hut with boughs, interlacing more and more stuff down the sides to give shelter, and on top we put our ground sheets to help to keep out the rain. Then went off for more straw—the only stack was about half a mile away, but we staggered back with about three sheaves apiece, fairly dry. The small amount of straw from the night before had disappeared in the mud, but this made a fairly dry foundation. Brought in all my belongings for a pillow, took my boots off, and with one blanket (sleeping bags were unknown to most of us) and overcoat got sort of warm and wet. An absolute blessing was one of the Regulation Tommy's stocking cap—one simply pulled it right down over the head and face so that one could not see or hear at all, and forgot one's troubles! Still shelling.

Joffre forms a new army to the north, under General Castlenau. The misnamed "race to the sea" gets under way as each side tries to turn the other's flank, restore movement and end the war.

German New Guinea capitulates to an Australian Expeditionary Force.

In Constantinople the British Naval Mission leaves as the *Kaiserliche Marine* takes over control of the Ottoman Navy, anticipating the Porte's entry to the war next month.

September 18th.

A grey drizzly dawn, for which one was thankful after such a black drizzly night, followed almost immediately by the resumption of gun fire. Somewhere between six and seven o'clock got out of "bivvy" wet and sloppy, and took a message to Captain Shelton of the ASC 19th Brigade Horse Transport, and found him in a luxurious bed in a chateau at Septmonts. I came in, my boots squelching water and covered in mud, and all he had to say was, "I say, old man, you might shut that door after you, there is a beastly draught." I don't think he ever realised quite how near he was to death at that moment! Good fellow, Shelton, but he used to get very worried because transport by the very nature of the beast never arrived at the time or place expected.

Returned to Venizel and had breakfast with the Royal Welsh Fusiliers. Really got dryish at last, as they had a roaring fire going at the cook-house set up in the woods. The Royal Welsh Fusiliers have somewhere possessed themselves of the most splendid mess cart with sides that flap out, forming tables, like an ice-cream cart.

Took a message to Third Army Corps Headquarters. Roads quite impossible. Go on to Fère-en-Tardenois to see if I can raise another bicycle. Meet

Montague Tanner Rogers, who has not got a bicycle for me at the moment, so run back to Venizel again on the old Premier. The life of a motor cycle at this work is only a matter of weeks. The field workshops were not very accessible to most of us and if anything went wrong which one could not repair on the road it just had to run somehow without repairs.

In the dusk of the evening I went across with Fletcher to get straw. We found the stack being pulled to bits by crowds of Tommies, but we got about eight sheaves and put them on a hurdle and carried them back to our "bivvy." We stacked it up inside and out and made a priceless nest each, and, considering we were on an open hillside we were remarkably cosy.

At about ten o'clock, when we had already turned in, a rattle of rifle fire began on the far poplar-lined ridge. It soon developed into an absolute roar, and through it ran the continuous cadenza of two or three German machine guns, which became audible in the lulls. Now shrapnel began to burst over the ridge in white flashes, showing up for a moment the poplar trees along some road out there. There were no lights at first, but suddenly a German searchlight situated up a ravine somewhere to the north-west blinked out across the scene. We were all out of our various bivouacs by now—Captain Jack, the general, King, Major Haywood and the others—and looking out in the rain from the bluff to see what was happening. It was apparently too far to the west to concern us and must have been a French night attack. After about half an hour it died down, but was renewed at intervals during the night, and we rested in constant expectation of a sudden move forwards or backwards. Nevertheless, nothing happened except the rain. It had never really stopped raining for days, but this time it showed what it could do, and came down in a torrential downpour, playing a wild tattoo upon our ground sheets on the roof and slowly, alas, beginning to penetrate through the sides.

Already the trench system, especially on the German side, is growing elaborate. Today Colonel Ernest Swinton comments: "Their infantry are holding strong lines of trenches among and along the numerous woods which crown the slopes. These trenches are elaborately constructed and cleverly concealed. In many places there are wire entanglements and lengths of rabbit fencing."[275] Colonel Swinton will later play a critical role in developing the tank, designed to crush wire and cross trenches.

The war of movement has almost come to an end. From First Ypres until Ludendorff's breakout in March 1918 creates renewed demand for his unique services, the glory days of the despatch rider are at an end; cable communication relegates the motorcycle to a supportive role.

---

[275] http://www.firstworldwar.com/source/aisne_swinton.htm.

Supportive—yet always needed; merely no longer utterly essential to the BEF as it has been since the Battle of Mons. West's period of secondment as DR to the 19th Brigade is at an end; he's on his way back to the Intelligence Corps.

Appendix 1
Note on BG Drummond.

The story of what happened to General Drummond, who disappeared from our Brigade after Le Cateau, I had a month later from Lieutenant-Colonel Delmé-Radcliffe of the 2nd Royal Welsh Fusiliers and Lieutenant Irwin of the Veterinary Corps, and other sources. It was much as follows:

After the hammering we got at Le Cateau and the complete break up of all organisation, General Drummond apparently quite lost his head. He came across Lieutenant-Colonel Delmé-Radcliffe in the early dawn of August 26th on foot, and said to him, "You must take over the command of my brigade. I've been kicked by a horse and cannot ride."

Colonel Delmé-Radcliffe pointed out that he could not do this as he was not the senior colonel in the brigade, which position was held by Colonel Ward of the Middlesex.

"I can't help that. I can't walk and I can't ride, so you'll have to take command."

Thereupon the general turned on his heel, walked to his horse held close by, mounted and rode away. The last that was seen of him by any of our brigade was by Lieutenant Irwin. The Germans were by then close on Le Cateau and shells were bursting in the streets when General Drummond, taking his ADC with him, went dashing out of the town on horseback, accompanied by a rabble of loose horses terrified by the explosions.

I give the above stories as told me, and not as personal experiences, for what they may be worth. There seems little doubt, however, that the strain and the responsibility had been too much for General Drummond, as it probably was for many good men in those days.

Appendix 2.
March 8ᵗʰ 1916.

EXTRACT OF LETTER TO TDL, CAMBRIDGE.

.... Today I went and got decorated by George RI with the Distinguished Service Order. We went up feeling fearful knuts, swords, etc, into Buckingham Palace.[276] Not a bad sort of place inside, guess I'll buy it after the War. Ran across Com. Norman Thurston, RN, brother of the Royal Naval Air Service lieutenant, engaged to Evelyn Joan Teresa Evans, sister of Gordon's bride. He was a very nice fellow indeed, a typical RN, He was also receiving the Distinguished Service Order, having been minesweeping for eighteen months or more. The ceremony is very simple. We were simply lined up in a large colonnaded room according to seniority. I came last of the DSOs, being the only lieutenant—all the others being majors and people, except one captain.[277] Thence we all went singly into the adjoining reception room, whence one moves as politely as possible without tripping over one's sword to the King, who affixes the medal murmuring some remark, both inaudible and unintelligible. (Little hooks were previously affixed to the tunic, on which the medal was hung.) The King was not looking at all fit after his accident.[278] One then shook hands and backed out again without tripping over sword, and out into the Hall, where the medal was taken off and put in a box for one. Ergo, if you see people coming out of Buckingham Palace wearing the medal you may know it is pure swank, and that they have put it on again themselves. The article is really quite a pretty plaything....

---

[276] Knut: a well-to-do idler, or fashionable man about town.

[277] British Army officers confirm that it would be "most unusual" for a lowly second lieutenant to be awarded the DSO. Lieutenant-Colonel Jim Storr suggests that "the award of a DSO to a subaltern would be just short of the award of a VC", congruent with family testimony that West was nominated for the Victoria Cross. "People" is a curious word to use, as it cannot mean civilians; perhaps it had an in-meaning for West and his recipient?

[278] George V was quite seriously injured when thrown from his horse at a military review in France on 28 October 1915.

"The Man who saved Paris"

ROGER ROLLESTON FICK West was born in London, at 15 Wimpole Street, on January 12th, 1891. He had a quite illustrious ancestry, one quarter of it German. He was named after Johann Christian Fick, likely the son of a bailiff but who became Professor of English at the University of Erlangen and published an English-German dictionary that ran into many editions. Johann also wrote an account of his escape from Napoleonic forces after being shipwrecked off Denmark.

Long before the Napoleonic Wars, in about 1780, this commoner had fallen in love with Christiane von Olhenhausen, of the Holy Roman Empire nobility, and the last in her family line. Apart from the social chasm between them, Christiane was Roman Catholic and Johann Lutheran, so given the problems that marriage in the First Reich entailed, the couple eloped to England. Ten years later they returned to Germany to have their marriage ratified by Protestant prince and Catholic bishop; one of the agreed conditions was that boys be raised Lutheran, girls Catholic. In the words of family-archivist John Bucknall, Roger West's great-nephew: "The Fick family and their descendents are able, intellectual and enlightened. To this day the English descendents of Sophie retain close ties with their cousins despite the cataclysmic effects of the wars during which many Ficks died".[279]

Some sixty years after Johann and Christiane eloped their grand-daughter Sophie married Edward Frankland at the Anglican Church of St Martin in the Fields. Edward was the illegitimate son of a lawyer at a time when illegitimacy cast a very dark shadow; as a consequence he was secretive about his origins, refusing to cooperate with any would-be biographers; it was almost a century after his death before Professor Colin A Russell wrote *Lancastrian Chemist: The Early Years of Sir Edward Frankland* (1986) and *Edward Frankland: Chemistry, Controversy and Conspiracy in Victorian England* (1996).

Edward's was a life to fill at least two books. He was one of the most eminent scientists of nineteenth-century Britain; yet he owed a great deal of his success to Germany. He was the first Englishman to gain a PhD at a Germany University, Marburg, where he studied under Robert Bunsen, as famous in his own time for devotion to his students and gentlemanly sense of honour as he now is for the Bunsen burner.

After Marburg, Edward worked with Justus von Liebig, the "father of the fertiliser industry" for his discovery of the importance of nitrogen to the plant cycle, and began his own original research. Returned from Germany, he became the first professor of chemistry at what is now the University of

---

[279] Private correspondence.

Manchester; later he worked in London at the Royal School of Mines, St Bartholomew's Hospital, the Royal Institution and Imperial College. With his German experiences, he reformed the teaching of chemistry in Britain; but of greater importance for the health of his countrymen and -women, he was, for almost forty years, government advisor on urban water supplies. "There is no such thing as pure water, but we can have potable water." Among his publications are *How to teach chemistry* (1875) and *Water analysis for sanitary purposes* (1880). He was knighted in 1897.

Roger West was immensely proud of his grandfather and of his dual heritage, reflected in the name he bore in memory of Johann Fick. His paternal grandfather came of more humble English artisan-yeoman stock. He worked for the first Travelling Post Office operating on the London and North Western Railway Company before being promoted to Postmaster of one of the London postal districts. Here he strove to improve conditions for Post Office workers and also published at least two books of his own sonnets.

Roger's father, Samuel West, was a complex character, beloved of his three daughters (who always referred to him as "Darling Father") but feared and disliked by his three sons, of whom Roger was the youngest. "Sam" West inherited his father's artistic talent, quick mind and capacity for scholarship. He showed early promise at Westminster Public School, and after graduating in Classics from Christ Church, Oxford (like his father), he studied medicine and rose to the top of his profession as one of the senior consultants at St Bartholomew's Hospital and the City of London Hospital for Diseases of the Chest. He wrote *How to Examine the Chest: A Practical Guide for the use of Students*—"West on the chest" to generations of medical students—as well as a definitive two-volume work on respiratory diseases.

Sam was a fine singer and known for his sensitive rendition of Schubert's songs in particular. This talent he passed along to his children, notably Elsa, a professional musician, and Roger, who, according to John Bucknall, "had an innate musicality, a superb baritone voice and a rare gift to harmonise intuitively". Roger's niece and god-daughter Sally Steen recalls how "in California it was for me a poignant experience to hear [Uncle Roger] singing Schubert's *Lieder* with my aunt, or quoting Goethe".[280]

Despite his great gifts, Sam West was not a comfortable man to be around. He was not liked by his Frankland in-laws and social events organised for his students to meet his three daughters are remembered as "cold and difficult

---

[280] Personal correspondence. Strictly, Sally is the niece of Roger's wife Barbara, and incidentally founder of the charity, Help 4 Forgotten Allies, these being the Karen and Karenni peoples of Burma, allies of Britain in the last war and now persecuted by the Burmese junta.

occasions". Roger describes this impressive person as "a fierce Victorian parent" and stern disciplinarian. John Bucknall testifies:

> Roger told me of the regular beatings he received from his father and how he envied the [other] doctors' sons in Wimpole Street who had kind fathers who held their hands when walking. I remember Roger's great affection for my own father, his nephew Christopher. "How fortunate you are, John, to have a kind and loving father."

As if to ensure that his sons would endure harsh treatment away from home, Sam sent them to Rugby Public School. Morrice Man, who attended a few years before Roger, describes the tough regime and how a boy died after a gruelling cross-country run; "It was certainly in those days a hard, not to say rough, experience".[281] Sally Steen believes that it was "partly on account of his stormy relations with his own father" that Roger left England after the war.

At home in Wimpole Street, Victorian self-entertainment expressed itself in plays and music, as one might expect of such a talented family. Dr West also maintained a country home at Tring, Hertfordshire, a small Regency house leased from Lord Rothschild, the first Jewish peer of England and owner of Tring Park (where, as a professional if eccentric zoologist, Rothschild kept exotic animals and birds and successfully trained zebras to pull a carriage). After this house was demolished, Dr West built his own at nearby St Leonards, which he named Frankland House, after his father-in-law. Roger recounts calling there on August 7th to visit his mother before going off to war. He was "entirely devoted" to his mother, and John Bucknall believes that his kindness and capacity to endure so much he got from her.

Maggie West, the eldest child of Sir Edward Frankland, was a lover of music and an accomplished sketcher and water-colourist, a capable woman who scrupulously maintained a diary all her life. Roger inherited her talent and, inspired by boyhood love for the stories of Ernest Thompson Seton, he made drawings of wildfowl and other animals—as well as landscapes—into old age. His art reveals in its detail a synthesis of scientific observation and artistic sensitivity. "On the way to Utah" is a watercolour that counterpoises the bleak beauty of a desert landscape with the ugliness of battered cars and the stark desperation of victims of the Great Depression.

If Roger's father was cold and insensitive, his mother's family was affectionate and close. Sally Steen describes how Roger "once gave me a stamp album featuring many Victorian stamps from the colonies. In it is written 'For the children from their very affectionate Uncle Percy February 1892'"—this being Percy Faraday Frankland, Edward's son and an eminent scientist in

---

[281] Quoted in Fran Abrams, *Songs of Innocence: The Story of British Childhood*, p. 27.

his own right, named after another even more eminent, Michael Faraday, Sir Edward's colleague and friend. However too young to remember that avuncular gifting, Roger remained a stamp collector and passed that same album onto Sally inscribed, in his turn, "To my goddaughter Sally Mclean with love from Uncle Roger (West)". The album had been "sent out to San Francisco by Marjory in 1950; approx. 851 stamps and 69 removed"—apparently Roger's Aunt Marjory "had removed all the valuable stamps!" Among those that Marjory spared were four from Lord Rothschild.

Aunt Marjorie was another high achiever. The first woman graduate in Divinity in England, she had attended lectures at Oxford but, as a woman in those pre-emancipation times, could not graduate from there, so she took her exams at King's College, London. In addition to divinity, she studied history, and in 1918 she and her sister Elsie visited the Western Front to see what war was really like. Like Roger and most of the family, she spoke fluent German and in 1940, when she and Elsie wished to converse in confidence on a crowded bus, they did so in German—much to the consternation of their fellow-passengers! They report a "ticking off from the local policeman that evening" in Clun, Shropshire, where they lived during the Blitz. Inspired by a Housman line describing Clun as one of "the quietest places / Under the sun", Maggie West had bought a house there as a safe retreat in the previous war, but it was less quiet when her daughters moved there: it seems that Elsie and Marjorie spoke German on other occasions purely to wind up the locals.

After Rugby, Roger went up to Cambridge. Sally Steen describes "an oar on the wall in their dining room in Carmel [California] with all the signatures from his college, Trinity I think, of the team he rowed with". He was something of a wag in his youth: once "he and another student amused themselves by rushing up to a policeman directing the traffic in a busy part of London with a brick and saying 'here hold this a minute', and rushing off". When war broke out Roger was working for Tangyes of Birmingham, an engineering firm that made hydraulic cylinders and rams, and stationary engines. He had graduated from Cambridge in 1912 with an engineering degree and went on to study further at Bonn University, Heidelberg and Würzburg, so he had German friends as well as relations; thus he was deeply conflicted about the war. Duty, however, was a stern and sacred thing back then, and Roger never doubted where his lay.

This dissonance can be discerned early in his account. On August 27th he finds himself in excellent cover on a railway embankment, looking down the sights of a Lee Enfield on an enemy cavalry patrol:

> Eleven of them at least were sitting ducks, and as good as dead, and maybe all 21 before they could reach any sort of cover. It was my duty to kill them. Or was it? But for once in the impersonality of war

> I could see them close to as fellow men, such men as I had met and
> been friends with at Bonn University before the war.

His account reveals how troubled he is by this conflict between duty and humanity; "But I knew in my heart I could not have murdered those men." The next day he alludes to "frightful things ... of which it is almost impossible to write". On September 9th he describes how "The whole world seemed unreal and ghostly, and perhaps I was a bit light-headed from want of sleep, but I rushed to the [motor]bicycle in a meaningless panic and made off into the forest"—a flight perhaps from his internal conflict.

As an old man Roger discussed this "unreality" of war with John Bucknall. "One evening we would sit in the trench sickened by the common slaughter—they were young chaps like us on the other side. Then next day a shell would kill and maim half your friends and that night we would assist a gun crew to blow the hell out of them on the other side".

For all the assured tone he sustains through his diary, and the occasional dry wit of his observations, the war had a terrible effect on Roger. He was evacuated out of the combat zone suffering from shellshock, which was to afflict him for the rest of his life. He told Sally Steen how once when "coming over a hill he saw some German soldiers advancing towards him. One of them was a fellow student from Heidelberg!" He does not recount this event in his "Diary of the War", so it must have occurred between the Battle of the Aisne and First Ypres (for Roger was not on active service when trench-lock was broken in 1918). But could it have been a muddled memory? Perhaps of that episode on the railway embankment, which, John Bucknall says, "haunted" Roger. Or might it have been delusionary; the friend from Heidelberg a subconscious projection of the "enemy" as "Brother Boche?"[282]

After his seconded stint as despatch rider with the 19th Brigade, Roger was returned to the Intelligence Corps. Though his memories were blighted by the awful thing that war is, he retained a great deal of affection for his old unit (he visited the IC HQ and museum every time he came home in later life) and was proud of the fact that his DSO was the first decoration earned by that Corps—which for its part seems to have overlooked the honour until 1962, when the Intelligence Centre enquired of the War Office for details of the award: "this would be of considerable interest for the Corps Journal and would be of use in the compilation of a Corps History".[283]

---

[282] In another splendid memoir of those years Charles Carrington warns that "Long memories ... are treacherous", acknowledging that he had been "dining out" ever since the war on stories that scrupulous checking while preparing his manuscript proved he never actually witnessed; *Soldier From the Wars Returning*, p. 12.

[283] National Archives, WO 339/10405.

Roger's award is evidence of his courage, and he was again mentioned in despatches after being promoted to full lieutenant on January 21st, 1915;[284] at some point he was recommended for the VC.[285] In September 1915, however, he left the Intelligence Corps and returned to England the following December suffering from neurasthenia—what shellshock was called when it afflicted officers. Just what prompted his breakdown is not clear, but he was on sick leave from January to April 1916 and in March that year paymaster solicitors, Messrs Cox & Co of Charing Cross, were advised that he was "not entitled to staff pay beyond 23rd December, 1915, and that the amount overissued should be recovered". Roger accordingly was informed on April 3rd that he owed the War Office £46.4.9, as well as £11.17.11 to Cox & Co, who "shall be glad to receive a remittance in respect of this amount also".

The following day—April 4th—Roger responds, explaining that his loss of entitlement to staff pay needed to be seen in light of the fact that as he had volunteered and been accepted directly into the Intelligence Corps he had "no ordinary regimental pay ... to revert to", which normally would have happened after three months' absence from Intelligence Corps duty (dating from Sept 24th, 1915). He sounds both wounded and indignant, and his War Office file contains much correspondence on the subject of his pay and pension, the tone growing increasingly acrimonious.

After his recovery Roger was seconded to civilian employment on February 28th, 1917. This does not imply discounting of his martial value, for by now the British government had committed to "total war" and was investing all the Empire's resources toward the Entente's best return. Specialists were recalled from active military service in order to make the most of their merits, and as a highly-qualified engineer, Roger was best deployed at home.

He was sent to the Aircraft Manufacturing Co, Hendon, where he became Geoffrey de Havilland's chief of research and directed his engineering skills toward important discoveries in wind-tunnel development. The War Office poorly appreciated his efforts, for after his demobilisation it argued that because he had been seconded to Airco he was "entitled to have [his] gratuity assessed only on the rate of pay received on 27th February 1917, i.e. 8/6 per diem."

Roger refuted this. On November 7th, 1920 he wrote to the WO to point out: "I was demobilised on April 7/19. Army order 406/1915 says: 'The gratuity is issuable on termination of service & will be calculated at the rate of pay issuable on the last day of service'.... The unfairness of issuing gratuity in 1919 at 1917 rate is obvious & penalises me moreover for having volunteered to go out so early". The per diem rate when Roger was demobilised was 11/6,

---

[284] *London Gazette*, 22 June 1915.

[285] Barbara Horder, "Memories of a Long Life", Chapter Six.

three full shillings above the 1917 rate, a significant sum over his four-and-a-half-year period of service.

A measure of his disgruntlement may be gauged from a letter he sends to the WO from Asiatic Petroleum Co at Shanghai, on November 8th, 1921. The ostensible reason for this letter seems to be a query regarding medals outstanding but Roger's real concern is with the money he feels he is owed:

> When forwarding these valued Medals I would esteem it a favour if you would *enclose some small portion of either the gratuity, the pension in lieu, or military income tax* rebate due to me for some $4\frac{1}{2}$ years service about which I have had much fruitless correspondence, and which would be even more highly valued.... I can only assume that the grateful country is waiting to enclose the above dues as a great surprise with the last medals it will have any occasion to forward me.

The emphasis is Roger's own; his bitterness is clear.

By now life has taken Roger far away from the country in whose cause he had volunteered and fought and risked his life and wrecked his mental health. Sally Steen thinks that he felt impatience toward "our island xenophobia and narrow vision". John Bucknall, however, feels that Roger "*loved* England", but that personal and national bereavement had left his *patria* a place of too-painful memories for him to remain. Decades later, on a visit to Christ Church Cathedral, Oxford, John watched tears trickle down his great-uncle's cheeks as he read the commemorated names of school-friends whose days had numbered but a quarter of his own.

Like many another anguished and disillusioned veteran, Roger left England. He ventured into petroleum geology and went on to make a successful career with Shell in China and the East Indies. In 1923 he was in Japan when the worst earthquake in Japanese history struck. This experience prompted an interest in seismology and he went on to make original discoveries in the field. Later he lectured at the University of British Columbia but remained an outdoors man and took great pleasure, and perhaps some therapeutic refuge, in the wildness of that mountainous province of Canada. He was still climbing there into his eighties. Later, in Carmel, he would walk the marshes near the Mission and watch the pelicans and other wild birds.

His love of the wilderness, and mountaineering, went back to his childhood captivation by Ernest Thompson Seton and the achievements of his grandfather, Sir Edward Frankland, who as a boy had climbed in the Lake District and as a scientist bivouacked on Mont Blanc while conducting experiments (on, among other things, the boiling point of water). When at Rugby Roger attended a lecture and bought a book on the Rocky Mountains (which, with his annotations, survives). He was absorbed by the world, its natural history, its peoples, and he and his wife later spent much of their time and money exploring it.

He did not, however, entirely absent himself from England. At some point he had met Barbara Horder, daughter of Percy Morley Horder, an eminent architect who, according to Barbara's cousin Mary Horder Friedel,

> did everything he could to prevent Barbara from marrying Roger West. Roger had made it clear that he had no intention of living in England, partly on account of his stormy relations with his own father, who seemed to have had a character similar to the father of Elizabeth Barrett Browning. He recognised also that Percy could ruin their marriage and that Barbara must take this into consideration before making up her mind. Roger seems to have made somewhat will-o-the-wisp appearances in England as he was mostly working abroad, but he did not leave Barbara in peace, nor did other candidates. It took her a long time to make a decision, but in 1930 she accepted her persistent suitor and they were married in St George's Church, Hanover Square, in London. It was a big wedding but somehow a sad occasion. I remember GK Chesterton, very stout, standing behind the refreshment table, with a glass in his hand, drinking and eating and talking without cease. The newly married couple left after the reception and were soon on their way to Canada. [Barbara] returned very occasionally for short visits. Roger visited England and his sisters only when he was an old man, a short time before he died.[286]

The wedding took place on July 18th, 1930, and among the presents was a drawing of Don Quixote inscribed by the artist Edmund Sullivan, a well-known book illustrator.

Both Sullivan and Chesterton would have been friends of Barbara, a talented artist and actress. She was a striking-looking woman, too patrician by her photographs to be called *pretty* and with too much character in her expression for even a clichéd *beautiful* to do her justice. No wonder many "candidates" couldn't "leave her in peace".

Barbara has left her own account in "Memories of a Long Life":

---

[286] *Mary Horder Friedel 1911-2005* by Mary Horder Friedel, privately printed. Chesterton was, famously, very stout. During the war he was accosted by a woman who asked, "Why aren't you out at the front?" He replied, "Madam, if you observe from the side you'll see that I *am* out at the front."

I had met Roger West off and on at the Fletchers' dances.[287] His hair-raising exploits intrigued [us all].... He had a useful technique with the girls; he phoned asking them to lunch and if they did not accept, he said casually, "Oh! It doesn't matter. I'm off to Singapore tomorrow". (Or it may have been Australia.) They usually accepted. He had wonderful blue eyes which seemed to look at far horizons....

Theirs would have seemed an unlikely match—quite apart from Barbara's father's opposition. Roger's interests were "Scientific, open air, wide open spaces and mountain climbing ... he even told me he disliked the theatre. We differed on practically everything. After his marvelous exploits in World War I and his pioneer work with de Havillands, he went to the Orient and I hardly ever saw him".

Roger courted her "for some years" according to Sally Steen, who thinks that part of Barbara's father's reluctance to see his daughter married was that "he relied on my aunt's charm and theatrical style at social events and when entertaining clients". Barbara would seem to expand on this supposition: "Father and his friends ignored the fact that [Roger was awarded] one of the first DSOs of the war, was recommended for the VC and was twice mentioned in despatches.... Someone at a party remarked: 'Do you know that your fiancé is the man who saved Paris?'"

Forced to concede to the power of love, Percy Horder "instructed his chauffeur to polish their Bentley till it shone for the event. Uncle Roger however had the great idea of hiring the last [horse-drawn] hackney cab in London for them to ride off in after the wedding. My grandfather was appalled," writes Sally.

Percy must have been less appalled than stricken when Roger whisked his daughter off to British Columbia, whose mountains he loved. Sally's mother, Joanna—Barbara's sister—visited the couple there and they brought her to parts of the province that were still unmapped and had a small lake, "somewhere far north of Victoria", named after her. Barbara taught her little sister to play the guitar and later Joanna "sang at the Players Theatre in London all during the [Second World War] years, but"—as her daughter says—"that is another story".

Later the Wests moved to Carmel, California. Roger's work in seismology may have drawn him here, his interest possibly piqued by the disastrous earthquake of 1906, and he worked on improving building construction in order to limit structural damage in any future 'quake; but he also had worked in California, perhaps as early as the silent film era, on special effects. He and Barbara went to live there around the turn of 1939; Sally records that her "aunt

---

[287] Might this Fletcher family have been related to Roger's old IC colleague, Lieutenant WG Fletcher?

had to give up her British nationality in order to do war work there" and his War Office file records that, writing from Vancouver in October 1938, Roger requests his "certificate of Honourable discharge" which he requires "immediately". He follows this up the following month for a duplicate, explaining that he needs two such certificates "for getting into the [United] States" and that "I require these now urgently". Obviously he was not visiting this time, but immigrating.

In California Roger became advisor to Paramount Pictures; Barbara advanced her own career (among her roles, she played Lady Montague in Sir Laurence Olivier's 1940 Broadway production of *Romeo and Juliet*). Frequently they were invited to Hollywood parties where they might sing together, in perfect harmony, Barbara playing the guitar. Roger's would have been an unknown face at most of these gatherings, but not at them all: Olivia de Havilland and Joan Fontaine were cousins of his old boss Geoffrey de Havilland, and it seems improbable that he didn't meet one or both of these famous sisters at such soirees.

In his mischievous way, though, Roger may have relished anonymity at Hollywood parties. He had a habit of stepping up to some star of the screen, reaching an enormous hand and proclaiming, dead-pan: "Roger West, engineer. What's your racket?"

His hands were very large: John Bucknall remembers being impressed by their size and Sally Steen describes how "Uncle Roger had large capable hands which when he was older he held rather out from his body as he walked".

Sally lived with Roger and Barbara when she was thirteen and Roger was in his early seventies, using his retirement to build houses which he then sold to finance the many long trips across the world he and Barbara took. There were shorter trips too: "He liked to get out of the car and walk in remote parts of California and say perhaps nobody in the history of the world had ever actually walked there, as it was such a vast country unlike England, that 'misty little island with bad plumbing', as he called it." He brought Barbara and Sally hunting for jade along the Californian coast and once returned to the car to find the tyres shot out, but was undeterred by the menace of this gesture in the land of the free and the private beach, and home of the brave intruder. "I think he thought it was wrong that only one third of the beach was legally accessible to the public and so he just ignored the ruling as ridiculous!" says Sally.

Once "He gave me a lecture on not being afraid", and "we had a great joke about the bears at Yosemite national park, which as a 13 year old had alarmed me. He found a Victorian engraving of a girl sitting on a grizzly bear's lap and wrote a poem to go with it, which of course I kept. He was full of that sort of fun." He used to call his god-daughter his "devil-daughter" and "his letters repeat that joke". He "adored cats" and there were many around the house, with idiosyncratic names like Percy, Nonsense and Rubbish (greatly given to assassinating hummingbirds). After the birth of one of Sally's children he enquired as to what name her daughter was to be given, suggesting Barbara, but "As an alternative what about 'Hopscotch' or 'Patent steam carpet beater'? I once had a terrier who wouldn't answer to either of these."

On another occasion he wrote: "We miss our Sally and the rest of the family [Sally's brothers and sisters, who also visited] out here, but more particularly you, so we hope you and family will one day migrate out to this rather horrible country"; he was discouraged by "the scandals and crooks and cheap money politics which seems an essential of American life."

Sally gives more detail on his musicality. She remembers Roger "singing with my aunt as we drove along in California and the way he harmonised as they sang."

Roger and Ba went to a lot of parties; they were very popular and sang together. Auntie Ba played the guitar. Uncle Roger enjoyed a drink and once mixed a cocktail which he called a "MOBC", we thought it was a reference to British Columbia but it turned out to stand for "My own bloody cocktail". It was such a stiff one that it caused some problems at a party my mother gave for them in Clevedon, many years later, when he finally made a visit to Britain in his eighties, with guests becoming more inebriated than they could cope with.

John Bucknall, who also visited Roger and "Aunt Ba" in the 1970s, recalls how Roger always carried a flask of gin in his pocket and how he regularly sipped from this—yet he also records how Barbara testified that she never in her life saw her husband actually drunk. Perhaps along with Roger's unusually large hands went a large liver? John describes the stern proclamation on the door of the house in Carmel: "No drinking before 5:00!"—and the trick clock across the threshold, whose every hour was marked "6".

But while the waggishness of youth survived, behind the light-heartedness and ready wit Roger could get depressed, a consequence of his shellshock, dark memories of the war and lost friends like the enigmatic Alfred Sang, mortally wounded at the Marne. At such times external anxieties could have a debilitating effect, and one may wonder how much of Sang Roger unconsciously took on: "His quick amusing conversation should have been a key to his character, but one often sensed a dark cloud hanging over [Sang] and a kind of bitterness against the world."[288]

Though he and Barbara were avid travellers, and Barbara did visit her family from time to time, until old age Roger felt unable to return to England, so painful were his memories. In his dark moods he must have reflected on "The Voyage", a sonnet written many years before by his grandfather, John West:

---

[288] Diary entry for August 23rd.

I did not think, when setting out, so long
And far a voyage I should make as this.
For tho' I did embark with joyousness
And hand in hand with Hope, amid the throng
Of those who sailed with me, scarce one, among
Them all, Life's risks and hazards did impress
As me, or seemed to know the dangerousness
Of winds and waves, and of the Siren's song.
Yet some the wind soon caught, and blew to sea,
And some sank down in sense, and in a lurch
Were rolled into the waves, and some, attent,
Sate listening to the witching melody
That came from off the rocks, and plunged in search,
And few did reach the ports whereto they went.

Roger was one of the lucky ones of his generation who did reach port, with all his limbs intact and both eyes and good looks spared by the war, a successful career and happy marriage following that, and the enduring love of his wife and "devil-daughter." When late in life he was able to bring himself back home to England the admiration and affection of great-nephews and -nieces was added to his stock of love. Those who got to know him then retain fond memories to this day. Sally, revisiting Carmel as a grown woman, remembers how he returned to the subject of fear, out of which he had cajoled her as a girl: "Uncle Roger's kindly lecture on not being afraid lest it hold me back from living fully." John Bucknall recalls Roger saying, shortly before his death, "You do that which you fear most."

This remark prompts re-examination of Roger's estimation of his colleague Fletcher: "one felt that he had innate courage, and all the more to be admired in that he was afraid". Might this also be unconscious projection? How fearful must Roger have been through those weeks he describes so insouciantly in his "Diary of the War"? How terrified as he rode those miles back toward the Oise and scaled the pillar of that bridge to lay those explosives with his lame foot hobbling him and the Germans marching up on him? How insouciant could he really have felt "riding I thought straight into the German army"? Behind the *sang froid* of his account is the palimpsest of understandable terror: "the hints of our impending suicide did not add to my peace of mind". Courage is never the absence of fear but the overcoming of it, and for Roger's generation, duty demanded not just courage but modesty in its discharge.

Roger and Barbara's marriage was, by every account, enviably happy. John Bucknall, who met his great-uncle only in Roger's old age, remembers Roger holding his wife close and murmuring "Bara-wara-wara"—his pet name for

Barbara. Sally Steen, who spent part of her youth with her aunt and uncle, remembers their affection too:

> There was always between them a great love. Often I would be thrilled to watch Uncle Roger stroke her arm and say "Bara-wara-wara" looking at her so softly. Despite being such a masculine man, he was not ashamed to show affection. In the mornings in Carmel they would have breakfast in bed and sit and read together for a long time. In many ways I was sent to witness this loving marriage since my parents had recently got divorced. It had been very acrimonious and painful. There were six of us children. Roger and Ba never had children and perhaps for this reason they were very attentive as aunt and uncle.

For all the tragedy and terror that it encompassed, Roger's was a happy life, all told. It certainly was successful. It even may have changed history.

Roger West died at Eskaton Monterey Health Centre on November 18th, 1975, aged 84. After a service at All Saints Episcopal Church, his remains were cremated. According to John Bucknall he did not believe in an afterlife, yet he attended Church, one might say religiously, every Sunday: "I couldn't do without it". Barbara died eleven years later, on November 8th, 1986, her eighty-seventh birthday.

One cannot leave this brief account of his life without further consideration of the accolade that was bestowed on Roger West in September 1914: *The man who saved Paris.* How valid was this, from the perspective of a century of scholarship?

For a start, the accolade appears to have been spontaneous and hyperbolic, as West himself admits: "a gross if enthusiastic overstatement". The French gave no official recognition of what happened at Pontoise. Two days later the government evacuated Paris and moved to Bordeaux, from where it could continue to direct the war. A week after the destruction of Pontoise Paris was still vulnerable; it was Gallieni and Manoury who saved it.

But what was at stake on August 30th was not the French capital but the French armies, for German victory could only come following military defeat and surrender, and if the Fifth Army could be knocked out of the fight a gap would open in the Allied defence which the enemy could infiltrate. It was just such an attack that was exercising General von Kluck as General Lanrezac was disengaging from his battle with General von Bülow at Guise. If the German First Army could get across the Oise and hit the French in the flank the result could have been calamitous.

It's often asserted today that the Schlieffen Plan could not have worked, for logistical reasons and because Moltke had fatally weakened the right wing. That is certainly plausible. But until the first days of September the Germans were rampant. They had had one victory after another and were probing hard for the decisive defeat that would knock France out of the war. Had that bridge over the Oise been open to them, might they have succeeded?

There is no way of knowing, of course, but destruction of that bridge was critical to subsequent events. Kluck was well aware that "the section of the Oise below [la Fère] is very important from a military point of view".[289] General Lanrezac was no less conscious of the danger posed by any German assault on his flanks, and the value of the Oise as a long defilade, one that allowed him to deploy his cavalry on his right flank, to guard this against any attack by both the German Second Army, from which he had just disengaged, and the Third; for Lanrezac's two flanks were in the air, the French Fourth Army being more than a day's march behind him and retreating at all speed, as were the BEF on his left. His position was "most dangerous", with elements of von Hausen's forces probing the twenty-mile gap between the Fifth and Fourth Armies to the east, while "West of the Oise and beyond it the First German Army was swerving south-eastwards at von Bülow's request to hurl itself against the left flank of the Fifth Army".[290] On the day that West demolished the bridge at Pontoise, Lanrezac sent an urgent request to Sir John French to destroy the one at Bailly, farther downriver, in order to neutralise the threat posed by Kluck to his left flank, but delays in despatching a demolition team meant that the Germans beat the British to it and the sappers of the expedition were all killed, so that enemy cavalry was able to cross the Oise early on August 31st.[291]

The BEF went to France with aggressive intent—but this of its very nature caused problems. Field officers and despatch riders were chronically handicapped by a lack of maps right through the Great Retreat because, in the spirit of offensive, all maps of France had been returned to the War Office after the BEF crossed into Belgium, the belief being that the Hun would quickly be set on the run.[292]

For a similar reason, the Royal Engineers were better prepared and equipped to build and repair bridges sabotaged by retreating Germans than to demolish them in any British retreat: "since the prevailing doctrine envisioned a war of movement—and forward, not back—demolitions were seen as secondary to river crossings". West is impressed by the pontoon bridge he observes on September 10th, "a wonderful piece of work on the part of the

---

[289] Alexander von Kluck, op cit, p. 71.

[290] Edward Spears, op cit, pp. 285-86.

[291] Max Hastings, op cit, p. 292: Ian Senior, op cit, p. 164; Spears, op cit, pp. 294-96.

[292] Michael Carragher, *San Fairy Ann? Motorcycles and British Victory 1914-1918*, p. 186.

Royal Engineers"; but budgetary constraints over many years had left the Army "The Absent-Minded Beggar" of Kipling's poem, and the *Field Service Pocketbook* (1914) implies the need to find and obtain explosives locally. The recklessness of so "muddling through" was evident on the very first encounter with the enemy—in a mining district where, of all places, it should have been easy to obtain black powder or dynamite, and all the detonators and fuse a small army could need. Instead, the unsuitability of the BEF's equipment was tragically made evident at the bridges over the Mons-Condé Canal where, despite the courage of Captain Wright and Lieutenant Dease, Corporal Jarvis and Private Godley and countless others overlooked by history, only one of the five bridges was blown, and the Germans were able to cross.[293] As late as the Marne "There were not enough engineers [or] explosive" to demolish all bridges.[294] The first failed attempt to blow up the one at Pontoise-lès-Noyon may be put down to the same sort of problems, and that West could obtain guncotton the next day, when sappers apparently could not earlier that morning (or didn't bother), says a great deal about the British government's dependence on its army's "muddling through" and the confusion this promoted, a confusion that was exacerbated by the pace of the Retreat.[295]

West summarises the effect of his demolition of the bright: it "threw the German Guard Cavalry far to the west to find a crossing. The crucial moment was lost to the Germans and the French army escaped". But this self-effacing summary camouflages the importance to the outcome of the campaign, of the war itself, if the French Fifth Army had *not* escaped.

Anglocentrism can blind one to the fact that the BEF was a minor player in 1914; in numbers it comprised not more than 7-8 percent of all Allied troops in the West. As Plan XVII rapidly unravelled salvation of the Western Allies devolved onto the French Fifth Army, originally designated as a buttress to the others in their offensive in Alsace-Lorraine. Now, with those other armies battered by German artillery and in retreat, and the bulk of the German forces swinging through north France, if the Fifth could be knocked out the entire French line, the whole way to Verdun, was vulnerable to enfilade attack and might be rolled up, the war in the West won, Schlieffen's plan accomplished. The tiny BEF was no more than a flank guard to the French armies, a minor

---

[293] Allan Mallinson, op cit, pp. 91-92, 305-06, 312. Destruction of even this bridge was at the second attempt, "the [initial explosive] charge having proved insufficient". See Martin and Nick Shelley, op cit, p. 177.

[294] Macdonald, op cit, p. 273.

[295] Colonel Huguet, Head of the French Mission attached to the BEF, in a telegram to GQG early in the very morning of the destruction of Pontoise, reports "great danger of blowing up bridges". His meaning is unclear (words from the text are missing) but he likely means "danger of *not* blowing up bridges", as several upriver from Pontoise had been blown in the hours and minutes before he transmitted his telegram. See Spears, op cit, p. 280.

irritant to the Germans, and by the end of August Kluck believed the British to be beaten and the French Fifth Army close to collapse. "It was therefore essential to defeat the enemy [the French] before he could gain time to reorganise his masses"—which Joffre was frantically trying to do (if *frantically* is the word for anything that phlegmatic commander did). Kluck goes on: "With this object in view, the attack was to be continued on the 30th August"—in the morning of which West blew up the main bridge over the Oise.

The importance of the trans-Oise assault Kluck leaves in no doubt: "an attempt might be made to take the retreating enemy in the flank by an energetic pursuit in a southerly and south-easterly direction", it being "of decisive importance to find the flank of this force, whether retreating or in position, force it away from Paris, and outflank it", so he proposes to "advance on the 31st by Compiègne and Noyon [whose bridge at Pontoise he will find broken] to exploit the success of the Second Army" at Guise. Cavalry was essential to this operation, and General von der Marwitz, commander of the First Army's cavalry, was assisted by General Manfred von Richthofen, whose cavalry was attached to the Second Army;[296] it was Richthofen's Guard and 5th Cavalry Divisions that would prove the main threat to the Fifth Army, the aims of Marwitz's forces being to locate and engage the BEF (which they did, to their cost, at Nèry); Richthofen's task was to hit the French flank and seize the Aisne crossings to cut off their retreat. (West's Map IV illustrates the German plan; see also Map V.)

The Battle of Guise was less the "success" that Kluck claims; rather, it was the first serious setback the Germans had received in the West and Bülow had called on Kluck for assistance. A delaying action, it successfully bought a hard-pressed force time to break contact with its pursuer, making operational concessions for longer-term strategic advantage, so that Lanrezac's Fifth Army was able to disengage and fall back in compliance with Joffre's General Order No 4. But now the Fifth's left flank had been exposed by Sir John French's uncoordinated retreat and was protected only by the natural obstacle of the River Oise. If this flank could be assaulted, if Richthofen's cavalry could cross the river in time to tear or even threaten it, what damage could the German horsemen have inflicted on the retreating French?

After decades of denigration, it's far too easy to lose sight of the devastating power of cavalry a century ago. Horsemen were the only shock troops then, and they had the potential to win the war for Germany in the last two days of August 1914. A couple of weeks before West's action at Pontoise, Belgian infantry, after a successful counterattack from Fort d'Embourg (at Liège), "could not follow up their success. Apparently they feared operating in the open in the face of large

---

[296] Kluck, op cit, pp. 75, 81-83, 86. The cavalry commander was great-uncle to his more famous namesake, the Red Baron.

numbers of German horsemen hovering in the vicinity".[297] On August 23rd West was sent to find the 19th Brigade's Transport which "would get massacred if not warned" of rampaging enemy cavalry. Horsemen could range far ahead of the main body of infantry and were by no means dependent on swords or sabres and carbines: light artillery accompanied them. It was partly fear that hostile cavalry might cut railway lines to the south of Paris that prompted Gallieni to urge the French government to evacuate the capital on the very day that West blew up the bridge. In the Spring Offensive of 1918, after a virtual revolution in warfare, a British officer could still report: "It was a crowning glory that [the Germans] had no cavalry. How many times during the retreat did we thank heaven for this!"—for had they taken Amiens the Germans could have divided the Allies and possibly defeated them in detail, as in 1940, before the Americans could fully deploy. "Cavalry was the one factor which would have smashed the morale of the defence in a twinkling".[298]

What must cavalry's effect have been, then, on an army that was at the very limit of its endurance, after two hard battles—Charleroi and Guise—and virtually without rest for ten days? The morale of the French Fifth Army did not have to be "smashed": it was on the canvas already, exhausted soldiers casting away their weapons as they were forced-marched toward the Aisne, and Kluck was aware of their "extreme depression".[299] What must Lanrezac and his *poilous* have thought if they had seen the terrible Uhlans riding in on their flank? Perhaps Desperate Frankie might have found himself a "stranger to depression" no longer.

Even if weariness or weakness of the German cavalry prevented an *arme blanche* charge, the very appearance of the enemy would have been enough to force the Fifth Army to deploy to face this threat. Lanrezac had lost a precious day in turning to attack at Guise, and this is a measure of an army's inertia. Even such a critic of the general as Lieutenant Spears acknowledges that "The difficulties of the manoeuvre now being carried out by the Fifth Army have not been sufficiently recognised.... [It] redounds greatly to the credit of both staff and troops, all the more so as it was not unhampered by the enemy."[300] Meeting a flank attack would not have been so taxing an operation but it still would have taken time, and even had the attack been seen off more time would have been lost in resuming the retreat, and all that time would have allowed Kluck's infantry to come up closer. If the Fifth Army could be trapped between

---

[297] David R Dorondo, *Riders of the Apocalypse: German Cavalry and Modern Warfare, 1870-1945*, p. 50.

[298] Sidney Rogerson, *The Last of the Ebb: The Battle of the Aisne, 1918*, p. 112.

[299] Hastings, op cit, p. 302; Kluck, op cit, p. 78.

[300] Spears, op cit, p. 254.

the Oise and the Aisne, a gap would be opened in the Anglo-French defensive line that would have been impossible to string.[301]

The Germans were no less tired than the British or the French but their morale was higher. "The certainty of early victory and of the triumphal entry into Paris keeps them going and acts as a spur to their enthusiasm. Without this certainty of victory they would fall exhausted." One last effort, for such men, might end this war; one more, for their enemies, just here and right now, might prove one too many to sustain. Furthermore, the units that were immediately endangered by a German flank attack were the least reliable of the entire Fifth Army. With Rupprecht's forces hammering the fortress line to the east, a defeat in the west would be fatal: "The French could never withstand such a double blow. In days, even hours, they would be squeezed into submission."[302]

To bolster cavalry's flank-attack on the Fifth Army, Kluck determined to lorry "mixed detachments" of cavalry, infantry and artillery straight to the Aisne to seize or destroy the crossings there, the motor-lorries cutting time and conserving troops' energy. Lanrezac's vanguard was "in an extremely fragile condition and might fall apart at the slightest blow, leaving the Germans to move along the Aisne valley, destroying the bridges and cutting off the rest of the [Fifth] army".[303] The blow to French morale at finding their retreat cut off, and pursuit close on their heels, would have been a powerful factor, especially given the state of the French Fifth commander's nerves.

Kluck was urgently aware of this opportunity, as Lanrezac's men stumbled, stupefied by want of sleep, toward the Aisne crossings.

> They looked like ghosts in Hades expiating by their fearful endless march the sins of the world[;] bumping into transport, into abandoned carts, into each other, they shuffled down the endless roads, their eyes filled with dust that dimmed the scalding landscape, so that they saw clearly only the foreground of discarded packs, prostrate men, and an occasional abandoned gun.[304]

---

[301] This counterfactual consideration must acknowledge that the German Second Army, far from being in hot pursuit, was rather resting and recuperating after Guise and ill-advisedly investing the minor fortress of La Fère—all much to Kluck's disgust. But Kluck's First Army was pressing Lanrezac hard and had his sometime-subordinate brought the French to battle military opportunism—and jealousy—would have stimulated Bülow to get his men moving to deal the fatal blow, and make up for the Second Army's indifferent performance at Guise.

[302] Macdonald, op cit, p. 246-47.

[303] Senior, op cit, p. 164.

[304] Spears, op cit, p. 318.

Kluck barely failed in his objective. Had Richthofen's cavalry been able to delay the Fifth Army by menacing its flank those "mixed detachments" could have beaten the French to the Aisne crossings and Lanrezac's forced night march could not have been sustained to its objective.[305] Imagine the effect on exhausted, demoralised men of broken bridges or muzzle-flashes in their faces just as they're about to reach some sort of safety? They would have had to regroup in the dark, improvise plans for an attack at first light, then ... see in the sunrise Kluck's main force on their flank and rear, and knowing that Bülow's army was following up. It's difficult to see how they could have survived.

"For want of a nail the shoe was lost ..."—and so the horse, the rider, the battle, the kingdom: all lost for want of a horseshoe nail.[306] To understand how close the outcome was it is necessary to examine in detail the events of August 30-31st. On the 30th, the Fifth Army was in a "very dangerous situation", in no small part due to Sir John French's persistence in maintaining the BEF's retreat. This imperilled the BEF itself—and Britain's very position in the war and in the world—should the Fifth be defeated. However, the I Corps, on the right of the BEF, was relatively close (see Map V), and in a position to ease pressure on the French left wing. When a report came in that the Germans were attacking from Noyon across the Oise toward the south of Lanrezac's HQ at Laon, clearly intending to cut the French off from retreat, the I Corps "was ordered to turn north-east so as to cover the left flank of the Fifth Army".[307]

The report was in fact false, probably emanating out of intelligence cobbled together from intercepted wireless messages (upon which the Germans unwisely had placed disproportionate reliance) regarding Kluck's *plans* to cross the Oise at Noyon—messages broadcast before he learned of the destruction of Pontoise—but the intentionality behind the report reflects the importance Kluck placed on that bridge for fulfilment of his plans.

The false report was fortuitous in that it allowed Haig, after being denied permission to assist Lanrezac at Guise, to make some amends—and any help the British could give was sorely needed. The Fifth Army was in a fragile state after the Battle of Guise. While on the right wing d'Espèrey's I Corps had driven the Germans back, on the left the XVIII Corps and adjacent Reserve divisions had been very roughly handled and had failed to prevent elements of Kluck's IX Corps from crossing the Oise. As a consequence, the situation on the left, along the river, "was precarious in the extreme"; the "Reserve Divisions on the left of the Army ... were far too shaken and exhausted (their

---

[305] Hastings, op cit, p. 302; Senior, op cit, p. 166.

[306] See Lyn Macdonald's horseshoe-nail analogy of Néry and the Marne; *1914*, p. 257.

[307] Spears, op cit, pp. 282, 289.

rearguards had been fighting and marching incessantly for three days) to put up any serious resistance.... There was not a single unit capable of marching to the threatened point" to anticipate the German cavalry.[308]

As yet none of this was obvious. Rather, as the sun rose on France on the last day of August 1914, "there was optimism in the air at Laon", Fifth Army HQ. To add to the euphoria of d'Espèrey's victory on the right wing came news of the transfer of two German corps to East Prussia. The odds were being evened.

Then, at 9:15 AM, came alarming "news that an enormous body of swiftly moving German Cavalry was making straight for the gap between the British and the Fifth Army, advancing towards the latter's open and undefended lines of communication". The Germans had beaten the British to the bridge at Bailly the night before and pushed horsemen across that morning. "Shortly after noon it became known that the German Cavalry had already reached Nampeel, some 12 kilometres east of Bailly.... At 5 pm it had almost reached the Aisne".[309]

Lieutenant Spears explains:

> The seriousness of this will be realised when it is remembered that the Fifth Army was isolated, nearer the enemy than any of its neighbours, its left flank in danger of an attack by von Kluck; and that from this situation there was only one means of escape, an immediate and rapid retreat, which the German Cavalry was now threatening to cut off.

The enemy cavalry's target was Vauxaillon

> which lay some fifteen miles south-west of Laon where we were sitting at that moment. If the enemy cavalry moved at any speed they would reach Vauxaillon hours before the retiring French infantry, completely outflanking our left. They would cut the Laon-Soissons Railway [along which Lanrezac was railing men to meet the threat on his left wing] and be only a short distance from the Aisne, from which the main body of the Fifth Army was separated by many miles of difficult hilly country. If the Germans occupied the passages of the river before the Fifth Army, they would cut off its retreat to the south.[310]

---

[308] Spears, op cit pp. 285, 296.

[309] Spears, op cit, pp. 300-01.

[310] Spears, op cit, p. 294.

Spears fails to mention what Roger West had accomplished the previous day, but what he laments highlights the importance of West's achievement: "It was extremely unfortunate that the bridge over the Oise at Bailly had not been destroyed." Had that at Pontoise not been destroyed how far more "extremely unfortunate" might have been the outcome for the Allies? For contemporary photographs show Pontoise to be, apart from closer to the French line of retreat, a stout and full-size bridge, not a "precariously swaying affair" as at Bailly, which cavalry had to cross in single file.[311]

The distance between Bailly and Pontoise is about fifteen kilometres—no more than minutes in the plush seat of a rented Renault over tarmac roads in 2014, but a great deal longer when you're swooning with fatigue and pulverising heat in a hard saddle on the back of a jaded horse along the dusty roads of a century ago. Furthermore, its direction was at right-angles to that in which the Fifth Army lay. In August 1914 time could mean the difference between victory and defeat, and the German armies, the First in particular, were straining every sinew to make the deadline for victory in the West: the fortieth day, now close upon them.[312] The extra distance imposed by having to cross the Oise at Bailly meant distance and time the Germans absolutely could not afford. On top of that, destruction of Pontoise meant an end to Kluck's plans to lorry "mixed detachments" to seize the Aisne crossings ahead of the French.

As Richthofen's Cavalry Divisions moved eastward toward Vauxaillon,[313] the French 4th Cavalry Division was raising as good a trot as it could from the Fifth Army's right flank—where it had been deployed against attacks from the German Second or Third Armies—along the north bank of the Aisne to meet the now more urgent danger of enemy cavalry seizing the river crossings, and elements of the French III Corps were entraining westward to meet the main flank attack. But by 5:00 PM Richthofen's cavalry "was ... within striking distance of the main Laon-Soissons Railway", along which that emergency force was moving, threatening to cut the line, as Spears describes. The Fifth Army's reserve divisions already had their line of retreat partially cut off, and "the country between Vauxaillon and the Aisne was entirely open to the enemy pending the arrival of the 4th Cavalry Division", which was "still 25 miles from their destination". The prospect was bleak: "it looked as if the enemy would be across our [the Fifth Army's] communications before nightfall", cutting the French off from the Aisne.[314] At British GHQ "it seemed even to the most

---

[311] Senior, op cit, p. 164.

[312] There was a certain flexibility to Schlieffen's plan, but the fortieth day remained the German target for victory in the West.

[313] As already noted, at least part of the Guard Cavalry had to be left behind at Noyon.

[314] Spears, op cit, pp. 316, 300-03.

stout-hearted folk that we had lost the War.... For two dreadful days all seemed lost".[315]

Earlier on the 31st Spears had been making frantic phone calls to post offices to which he hoped the British I Corps might be adjacent and by great good luck he got to speak with his former superior in the 8th Huzzars, the Royal Irish (Spears was half-Irish), Colonel Burns-Lindow, now with the South Irish Horse, the I Corps' Cavalry.[316] Sir Douglas Haig authorised Burns-Lindow to advance toward Venizel, on the Aisne, and this the South Irish Horse did, fending off German attacks through the afternoon. Thus Haig was able to make up a little for having had his offer to support Lanrezac at Guise countermanded by his superior. "Their [the South Irish Horse's] timely intervention played a considerable part in saving the Fifth Army, and was probably the main factor in blinding the enemy to the open gap behind the left flank of Lanrezac's command."[317]

Through that parlous gap the Fifth Army kept stumbling toward the Aisne, half starved, worn out, their waggons breaking under the weight of wounded and exhausted troops and the pace of the retreat, bombarded by pursuing German artillery. Kluck hoped to have at least one corps across the river early on September 1st to cut off the French escape,[318] and the need to shift the axis of retreat toward the east to evade Richthofen's thrust added to the distance and management of Lanrezac's footsore route. All that night of August 31st and through the next day the French slogged on, but they beat the Germans to the river and by the evening of September 1st their rearguards were holding the heights south of the Aisne.

The critical danger was past. The next day Richthofen again moved against the Fifth Army's flank, hoping to delay it until Kluck's IX Corps could cut off its retreat by seizing the Marne crossings this time, but he failed to disrupt the retreat significantly, and next day the enemy was contained to a bridge-head at Chateau-Thierry.[319] French and British forces continued to fall back in accordance with Joffre's strategic plan and by September 5th the Fifth was fully integrated into the Allied defensive line.

The French, indeed the Allies, had had an almost unbelievable lucky escape. If on August 31st "the German Cavalry had had real dash and been

---

[315] Jack Seely, op cit, pp. 67, 69.

[316] This simple strategy had been employed to potentially excellent effect by West's IC colleagues the previous week, when they had telephoned post offices across Belgium from Mons railway station and thereby built up a profile of the enemy advance, valuable intelligence that was discounted by Sir John French. See Charles Messenger, op cit, p. 52.

[317] Spears, op cit, p. 299.

[318] Kluck, op cit, p. 87.

[319] Senior, op cit, pp. 175-77.

well-led, it is difficult to see how the Fifth Army could have escaped without serious loss"—possibly fatal loss. Perhaps Spears is being unduly harsh here: the Germans' horses were utterly spent, their horseshoes "almost completely worn out".[320] Those extra miles imposed by having to cross so far downriver had taken their toll. But had Pontoise been unbroken the outcome might have been different; possibly very different. For apart from its closer proximity to the vulnerable Fifth Army, Pontoise was no glorified *passerelle* that cavalry must cross in single file, but a broad highway capable of carrying those lorry-mounted "mixed detachments" and infantry spread in broken step the width of the way, all forces focused on the fragile flank of the French Fifth Army.

As the Official History acknowledges, at this point there was little that "could hinder Kluck from wheeling south-east against the open left flank of the French Fifth Army, annihilating it in conjunction with Bülow, and then rolling up the French line from west to east".[321] If the Fifth could even be cut off and contained, this would put an end to Joffre's plan to consolidate his line and launch a renewed assault, and possibly lead to defeat of the Western Allies that way. "If ever a plan deserved victory it was the Schlieffen Plan", Lord Wavell remarks, it was so audacious—and Wavell, one of West's colleagues in the Intelligence Corps, watched it unfold in 1914. Perhaps but for a bridge Schlieffen's plan might have proved as successful a daring endeavour as Lee's strategy at Chancellorsville in 1863, or Manstein's in 1940.

It's impossible at this remove to calculate exactly how much time and distance the loss of Pontoise cost Kluck, but at very minimum the enemy had ten kilometres added to his journey. The distance seems modest, but it was a great burden on tired horses and men, especially when time was at such a premium. Cavalry could sustain a speed of about 8 miles an hour at a trot, but less than half that at a walk, and "posting" at a trot, while it spared horses, was hard on riders, who were as worn out as their steeds. At the start of the campaign 35 miles was a good day's ride for a cavalryman, so the minimum distance added by destruction of Pontoise was about a sixth of a good day's travel, and everyone was now far from the start of the campaign. "In just one German cavalry division seventy horses died of exhaustion in the first fort-night of the campaign, and most of the others could scarcely raise a trot".[322] On August 27th West observed enemy cavalry "very tired.... The horses slopped along with heavy feet, and the leader's head was bowed on his chest from sheer exhaustion." By the end of the month Moltke admitted, "we've hardly a horse in the army which can go faster than a walk". From Noyon, facing his critical crossing at Pontoise broken and forced to halt part of his cavalry,

---

[320] Spears, op cit, pp. 307, 301.

[321] James E Edmonds, *Military Operations: France and Belgium 1914*, p. 244.

[322] Dorondo, op cit, p. 48.

Kluck pleaded for "three lorry-loads of horseshoes and as many nails as could be found".[323] Apart from the time the extra distance imposed on horses and riders, and the impossibility of deploying lorry-mounted forces to support them, the broken bridge must also have been demoralizing.

It was as much the mathematics of time and distance as that of divisional strength that frustrated the Schlieffen Plan. Given the state of cavalry at the end of August destruction of Pontoise added at least two hours and likely more to Richthofen's journey, enough to make a difference to the outcome of events, and had the bridge been open and Kluck pushed the horsemen across on the evening of the 30th rather than at dawn on the 31st the time saved would have been greater. Kluck does not say in his account at what time his forces reached Pontoise, but the bridge was demolished at about 8:00 AM, and West reports rifle-fire across the river; upriver demolition teams had been fired upon during the night so the enemy could not have been far away. Later that day a driver was fired upon a few kilometres south of Noyon and learned that "the Uhlans had been quartered in some strength all the morning" there.[324] Given these facts, and Kluck's sense of urgency in "energetic pursuit", it seems likely that Noyon and Pontoise were occupied quite early in the day.

A sixth of the distance a *fresh* horse could be expected to cover in a day was the very minimum West's destruction of Pontoise imposed on jaded enemy cavalry. How many nails were lost out of clinking horseshoes over all those miles? How many horses went lame or died, and how many enemy troopers perforce were left behind? How many might have mustered on the Fifth Army's flank had that bridge been open to them, in time to force battle on the demoralised Lanrezac? General Douglas MacArthur once remarked that all military defeat can be explained in two words, "Too late", and the critical defeat the Germans suffered at the Marne, and all that stemmed from that, in significant part followed from their cavalry crossing the Oise too late to cut off the Fifth Army. Lanrezac's shifting his own cavalry and elements of his III Corps toward his imperilled left wing accomplished less than the South Irish Horse did in menacing the German thrust, but it was more luck than command that saved the day. As a modern researcher points out, "it was a close run thing".[325]

It would be hyperbolic to pretend that the outcome of the Great War hinged on the oversight of a fevered despatch rider who happened to forget his maps or on his dutiful return to recover them, and all that followed from that. Any counterfactual consideration has to be beset with caution, and war is notoriously disruptive of all plans and projections. Had Pontoise been open to Kluck

---

[323] Dorondo, op cit, p. 48; Hastings, op cit, pp. 165, 202, 305.

[324] Frederic Coleman, op cit, pp. 60-61.

[325] Kluck, op cit, pp. 85-86; Senior, op cit, p. 166.

it does not necessarily follow that he would have been able to bring Lanrezac to battle—but it would have improved his chances, and such a ruthless task-master as Kluck could hardly have failed to take advantage. Equally, denial of that bridge to the enemy immensely improved the Frenchman's chances of escape. Had it been assaulted the Fifth Army would have been mauled but it need not have been defeated; unless the Germans were able to seize or destroy the Aisne crossings, the I, III and X Corps, and maybe elements of the XVIII Corps, might have sustained a fighting retreat across and dug in on the slopes south of the river. But had the isolated Fifth Army been stalled and its retreat cut off, both the German First and Second Armies could have engaged, with a cauldron battle like Tannenberg the possible outcome.

Even to presume a fighting retreat across the Aisne, with the enemy in hot pursuit a defence along that river rather than the Marne would have opened the great defensive battle before the French line was fully consolidated and dangerously open to enfilade, with both of the Fifth Army's flanks vulnerable, the right wide open. Defeat would have opened a fatal rent in the Allied line.[326]

Such a German victory need not have ended the war. The scale of the battlefield and the size of the French forces—six armies now, and another being assembled—meant that the outcome would have been closer to that of 1870 than that of 1940. French resistance would have continued, though forced back and isolated from the capital. Screened-off from the main battle, the Sixth Army would have retired to reinforce the Paris garrison out of which it had been formed and help sustain defiance as the Commune had in 1870. The BEF would have retreated, footsore but unmolested, to St Nazaire and been evacuated with much less drama than at Dunkirk, and Britain could have fought on, as in 1940.

But with France no longer able to sustain the offensive, for how long could Imperial Russia withstand the combined might of Austria-Hungary and several German armies—as well as Ottoman assaults across the Caucasus and the Black Sea? And with Russia defeated what Continental allies could Britain sponsor, as in past wars, while blockading an enemy that had established Continental hegemony? Blockade is a long-term strategy, and with the war effectively over, as the Kaiser bragged, "before the leaves fall", embargo of British goods by the new *zollverein* would have economically sapped a trading nation that already had suffered military defeat.

Counterfactual speculation ultimately must butt up against empirical reality and what actually happened is that on August 30th, 1914, Roger West, a man not quite three weeks in uniform, went over and beyond his duty when

---

[326] Joffre's observation on how close things came even on the Marne seems relevant in this counterfactual consideration: "I don't know who won the Battle of the Marne, but if it had been lost, I know who would have lost it".

he volunteered to destroy a bridge and succeeded in doing so. The ultimate consequences are inestimable, but the immediate result was critical. "The Fifth Army owed its extraordinary escape partly to a lucky accident and the lack of initiative of the Germany Cavalry, and partly to the action of the British I Corps Cavalry".[327] Spears' analysis leaves out what West and Pennycuick accomplished at Pontoise. Had Kluck secured that bridge, August might have ended in calamity, and September marked the end of the war in the west.

But if that bridge really was so important, how did the action at Pontoise come to be overlooked by historians?

The most obvious possibility is that it really wasn't all that important; the action of those who went beyond the call of duty in destroying it merely another instance of such conduct in the BEF at the time. No one would claim that Dease and Jarvis and their chums affected the outcome at Mons by their bravery, or that the wounded Julian Grenfell's assistance in saving British guns next day was more than acts of impressive courage. A few field guns more or less could not have made a difference to the outcome of the war.

But a large suspension bridge over the Oise could not *but* have made a difference a week later. The most comprehensive account of the campaign, Spears', makes perfectly clear how critical was the Oise as a natural defilade, and how grave was the failure to destroy the bridge at Bailly. The importance of destroying that at Pontoise was recognised at the time, with a lengthy mention in the Official History and DSOs for West and Pennycuick. Yet Spears, in his otherwise comprehensive detailing of every day's events, doesn't even mention the episode.

In this omission may be a clue; a Holmesian dog that didn't bark. In his account West describes himself as "the last of the DSOs [at the award ceremony], being the only lieutenant" (Pennycuick was absent, possibly wounded and indisposed; eventually he got a bar to his DSO). There was only one captain there too, for the DSO is very seldom awarded to junior officers, being all but reserved for those with the rank of major and above. A career officer writes: "I've never heard of a 2/Lt being awarded a DSO".[328] West was not merely a junior officer, he was what the old professional army looked down on as a "temporary gentleman", and when he was commissioned "those in authority had impressed us with the fact that, though we had received commissions, we were never under any circumstances to consider ourselves officers".[329]

His decoration proves that the importance of what West did was not in doubt at the time and one cannot but wonder whether, with acknowledgement and appreciation magnanimously granted, and with the time now come for

---

[327] Spears, op cit, p. 307.

[328] Lt-Col Jim Storr; private email.

[329] Diary entry for August 21st.

serious historical analysis and evaluation, professional jealousy may have been a factor in discounting the achievement of a temporary gentleman who'd barely worn the sharp creases out of his King's uniform. Apart from Smith-Dorrien, British generals gave an indifferent account of themselves in the Great Retreat so it would be understandable if, in their memoirs and interviews, they omitted to mention an action instigated and carried out by a "wart", aided by another lowly subaltern, if the importance of this action might highlight their own ineffectiveness and even shortcomings.

The very need for the bridge to be destroyed by West and Pennycuick reflects poorly on what the Official History famously described as "incomparably the best trained, best organised and best equipped British Army which ever went forth to war"—though it admits: "Throughout the retreat there was considerable confusion with regard to the responsibility for the demolition of bridges".[330] Pontoise had been prepared for demolition the night before and a sapper detailed to do the job early that morning but "the effect was only partial",[331] so there was failure somewhere, in matériel or personnel, and this failure is compounded by the evident alacrity with which the professionals abandoned their task when the explosives failed. The bridge at Bailly too was wired for demolition but blurred command led to the order for its destruction not being issued in time and men lost their lives as a result. A few miles downriver at Compiègne the bridge was demolished "literally in face of the advancing enemy, and two RE officers who were doing the work were killed by enemy bullets".[332] All this indicates confusion, incompetence and perhaps general nervousness at proximity of the enemy, something to which no professional soldier would wish to draw attention. When their explosives failed West and Pennycuick did not abandon their task, though the Germans were much closer now, but re-primed and re-fused the guncotton and completed their mission.

With good reason Spears' *Liaison 1914* is regarded as something like the "holy writ" of the Great Retreat—but perhaps as holy writ it cannot contain anything like military heresy. It is impossible that Spears could not have known about the action at Pontoise, but he fails even to mention it. On August 30th he reports the false intelligence that "a German force was advancing from Noyon" and, next day, the "terrifying development" at Fifth Army HQ at Laon, when it was learned that enemy cavalry had "cross[ed] the Oise at Bailly".[333] Spears became a major-general, testimony to his military acumen, so by the time he set his account down in 1930 he simply could not have failed

---

[330] Edmonds, op cit, pp. 10, 242-43.

[331] JC Dunn, *The War the Infantry Knew*, p. 37.

[332] A Corbett-Smith, op cit, p. 205.

[333] Spears, op cit, p. 294.

to realize the significance of the destruction of Pontoise-lès-Noyon, and how much more "terrifying" the outcome must have been had Kluck's plan to cross there not been frustrated. His criticism of enemy cavalry for its lack of "real dash" and good leadership may be in part deflection from the reason for its tardiness. He makes no mention of how the destruction of Pontoise not merely blunted Kluck's cavalry thrust but frustrated completely his plan to send lorry-mounted detachments in support and to seize the Aisne bridges.

Churchill's introduction to *Liaison* quotes Sir John French's mention of Spears' "reckless, daring courage",[334] and Spears was only human. His military acumen was matched by professional ambition, so to neglect to mention that the "reckless, daring courage" of another subaltern might have matched or exceeded his own would have been tempting, especially as West was a mere "temporary gentleman", while Spears had joined the Kildare Militia in 1901.[335]

John Terraine claims that in 1914 "The British Army was saved by the skin of its teeth, more by the efforts of Spears, a subaltern, than by any other single man".[336] But there was another subaltern who also played a crucial role and who has been forgotten. The extent to which Lieutenant Roger Rolleston Fick West delayed the Germans' homecoming and robbed them of laurel garlands can never be evaluated. But we can be grateful that he rode back to Pontoise.

---

[334] Spears, op cit, p. viii.

[335] The Kildare Militia became the 3rd (Reserve) Battalion, Royal Dublin Fusiliers, after the Haldane reforms.

[336] John Terraine, *Mons: The Retreat to Victory*, p. 98.

Glossary

AOK	*Armeeoberkommando*: Austro-Hungarian Army High Command
APM	Assistant Provost Marshal
BEF	British Expeditionary Force
Cran	Guts; courage
Élan à outrance	Forward movement even to the point of excess
GHQ	British General Headquarters
GQG	*Grand Quartier Général*: French Supreme Headquarters
Großer Generalstab	German Great General Staff
GS waggon	General Service waggon
IA	Indian Army
IC	Intelligence Corps
Kaiserlichen Marine	Imperial German Naval Service
Kindermord zu Ypern	The mass-slaughter of ill-trained German reservists at Langemarck, north of Ypres, in October 1914
LC	Lines of Communications
OHL	*Oberste Heerestleitung*; German Supreme Army Command
Pavé	Strong, deeply constructed French and Belgian highways, surfaced with large cobblestones
PBI	Poor Bloody Infantry
Piou piou	Slang for French soldier
Poilou	Literally, a hairy-faced one; slang for French infantryman (Gallic equivalent of Tommy Atkins)
QMG	Quartermaster General
RWF	Royal Welsh Fusiliers
SMLE	Short Magazine Lee Enfield rifle
Soixante-quinze	French 75mm field gun, which set a new standard when introduced in 1897
Taube	Dove—whimsical name for German monoplane
Tommy Atkins	British infantryman

Uhlan	Originally Polish light cavalryman; by 1914 a generic name for German cavalryman
Wart	Disparaging name for a new, junior officer
WO	War Office

Bibliography

Abrams, Fran. *Songs of Innocence: The Story of British Childhood* (London: Atlantic Books, 2012).

Badsey, Stephen. *Doctrine and Reform in the British Cavalry 1880-1918* (Farnham: Ashgate, 2008).

Barnett, Corelli. *Britain and Her Army* (Middlesex: Pelican, 1974).

Beach, Jim. *Haig's Intelligence: GHQ and the German Army, 1916-1918* (Cambridge: Cambridge Military Histories, 2013).

Beatty, Jack. *The Lost History of 1914: How the Great War was not Inevitable* (New York: Bloomsbury, 2012).

Bilton, David. *The Germans in Flanders 1914-1915* (Barnsley: Pen & Sword, 2012).

Bourne, JM. "Major General Sir Archibald Murray" in *Stemming the Tide: Officers and Leadership in the British Expeditionary Force 1914*, ed. Dr Spencer Jones (Solihul: Helion and Company, 2013).

Bridges, Tom. *Alarums and Excursions: Reminiscences of a Soldier* (London: Longman, Gree and Co, 1938).

Burns, Max and Ken Messenger, *The Winged Wheel Patch: A History of the Canadian Military Motorcycle and Rider* (Ontario: Vanwell, 1993).

Carragher, Michael *San Fairy Ann? Motorcycles and British Victory 1914-1918* (Eastbourne: FireStep Press, 2013).

---. "'Amateurs at a professional game': The Despatch Rider Corps in 1914", in *Stemming the Tide: Officers and Leadership in the British Expeditionary Force 1914*, ed. Dr Spencer Jones

Carrington, Charles. *Soldier From the Wars Returning* (Barnsley, S Yorks: Pen & Sword, 2006).

Casson, Stanley. *Steady Drummer* (London: Bell & Sons, 1935).

Clayton, Anthony. *Forearmed: A History of the Intelligence Corps* (London: Brasseys, 1996).

Corbett-Smith, A. *The Retreat from Mons* (New York: Houghton Mifflin, 1917).

Coleman, Frederic. *From Mons to Ypres with French* (Toronto: William Briggs, 1916).

Coward, George. *Coward's War: An Old Contemptible's View of the Great War* (Leicester: Matador, 2006).

Diary of the Argyll and Sutherland Highlanders; the National Archives, Catalogue Reference: WO/95/1365.

Denore, Bernard John "The Retreat from Mons", in CP Purdom (ed), *On the Front Line: True World War I Stories* (London: Constable, 2009).

Dorondo, David R. *Riders of the Apocalypse: German Cavalry and Modern Warfare, 1870-1945* (Annapolis, MD: Naval Institute Press, 2012).

Dunn, Captain JC. *The War the Infantry Knew 1914-1919: A Chronicle of Service in France and Belgium* (London: Abacus, 1994).

Emden, Richard van (ed.). *Tickled to Death to Go: Memoirs of a Cavalryman in the First World War* (Staplehurst, Kent: Spellmount, 1996).

---. *The Soldier's War: The Great War Through Veterans' Eyes* (London: Bloomsbury, 2009)

Fermor, Patrick Leigh. *A Time of Gifts: On Foot to Constantinople: From the Hook of Holland to the Middle Danube* (London: John Murray, 1977).

Firstworldwar.com, http://www.firstworldwar.com/source/aisne_swinton.htm

Fischer, Fritz. "World Policy, World Power, and German War Aims", in Koch, HW (ed). *The Origins of the First World War: Great Power Rivalry and German War Aims*, Second Edition (London: Macmillan, 1984).

French, Sir John, *1914* (New York: Houghton Mifflin, 1919).

Gegg, Martin. *War Bike: British Military Motorcycling 1899-1919* (ISBN 978-1-326-40667-7, 2015)

Gilbert, Adrian. *Challenge of Battle: The Real Story of the British Army in 1914* (Colchester: Osprey, 2014).

Gilbert, Martin. *The First World War: A Complete History* (New York: Henry Holt, 1994)

Hart, Peter. *Fire and Movement: The British Expeditionary Force and the Campaign of 1914* (Oxford: Oxford UP, 2015).

Harvey, AD. "Taken in the First Few Weeks: Five First-Hand Accounts of British Prisoners of War" in *Stand To!*, June 2014.

Hastings, Max. *Catastrophe: Europe Goes To War 1914* (London: Collins, 2013).

Hesketh-Pritchard, H. *Sniping in France: With Notes on the Scientific Training of Scouts, Observers and Snipers* (New York: Dutton and Company, 1920).

Holmes, Richard. *Riding the Retreat: Mons to Marne: 1914 Revisited* (London: Pimlico, 2007).

Hopkirk, Peter. *On Secret Service East of Constantinople: The Plot to Bring Down the British Empire* (London: John Murray, 2006).

Horder, Barbara. "Memories of a Long Life" (unpublished memoir).

Horder Friedel, Mary. *Mary Horder Friedel, 1911-2005* (privately published memoir).

Horne, John and Alan Kramer. *German Atrocities 1914: A History of Denial* (New Haven: Yale UP, 2001).

Jackson, Jolyon. *Family at War: The Foljambe Family and the Great War* (Yeovil: Haynes, 2010).

Joll, James. "The 1914 Debate Continues: Fritz Fischer and his Critics", in HW Koch (ed): *The Origins of the First World War: Great Power Rivalry and German War Aims*, Second Edition (London: Macmillan, 1984).

Jones, Spencer and Steven J Corvi, "'A Commander of Rare and Unusual Coolness': General Sir Horace Lockwood Smith-Dorrien", in *Stemming the Tide: Officers and Leadership in the British Expeditionary Force 1914*, ed. Dr Spencer Jones (Solihul: Helion and Company, 2013).

Keegan, John. *The First World War* (New York: Knopf, 1999).

Kelleher, JP. *The Royal Fusiliers (the City of London Regiment) and the Intelligence Corps 1914-1920* (Internet: Community Texts, 2010,

http://archive.org/stream/RoyalFusiliersIntelligenceCorps1914-18/
TheRoyalFusiliersAndTheIntelligenceCorps_djvu.txt, accessed 29 April
2014).

Kenyon, David. *Horsemen in No Man's Land: British Cavalry and Trench
Warfare 1914-1918* (Barnsley: Pen & Sword, 2011).

Kerr, Alastair. *Betrayal: The Murder of Robert Nairac GC* (Cambridge:
Cambridge Academic, 2015).

Kildare Observer, 12 September 1914.

Kluck, Alexander von. *The March on Paris and the Battle of the Marne, 1914*
(London: Edward Arnold, 1920).

Koch, HW (ed). *The Origins of the First World War: Great Power Rivalry and
German War Aims*, Second Edition (London: Macmillan, 1984).

Laws, Felicity Jane (ed). *War on Two Wheels: A Diary of Overseas Service*
(private publication).

Lipkes, Jeff. *Rehearsals: The German Army in Belgium, August 1914* (Leuven:
Leuven UP, 2007).

London Gazette, 22 June 1915.

Macdonald, Lyn. *1914-1918: Voices and Images of the Great War* (London:
Michael Joseph, 1988).

---. *1914* (London: Penguin, 1989).

---. *Ordeal by Fire: Witnesses to the Great War* (London: The Folio Society,
2001).

Mallinson, Allan. *1914: Fight the Good Fight: Britain, the Army & the Coming
of the First World War* (London: Bantam, 2013).

Maurice, Sir Frederick. *Forty Days in 1914* (New York: George H Doran, 1919).

Maze,Paul. *A Frenchman in Khaki* (London: Heineman, 1934).

McMeekin, Sean. *The Berlin-Baghdad Express: The Ottoman Empire and
Germany's Bid for World Power, 1898-1918* (London: Allen Lane, 2010).

Messenger, Charles. *Call-to-Arms: The British Army 1914-1918* (London:
Cassell, 2005).

Minton, David. *The Triumph story: Racing and production models from 1902
to the present day* (Yeovil: Haynes, 2002)

Morris, Ian. *War: What is it Good For: The Role of Conflict in Civilisation, from
Primates to Robots* (London: Profile Books, 2014).

Motor Cycle, The, July 9th, 1914. (Archives held by The Vintage Motorcycle
Club Ltd, Allen House, Wetmore Road, Burton Upon Trent, Staffs.,
DE14 1TR).

Motor Cycling, 5 October 1915. (Archives held by The Vintage Motorcycle
Club Ltd, Allen House, Wetmore Road, Burton Upon Trent, Staffs.,
DE14 1TR).

Neillands, Robin. *The Old Contemptibles: The British Expeditionary Force
1914* (London: John Murray, 2005).

Reisler, Kurt. Letter to his fiancée, Käthe Liebermann, August 29, 1914; Jaffé-
Richthofen family correspondence, Leo Baecke Institute, New York.

Richards, Frank. *Old Soldiers Never Die* (Uckfield: Naval and Military Press, 2001).

Rimington, Major-General MF. *Our Cavalry* (London: Macmillan, 1912).

Robertson, William. *From Private to Field-Marshal* (London: Constable and Co, 1921).

Robinson, Janet & Joe Robinson. *Handbook of Imperial Germany* (Bloomington, IN: AuthorHouse, 2009).

Rogerson, Sidney. *The Last of the Ebb: The Battle of the Aisne, 1918* (Bernsley: Frontline, 2011).

Scott, Brough. *Galloper Jack: The Remarkable Story of the Man who Rode a Real War Horse* (Newbury: Racing Post Books, 2012).

Seely, Jack. *Warrior: The Amazing Story of a Real War Horse* (Newbury: Racing Post Books, 2013).

Senior, Ian. *Home Before the Leaves Fall: A New History of the German Invasion of 1914* (Oxford: Osprey, 2012).

Shelley, Martin and Nick. *Two Wheels to War* (Solihull: Helion, 2017).

Smith-Dorrien, Sir Horace. *Memories of Forty-Eight Years' Service* (New York: Dutton and Co, 1925).

Spears, Edward. *Liaison 1914: A Narrative of the Great Retreat* (Barnsley: Pen & Sword, 2014).

Sproston, AJ. "Four Months Under Fire" in the *Daily Mail*, 14-19 December 1914.

Statistics of the Military Effort of the British Empire during the Great War 1914-1920 (London: HMSO, 1922).

Stewart, Herbert A. *From Mons to Loos* (Edinburgh: Blackwood, 1916).

Strachan, Hew. *The First World War: A New Illustrated History* (London: Pocket Books, 2006).

Tait, WH. IWM document PP/MCR/161.

Terraine, John. *Mons: The Retreat to Victory* (Ware, Herts: Wordsworth Editions, 2002).

Tuchman, Barbara. *The Guns of August* (New York: Bantam, 1976).

Vivian, E Charles. *A History of Aeronautics* (New York: Harcourt, Brace and Company, 1921)

Watson, Captain WHL. *Adventures of a Despatch Rider* (Edinburgh: Blackwood, 1915).

Young, Peter. "The Great Retreat" in *Purnell's History of the 20th Century* (London: BPC Publishing, 1968).

Zuber, Dr Terence. *The Mons Myth: A Reassessment of the Battle* (Stroud: The History Press, 2010).

Zuckerman, Larry. *The Rape of Belgium: The Untold Story of World War I* (New York: NYU Press, 2004).

Index

3rd Division (BEF): 60, 61, 88, 111, 112, 119.

4th Division (BEF): 26 (f/n), 59, 61, 121, 144.

5th Division (BEF): 60, 61, 70, 131, 191.

6th Division (BEF): 59, 60, 186, 187.

14th Brigade (BEF): 88.

19th Brigade (BEF): 21, 24, 26, 35, 37, 59-61, 63, 65, 69, 70, 71, 73-76, 79, 83, 84, 86, 88, 92, 117, 119, 124, 144, 145, 159, 168, 174, 178, 188, 190, 192, 194, 201.

I Corps (BEF): 25, 26, 30, 88, 112, 114, 148, 160, 215, 218, 222.

II Corps (BEF): 21, 24-26, 52-53, 59-60, 67, 71, 88, 92, 93, 112, 114, 124, 132 f/n, 134.

III Corps (BEF): 26 f/n, 61, 217, 220.

Aerial bombardment: 153, 156.

Aerial reconnaissance: 39, 61, 80, 152, 157, 161, 176.

Aisne, River: 26-27, 126, 129, 132, 135, 141, 158, 201, 212-18, 221, 224.

Aisne, Battle of: 21, 27.

Allenby, General Edmund: 59, 67, 82.

Alsace-Lorraine: 34, 41, 57, 94, 125, 211.

d'Amade, General Albert: 52, 54, 60, 70, 88, 113, 125.

Amiens: 33, 39, 43, 48, 49-50, 58, 68.

"Amiens despatch": 134.

Antwerp: 20, 53, 56, 162.

Ardennes: 41, 52, 54, 57, 62, 64, 81, 150.

Argyll and Sutherland Highlanders: 60, 67, 71, 78, 79, 84, 85, 87-88, 89-92, 110-11, 131, 170-71, 173, 178, 184-85, 191.

Army Service Corps (ASC): 89, 92, 111, 167, 184, 192.

Artillery: 47, 83, 85, 90, 96, 129, 144, 165-66, 170, 181, 189, 190-91.

ASC: see Army Service Corps.

Atrocities: 33, 38, 41, 54-56, 58, 64, 72, 82, 94, 145-46, 155-56, 173, 175, 180, 182.

Audreignies: 81, 86.

Bailly-Thourotte: 140-141, 210, 216-17, 222-23.

Bavai: 69, 74, 77, 87.

Beaudignies: 74-75.

BEF (British Expeditionary Force): 20, 23, 28-31, 33, 35, 38, 42, 47-48, 51-52, 54, 56, 59, 63-64, 71, 81-82, 87, 88-89, 93, 111, 113-14, 120-21, 125, 132-34, 140-41, 149, 157-58, 161-65, 167, 171-72, 175-76, 187-88, 194, 210-12, 215, 221-22.

Berlin: 32, 36, 52, 55, 89, 134, 162.

Bevan, Lt FH: 42, 44, 47, 148.

Blenner Hasset, Lt WL: 44, 46-47, 49, 97.

Blockade, naval: 32-33, 41, 221.

Bonn: 96, 200-01.

Breslau: see Göben and Breslau.

Bridges, demolition of: 26, 28, 124, 127-29, 178, 210-11, 220, 223.

Bridges, Major Tom: 47, 112.

Bridges, pontoon: 177-78, 210.

British Expeditionary Force: see BEF.

British Columbia: 19, 46, 106, 203, 205, 207.

British Neutrality Committee: 32.

British War Council: 32.

Brussels: 41, 54, 56, 57, 156.

Bucknall, John: 21, 197-99, 201, 203, 206, 207-09.

Bülow, General Karl von: 53, 61, 64, 89, 93, 101, 113-14, 120-21, 125, 132-33, 155, 157, 160-61, 166-67, 172, 176, 191, 209-10, 212, 214 f/n, 215, 219.

Burney, Alick and Cecil: 115, 119.

Burney, Lt E: 46, 123.

Cambrai: 53, 56, 63, 77, 84, 113.

Cambridge University: 20, 35-36, 56, 67, 123.

Cameronians (Scottish Rifles): 60, 65, 67-68, 70, 72, 90, 110, 115, 123,

137, 144-45.

Carlepont (Bois de): 124, 126-27, 129.

Carmel, CA: 22, 106, 200, 203, 205, 207-09.

"Case 3": see Schlieffen Plan.

de Castlenau, General Éduard: 192.

Cavalry, British: 28-29, 33, 40, 48, 50, 59-60, 63, 67, 71, 76-77, 81-83, 86, 88, 90, 112, 116, 129, 136, 139, 143, 145, 147-48, 172, 177, 189, 218, 222.

Cavalry, French: 25, 54, 60, 86, 95, 152, 156, 158, 165, 180-81, 210, 217, 220.

Cavalry, German (see also Uhlan, hussar): 21, 24, 26, 41, 43, 52-53, 55, 60, 67-69, 73-74, 77, 79-80, 82, 85, 88, 95-97, 101, 102, 114, 121, 125, 127, 134, 139, 140-41, 147, 150, 155-57, 167, 169, 200, 210-20, 222-24.

Chamicy: 145, 148.

Channel crossing: 31, 32, 35, 39-40, 114, 122, 176.

Charleroi, Battle of: 30, 61, 64, 81, 87, 213.

Chateau Thierry: 185, 188, 218.

Chatham: 34-36.

Churchill (Signals officer): 65, 69, 77, 82, 84, 126, 129-30, 164, 170, 173, 178, 180, 183.

Clayton, Anthony: 45-46.

Coblenz: 52, 134.

Communications: 20-21, 24, 28-29, 32, 35, 40, 52-54, 57-60, 63, 64, 81-82, 88-89, 113-14, 125, 131, 133-34, 139, 157, 160, 165, 168, 171-72, 175, 190 f/n, 193, 215-17.

Compiègne: 26, 129, 131, 135, 212, 223.

Congestion, roads: 80, 84-85, 87, 91, 143.

Coulomniers: 36, 185.

Cox, Captain EW: 37, 95, 111, 188.

Cunnynghame, Captain, APM: 123.

Dammartin: 151, 156.

Defence of the Realm Act (DORA): 34, 119 f/n.

Delbrück, Clemens: 175-76.

Delmé-Radcliffe, Colonel Charles: 112, 139, 142, 173.

Despatch rider (DR): 19-21, 23, 32-37, 40, 47, 51, 56, 60, 63, 65-66, 70-71, 79-81, 87-88, 111, 115, 119, 131, 134, 138-40, 147, 166, 171, 176, 180, 185-86, 189 f/n, 190 f/n, 193, 201, 210, 220,

Dinant: 52, 72.

Dispatch rider: see Despatch rider.

DR: see Despatch rider.

Drummond, General JG: 59, 65, 76, 84, 112-13, 195.

Drunkenness: [alcohol; wine] 148, 166, 175-77, 179.

Dury: 116, 146.

Dust (road hazard): 42, 49, 56, 77-78, 116-17, 129, 145, 162, 164, 169, 177, 180, 214.

Duty, sense of: 19, 20, 30, 70, 79, 86, 96, 200-01, 208, 221-22.

Duval, Captain Claude Raoul: 138-40, 164.

East Prussia: 41, 53, 55, 57, 64, 72, 82, 89, 115, 121-22, 134, 156, 161, 168, 181, 183, 216.

Edwards, Wynne: 146, 177, 178, 182, 191.

Eighth Army (German): 64, 72, 89, 115, 133, 183.

Enemy agents: see Spies.

d'Espèrey, General Franchet: 27, [desperate] 27, 30, 157, 165, 213.

Etreux: 114.

Eve: 151, 156.

Falkenhayn, General Erich von: 31, 135, 187.

la Fère: 210.

Fère-en-Tardenois: 188, 192.

la Ferte: 169, 173-74, 178, 188.

Fick, Johann Christian: 197-98.

Fifth Army (French): 20, 27-30, 41, 52, 61, 64, 87, 114, 120, 124-25, 131-33, 140-41, 149-50, 157-58, 161, 163, 172, 209-23.

First Army (German): 25, 28, 53, 125, 131, 134, 155, 163-64, 176, 209, 212.

First Army (Russian): 58, 156, 168.

Fletcher, Lt WG: 42, 58, 65-66, 69-70, 77, 78, 83-84, 94, 110, 115, 117-18, 120, 124, 126, 129-31, 135-38, 146, 164, 166, 170-71, 173, 178-79, 184-85, 187-88, 191, 193, 205 f/n, 208.

Foch, General Ferdinand: 27, 64, 158, 172.

Fourth Army (French): 57, 64, 210.

Fourth Army (German): 172.

Frankland, Sir Edward: 34 f/n, 66, 199, 203.

French, Field Marshal Sir John: 24-26, 29-30, 31, 33, 39, 51-54, 81, 88, 93, 100, 114, 121, 124-25, 132, 141, 149, 162, 163, 191, 210, 212, 215, 218 f/n, 224.

Fresnoy: 95-96, 145-46.

Frontiers, Battles of the: 31, 48, 54, 56, 61-62, 64, 88.

Galicia: 55, 94, 183.

Gallieni, General Joseph: 52, 88, 94, 122, 125, 134, 150, 155-56, 161, 167, 209, 213.

Garnier, General Otto von: 147.

GHQ (British): 40, 47, 52, 59, 82, 83, 84, 88, 93, 97, 111-13, 121, 123, 133, 186, 191, 217.

Göben and *Breslau*: 34, 38.

GQG (*Grand Quartier Général*): 29-30, 41, 52-54, 57, 61-62, 88, 93, 114, 120-21, 149, 157, 161, 211 f/n.

"Great Retreat": 19-21, 23-26, 56, 59, 61, 71, 79, 111, 120, 171, 180, 210-11, 223

Guise, Battle of: 25, 29-30, 114, 120, 125, 131-33, 141, 209, 212-13, 214 f/n, 215, 218.

Haig, General Sir Douglas: 30, 34, 88, 112, 122, 125, 167, 185, 215, 218.

Ham: 115-16, 135.

Hausen, General Max von: 54, 158, 210.

la Haute Maison: 165, 168.

de Havilland, Geoffrey: 119, 202.

Heidelberg: 200-01.

Hentsch, Colonel Richard: 163, 172, 176.

Hindenburg, General Paul von: 58, 72, 168.

Hitler, Adolf: 52, 156.

Hoffman, Major Max: 168.

Hollywood, CA: 19, 206.

Horder, Barbara: 103, 204-05.

Horder, Percy: 204-05.

Horne, General Henry: 160.

IC: see Intelligence Corps.

Intelligence Corps (IC): 17, 19, 21, 23, 27, 33 f/n, 37, 38, 40, 43-47, 50, 56, 57 f/n, 58, 60, 61, 65-67, 79, 119, 123, 143, 148, 149, 194, 201, 202, 219.

Jack, Captain (later General) James: 59-60, 65, 69-70, 86, 92, 110, 123-24, 129, 131, 137, 138-40, 142, 151.

Joffre, General Joseph Jacques Césaire: 24-25, 27, 29-30, 52, 54, 57, 61, 81, 88, 93, 114, 121, 125, 132-34, 141, 149-50, 157, 159, 161-63, 165, 181, 192, 212, 218-19, 221 f/n.

Johnson, Major, 19th Brigade: 65, 67, 76-77, 84, 123-24.

Kaiserliche Marine: 31, 35, 36, 94, 187.

King, Lt EH: 44, 63, 65-66, 78-79, 182, 193.

Kitchener, Lord Herbert Horatio: 33-34, 62, 114, 132, 140, 149.

Kluck, General Alexander von: 25, 27-29, 53, 56-57, 60, 120-21, 124, 131-35, 140, 147, 149, 153, 155, 157, 160, 163-67, 172, 175-77, 209-22, 224.

Lagny: 156, 159.

Laigle: 124, 126.

Landrecies: 88, 111.

Lanrezac, General Charles: 24-30, 39, 41, 48, 51-54, 57, 61, 64, 71, 81, 88, 93, 102, 114, 120-21, 125, 131-34, 141, 147, 149, 155, 157, 183, 209-10, 213-21.

Laon: 26, 215-17, 223.

"Learning Curve": 172.

Le Cateau, Battle of: 25, 28, 52, 59-60, 70-72, 83-89, 92-93, 110, 113, 118, 121, 123-25, 150, 195.

Lee Enfield rifle: 96, 111, 200.

Lichnowsky, Prince Karl Max: 32.

Liège: 24, 31, 33, 34, 36, 41, 52, 64, 120, 212.

Lody, Karl: 48 f/n, 162, 176.

Louvain: 55, 72, 94, 148, 155-56.

Ludendorff, General Erich: 34, 58, 64, 72, 82, 89, 94, 156.

MacCallum, Captain AEG: 43, 55.

Manoury, General Michel-Joseph: 114, 133-34, 141, 147, 158, 161, 163-64, 166-67, 172, 175, 209.

Manstein Plan: 134, 219.

Maps, problematic: 76, 79, 84, 116, 126, 136, 138-39, 142, 144, 151, 210, 220.

Marne, Battle of: 17, 20, 27, 28, 30, 45, 52, 66, 69, 115, 134, 141, 147, 153, 155-60, 162-63, 165-81, 183, 185, 187, 191, 207, 211, 218, 220, 221.

Marne, "Taxis of": 153, 155, 160, 167.

Marwitz, General Georg von der: 41, 101, 140, 147, 167, 212.

Masurian Lakes, Battle of: 168.

Maubeuge: 33, 51-52, 89.

Mauser rifle: 71, 111.

McClure, Ivor: 35-37, 186.

Meuse, River: 29, 52.

Middlesex Regiment: 60, 67-68, 71, 82, 84-85, 110, 112, 117-18, 123, 126, 138, 142, 148, 151, 165-66, 169, 178, 195.

Moltke, General Helmuth von (the Younger): 20-21, 64, 141, 155-56, 158, 161, 163, 166-67, 172, 181, 183, 187, 210, 219.

Moltke (the Elder): 133, 167-68.

Mons, Battle of: 20, 24, 28, 35, 47, 56. 59-60, 67-69, 71, 81, 82, 93, 111, 194, 222.

Mons-Condé Canal: 24, 67-68, 86, 186, 211.

Montay: 83-85.

Morhange: 56, 62.

Moulton-Barrett, acting-Lieutenant-Colonel EM: 91-92.

Mud (road hazard): 43, 56, 135, 157, 177, 184-85, 190, 192.

Mulhouse: 36, 38, 54, 57, 81.

Munster Fusiliers: 111, 114.

Murray, Sir Archibald: 112-13, 122, 162.

Namur: 62, 64, 81, 89, 120.

Néry: 142-48, 155, 212.

Ninth Army: 172.

Noyon: 19, 21, 93, 98, 111, 114, 117, 119, 131, 148, 211-12, 215, 219-20, 223-24.

OHL (*Oberste Heeresleitung*): 52-53, 57, 64, 113, 134, 155, 157, 161-63, 172, 175-76.

Oise, River: 26, 88, 114, 130-32, 134, 140, 208-10, 212, 214-15, 217, 220, 222-23.

"Old Contemptibles": 19, 23 f/n, 25, 51, 54, 71, 171.

Order No 2 (Joffre's): see Plan XVII.

Order No 4 (Joffre's): see Plan XVII.

Ostend: 27, 48, 114.

Ourcq, River: 153, 163-64.

Paris: 27-28, 52, 81, 93, 133-34, 149-55, 157-60, 167, 175, 188, 209, 213-14, 221.

Paris garrison: 93-94, 125, 150, 221.

Pennycuick, Lt JAC: 127-28, 222-23.

Plan XVII: 30, 56-57, 93, 150, 211-12.

Pontoise-lès-Noyon: 19, 25-26, 28, 79, 98, 117-19, 123-24, 126-28, 130-31, 134, 141, 148, 209-12, 215, 217, 219-20, 222-24.

Premier (motorcycle): 33, 39-40, 47, 49-50, 129, 131, 143, 151, 162, 164, 170, 179, 184, 187-88, 193.

Quarouble: 68, 76.

Quiévrechain: 68-69.

Quievrain: 67, 135, 186.

Railways: 26, 63, 114, 134, 161, 163, 168, 213.

Raray: 144.

RE: see Royal Engineers.

Red Cross: 94, 117, 136, 181, 183.

Refugees: 74, 80, 85-87, 95, 111, 142, 152.

Rennenkamf, General Paul von: 53, 72, 82, 115, 122, 156, 168, 181, 183.

Reservists: 60, 62, 120.

RFC: see Aerial reconnaissance.

Richthofen, General Manfred von: 52, 80, 114, 140-41, 215, 217-18, 220.

Roissy: 152-54.

Ross, Major: 142, 151, 178-79.

Rothschild, Lord: 199-200.

Royal Engineers: 26, 30, 56, 110, 116, 124, 127, 174, 178, 192, 210-11, 223.

Royal Navy: 32, 36.

Royal Welsh Fusiliers: 58, 60, 67-68, 70, 72, 89, 92, 115-16, 119-20, 135, 138-42, 146, 148, 159, 162, 171, 173, 177-79, 182. 190-92, 195.

Rudge (motorcycle): 33, 49, 126, 131, 138, 166, 170, 173, 177, 180, 184, 186-87.

Rugby (school): 20, 187, 199, 200, 203.

Rully: 145-46.

Rupprecht, General Prince: 46, 48, 53, 56-57, 62, 64, 72, 94, 120, 157, 161, 163, 167, 214.

"Russians with snow on their boots": 114-15, 122, 176.

Sambre, River: 52, 54, 57, 61.

Saintines: 142-44.

Samsonov, General Aleksandr: 53, 58, 64, 72, 82, 89, 94, 115, 122, 134, 168, 183.

Sang, Lt Alfred: 45, 58, 63, 65-66, 68-69, 78, 82, 84, 110, 115, 118, 124, 126, 129-30, 135-36, 145, 164, 169-71, 186, 207.

Schlieffen Plan: 20, 21, 28, 38, 41, 53, 57-58, 64, 72, 89, 113, 120, 133-35, 157-58, 161, 163, 167, 172, 175, 181, 187, 210, 211, 219-20.

Schrecklichkeit: 54-55, 80, 92, 111, 120, 156, 174-75.

Seabrook, Lt JT: 42, 45, 49.

Second Army (German): 61, 64, 89, 114, 120, 131, 133, 155, 166, 176 f/n, 210, 212, 214, f/n.

Second Army (Russian): 53, 58, 122, 156.

Seely, General "Galloper Jack": 48, 125 f/n.

Senlis: 145, 155, 159.

September Programme: 72, 167, 175.

Seventh Army (German): 53, 64, 72.

Signals Corps: see Communications.

Signy-Signet: 165, 168, 171, 173.

Sixth Army (French): 27, 93, 114, 133, 147, 150, 157-58, 161, 163-66, 175, 181, 221

Sixth Army (German): 46, 64, 72.

Smith-Dorrien, General Sir Horace: 25, 53, 59, 88, 93, 100, 124, 132, 172, 223.

Soissons: 26, 129, 191, 216-17.

Solesmes: 69-70, 73-74, 76-77, 84-85, 87, 88, 118.

Somme, River and Canal: 62, 81, 110, 114, 115-16, 135, 172.

Sordet, General André: 25, 54, 60.

South Irish Horse: 218, 220.

Spahis: see Zouaves.

Spears, Lt (later General) Edward Louis: 29, 48, 51, 54, 57, 113, 121, 124, 149, 213, 216-19, 222-24.

Spiers, Lt: see Spears.

Spies: 35, 47, 79, 115, 118, 120, 138, 145, 160.

Sproule, Lt JC, RAMC: 68, 135, 170.

Stallupönen, Battle of: 53, 55, 58.

St Aybert: 68, 73, 82.

St Nazaire: 125, 158, 221.

St Quentin: 25, 43, 55, 71 f/n, 82, 91, 93, 95-97, 110, 112, 114, 116, 118, 120, 125 f/n, 188.

Steen, Sally: 21, 107, 198-201, 203, 205, 206, 209.

Stragglers: 93, 97, 115, 128, 130, 137, 143, 182, 184-85.

Tait, Cpl WH: 47.

Tamines: 61, 64.

Tannenberg, Battle of: 134, 168, 221.

Third Army (French): 54, 61, 181.

Third Army (German): 24, 64, 113, 121, 158, 176, 217.

Torrie, Captain TGJ: 43, 46.

Trenches: 27, 78, 82, 174, 186-87, 189, 193, 201.

"Turcos": see Zouaves.

Valenciennes: 65, 67-69, 73-74, 77.

Vauxaillon: 216-17.

Venizel: 188, 190, 192-93, 218.

Verberrie: 138, 142-43.

Verdun: 27, 62, 133, 140, 211.

du Vignaux, Commandant: 65, 188.

Villers-Cotterêts: 26, 148.

Ward, Colonel: 110, 112, 117, 123, 126-27, 129, 142, 151, 195.

War Office: 32, 37-38, 40, 69, 183, 187, 201-02, 206, 210.

Watson, WHL: 34, 36, 70, 119.

Wavell, Captain (later General) AP: 46, 219.

West, Barbara: see Barbara Horder.

West family: 21, 34, 37, 66-67, 160, 197-200, 207.

West, Samuel: 198-99.

Wilhelm, Crown Prince: 72.

Wilhelm II, Kaiser: 23, 38, 39, 52-53, 54, 57, 161, 187, 221.

Wilson, General Sir Henry: 33, 63, 82, 112, 121 f/n, 162.

Wireless: 29, 52, 82, 89, 113-14, 134, 215.

Zouaves: 150, 174, 180, 182.

Zuber, Dr Terence: 21, 28 f/n.